BARRY

BARRY

The Story of
Motorcycling Legend
Barry Sheene, MBE

Steve Parrish and
Nick Harris

sphere

SPHERE

First published in Great Britain in 2007 by Sphere

Copyright © Steve Parrish and Nick Harris

The moral right of the authors has been asserted.

A CIP catalogue record for this book
is available from the British Library.

Hardback ISBN 978-1-8474-4033-4
C-format ISBN 978-1-8474-4034-1

Typeset in Caslon by M Rules
Printed and bound in Great Britain by
Clays Ltd, St Ives plc

Sphere
An imprint of
Little, Brown Book Group
Brettenham House
Lancaster Place
London WC2E 7EN

A Member of the Hachette Livre Group of Companies

www.littlebrown.co.uk

Nick:

To my wife Sheila and daughter Sophie, for their encouragement and patience when the going got tough, and to dear Jackie.

Steve:

To the next generation: Freddie and Sidonie Sheene, and Francesca and Joe Parrish.

CONTENTS

Foreword   xi

The Final Lap   1
The Beginning   23
Good Old Days?   44
World Champion   63
The Squadron   80
Kenny   101
My Way or the Highway   116
Just One of Those Days   134
Nigel Cobb   151
Retirement   166
Life After Barry   185

Race Results   206
Index   215

ACKNOWLEDGEMENTS

Thanks to:

Maggie Smart, Kenny Roberts, Giacomo Agostini, Phil Read, Angel Nieto, Valentino Rossi, Gary Nixon, Dr Martin Raines, Cathy Metcalfe, Nigel Cobb, Andrea and Barry Coleman, Lord Hesketh, Julian Seddon, Jeremy Paxton, Leigh Diffey, Greg Rust, Daryl Eastlake, Andrew Marriot, Linda Patterson, Marie Armes, Mick Woollett, Henk Keulemans, David Luxton, Tom Bromley, Barbara Daniel and everybody at Little, Brown for their enthusiasm and total support.

FOREWORD

I first met Barry in late 1975 and was introduced to my first motor-cycle race early in 1976, at the Paul Ricard circuit in France. I had absolutely no idea about racing at that point.

When I arrived at Nice airport Barry and his friend Gary Nixon met me. At the hotel I was told that the water was OK to drink. I never drank anything but bottled water on the continent, but Barry assured me he had been drinking it for days.

I spent the next three days hugging the toilet seat. The pain was so bad the doctor came to visit me twice. Despite still feeling queasy I was driven to the circuit where I was made welcome at the caravan of his teammate John Newbold. I think I ventured out into the garage once, where the only thing to sit on was a spare petrol can, once. After smelling the petrol amid all the noise I wondered if I would ever fit into this new world.

The press was rather curious about me at first but I soon fitted into the racing way of life. After a lot of coaching from Andrea, the wife of Tom Herron, and Linda Davies, Steve Parrish's girl-friend, I was even roped into being a timekeeper. It surprised me just how good I was at it – I had never been any good at maths but even people from other teams would check their times with me.

Barry was very much the star at that time and would spend hours with the fans after the races, signing autographs and chatting. Also, straight after the race the journalists would turn up for interviews and I soon learned who was who and who to let in first.

Nick Harris was one of Barry's favourites. I always remember Nick coming to the motorhome. Barry's mum would say, 'Cup of tea, Nick?' and he would always reply, 'I don't mind if I do Iris.' Barry would call Nick 'Nickel Arse'. The nicknames he had for members of the press that he didn't like were a lot worse.

Barry liked Nick and Nick certainly knew how to play Barry, by writing positive things about him. Barry knew that Nick would always write the good stuff and gloss over the bad, if there was any. Nick was one of my favourites too. He was always friendly and ready to congratulate when races went well or to commiserate if they went badly.

Stavros, or Steve Parrish, came into my life over the Christmas of 1976. Barry had invited him and Linda to Wisbech over the holiday break and we soon became firm friends. We were forever in and out of each other's caravans at the races. Linda and I soon developed a ritual after each race and practice: we would compare notes on time-keeping and results before having a chinwag over a gin and tonic and a packet of Twiglets while the boys sorted out their bikes.

Holidays also became a bit of a ritual. Every January we would go to Venezuela for four weeks. Linda would bring the tea bags and Twiglets and we would spend the time water-skiing, sunbathing and having fun before getting ready for the racing season to start.

Stavros and Barry got up to God knows what together and I really don't want to know. Their great friendship continued right until the end, when Stavros came over to Australia to say goodbye. Barry was really sick and it was a very emotional day for both of them. Linda also came over because Barry loved her to bits and always called her 'Bindy Bobblers'.

I once read that there are two kinds of people in the world, taxi drivers and bus drivers. Taxi drivers are told which way to go and are directed. Bus drivers are on their own route. If you are not going that way don't get on or, as Barry would say, it's my way or the highway.

PS – Since reading the draft of the book I've found out a few things that I didn't know about Barry. I bet he's up there, already preparing his excuses for when 'her indoors' pitches up to join him.

Stephanie Sheene
Surfers Paradise, Australia, December 2006

THE FINAL LAP

The giant rotor blades of the magnificent helicopter gently swayed in the warm Queensland breeze. The perspex cockpit glinted in the afternoon sun as the hangar doors were opened for probably the last time for quite a while.

It had been a long, tortuous 100-metre walk for Barry's frail body, which was now ravaged by the final stages of cancer, but he was determined to show his best friend his ultimate toy, even if he could not take him on the flight of their dreams. Tomorrow Barry Sheene and Steve Parrish would say goodbye for the final time.

Words would have been wasted because they both knew that a very special friendship was coming to a premature and tragic conclusion. Just six-and-a-half short months after Barry had been diagnosed with cancer of the oesophagus and upper stomach the end was in sight. Both Barry and Steve had finally accepted that time had run out.

'Barry had never once talked about dying but on the way down the garden he turned to me and said, "Stavros, at least we are not going to die wondering." Perhaps that was his way of indicating that he knew he was going. It was a great summary of his life and I will never forget it.

'He was struggling to even walk but he was determined to make it down the to the hangar because he was so proud of his helicopter and was desperate to show me the new avionics. We both knew each other well enough to realise the end was very close although we never said it. I left the next day, after my final goodbye.

'Since I had arrived in Australia, Barry kept saying he wanted to take me up in the helicopter. He had just bought this Agusta 109C, which he had found in Switzerland and then shipped back to Australia where he had got it completely refurbished with some amazing gear. It was the helicopter of his dreams, down at the bottom of his garden in this specially built hangar. It was his ultimate toy and something Barry had worked to get all his life.

'For the first couple of days Barry said he would take me on the trip the next day, if he felt better. It was always "tomorrow, if I feel better". I knew we were never going on that flight. Perhaps each day he thought he was going to wake up feeling better. He had not been out of the house the whole time I had been there but finally that day we walked down the garden to his helicopter that he had always dreamed of having. He finally got it back there, completely refitted and it was the dog's knob.

'It was both inspiring and emotional seeing something that Barry had always aimed to get. Generally, when Barry set his sights on getting something he got it, one way or the other. By hook or by crook, he got it and there it was. The Agusta had been parked there for some considerable time because he was not well enough to fly it. I dare say his licence was revoked by then but Barry had conveniently forgotten to tell anyone.

'Even at this stage I don't know if Barry knew that he would never fly it again. He did not want to tell me that he wouldn't, and I certainly did not want to tell him.'

The bronzed and generally relaxed inhabitants of the MotoGP paddock were in high spirits in August 2002 as they arrived in Brno for the Czech Republic Grand Prix. The long-awaited five-week summer break was over for the 1500 inhabitants of this travelling circus that circumnavigates the world. It was now time to prepare for the tenth round of the sixteen-round world championship.

Talk of sun-kissed beaches and long hard nights in Ibiza was soon drowned out by the roar of racing engines being prepared for action once again. Then, suddenly, the atmosphere changed. It was a simple fax from Australia, from one of the sport's favourite sons, that changed the mood so dramatically. The message from Barry Sheene was stark, simple and typically upbeat:

> On 22 July I was diagnosed with cancer of the oesophagus and upper stomach. Although this is a complete pain in the arse, it happens to a lot of people, and a lot of people get over it. I will do everything within my power to beat this thing. My family and I would appreciate privacy at this time so I can get on with fighting this in my own way. At this time I feel there is nothing more for me to add and I thank all my well-wishers for their thoughts.

People gathered in groups to discuss the news. Older members of the paddock simply could not or did not want to believe it. After all this was Barry Sheene, who had survived everything the sport had thrown at him and come out the other end smiling; Barry who never let anything get in his way once he had set his mind to something; Barry who would constantly remind us that he was invincible, even eighteen years after his retirement from one of the toughest and most demanding of sports.

Old rivals who had battled wheel to wheel with Barry round the famous old Brno street track thirty years earlier were quickly on the phone to check out the authenticity of the fax. Thirteen-time world champion Angel Nieto of Spain was the first to speak to Barry, his great rival and special friend. Typically, the American Kenny Roberts started with a joke, telling Barry he was glad he had answered the phone because it meant he couldn't be dead, but, like everybody else, Kenny was concerned and wanted to help.

'It was a real shock and brought back memories of Barry drilling a hole in his helmet to have a smoke although I have no idea if that [smoking] was the cause. Barry told me he was going the natural route to find a cure because they could not tell him if he was going to make it if they operated on him. I immediately spoke to my doctor after phoning Barry and he said, "I would trust science before I would trust nature".'

In fact, Barry had given up smoking five years previously and completely changed tack, castigating anybody who dared to smoke a cigarette.

'He tried a few times to give up but finally made it five years before he died,' explains Stephanie. 'He put all his packets of Gitanes in a black plastic bag and hid them in the roof for an emergency but he never used them. They were still there when he died. Typically, Barry could not stand the sight of anybody smoking or even just a cigarette packet after he'd given up. He went mad when he found out that our daughter Sidonie was smoking.'

Brno is not only famous for grand prix motorcycle racing and the early production of the machine gun, but also for brewing some of the finest beer in the world. Late into that summer evening, long after the sun had dipped behind the trees on the hillsides that surround the new purpose-built circuit, plenty of the city's finest was consumed. Talk was only of Barry. Those 500cc world titles, the Daytona and Silverstone crashes and, as more alcohol was consumed, the blowing up of the Imatra toilets, the destruction of hire cars and, of course, the women.

Brno beer or not, one thing was certain. Barry would survive this next challenge in his life the same way he had survived all the others.

Just six weeks earlier Barry had stood outside the Sports Café in London joking with world champion Valentino Rossi. The young Italian laughed with the man who had won that same 500cc championship twenty-five long years before. Four days later the pair of them would be performing at Donington Park, Rossi riding a Honda

to defend his lead in the new MotoGP world championship and
Barry a Norton in the Classic event. Both were to win their respec-
tive contests.

Even though he had retired eighteen years before, Barry's presence at the British Grand Prix preview event brought the media
flocking. Pictures of Barry, who had raced against Valentino's long-
haired father Graziano, and the new world champion filled the
sports pages the next day. A twenty-nine-year age gap made no difference. The two champions had great respect for each other and
the same insatiable appetite for life away from the track.

Despite the smiles, all was not well. As we watched Valentino
leave on a giant Honda Gold Wing machine en route to a public
appearance in Leicester Square, Barry told me he had had diffi-
cultly swallowing his food for the last couple of months. He would
see the doctor when he returned to Australia the following week.

A routine morning weigh-in on his electronic scales confirmed
Barry's worst fears, as Stephanie recalls.

'Barry would weigh himself every morning, and one morning
after he had got back from England he got on the scales and realised
something was wrong because he had lost so much weight. Barry
went to the doctor that morning and he immediately sent him to
a gastroenterologist.

'Barry was a hypochondriac, always telling me how he felt physically and now he was having difficulty swallowing his food. He
started chewing it whereas before he was a gulper, always wolfing it
down. He was also drinking a lot of water. It got worse when he
came back from the British Grand Prix at Donington Park.

'Earlier in the year he went to Mexico to look at a helicopter and
when he returned he said he did not feel well. You know men,
when they have a cold they tell you it's full-blown flu and can't get
out of bed. Of course, Barry would not ring the doctor and the next
day he was fine, but I was a little scared. It was strange that he
never checked out the swallowing problem earlier. It was as if sub-
consciously he knew that something was wrong.'

On 22 July 2002, Stephanie drove Barry to a hospital in Surfers Paradise. It's a day she will never forget.

'I took him to the hospital and Barry told me he would ring me on my mobile when he wanted picking up. I thought it was odd when the hospital rang asking me to come in.

'When I arrived Barry was sitting there as white as a sheet, giving blood. We went into the specialist's office who simply said to Barry, "You've got cancer, mate." He did a drawing to show us exactly where the cancer was. I burst into tears and Barry just sat there in complete shock.

'We went home. Barry got upset that night and got a lot of emotions out of the way, and then asked, "What's for dinner?"'

A month before he sent out the fax to Brno, Barry told his family and close friends of the diagnosis. It's a situation that everyone dreads.

Three times he phoned his sister Maggie before he could actually disclose the reason for the call.

'"I've got something to tell you, Maggie," he said. "It's not about Dad, Dad's fine." Then he told me about the cancer and also admitted he had phoned me two previous times to tell me but just could not force himself to say it.

'He went back to Australia after the British Grand Prix and he phoned up one day, we chatted and then he rang off. Two days later Barry rang again. My daughter Paula answered the phone, had a chat with him and I then spoke to him and he rang off. He rang again for the third time that week and my husband Paul answered. He talked with Barry for a while and then called upstairs that Barry was on the phone. I joked with Barry that it was the third time in a week that he had phoned while normally he called about once a fortnight. Then he just blurted it out.

'I was absolutely gobsmacked and just didn't know what to say. It was horrendous and could not be true because I thought that Barry was invincible. He was like my security blanket. By this time we were really big mates and I knew if I had any problems he would help sort them out. If I wanted to get away I could always go there.

'I thought, this will not affect him; he will get over it. I was convinced he would get over it. After all, he got over everything else. People said he would never walk again after the Silverstone crash, let alone ride a bike again. He did all that and so cancer was not going to kill him. I never had a doubt in my mind that he would get rid of it. I think he believed that as well.'

Barry and his sister Maggie had not always got on. After their parents moved to Australia to live with Barry and Stephanie, they fell out and did not speak for a couple of years. However, that was all in the past and long forgotten. Barry and Maggie were closer than they had ever been and enjoyed some very special moments together before Barry's torment began.

'We had had such a fun year. I had been out in Australia since about February until April. Barry and I flew back to England together when he came over to help promote the North West 200 race in Northern Ireland.

'Barry, Stavros, myself and a pilot nicknamed Large by Barry went to Northern Ireland in a helicopter we had borrowed. Barry flew it with Large in the co-pilot's seat with Stavros, who had his fake teeth and lifejacket on, and me giggling all the way in the back. They kept telling us off for making too much noise. We had two or three days there laughing a lot.

'While I had been in Australia, Barry had desperately been trying to find this particular helicopter – an Agusta 109. He had made phone calls all over the world and even been to see a couple that were not good enough or not the right thing. Just before we flew back to England, somebody contacted him and told him they had found one in Switzerland. Pictures and details came through and it was the perfect helicopter for Barry.

'After the North West he had to fly back to Australia because he had a commitment for Channel Ten and he planned to fly back a week later and then go to Switzerland. We had heard so much about this helicopter because he would sit there every night and go on and on. We would tell him to shut up about bloody helicopters. When

he actually found this one we were relieved. I told him if this is the
one I had better come with him because I had heard so much about
it.

'I met Barry and Large at Gatwick at five o'clock one morning
and we flew to Zurich where we got picked up and taken to a little
airport. The weather was horrendous, with the cloud base just above
your eyebrows, but there in front of us was this perfect, beautiful
helicopter. It was so nice to be with Barry the first time he saw it
because it really was something very special.

'We had to wait at the tiny airport for the weather to lift but
finally the clouds cleared and there was a window in the weather.
We got in the helicopter, which was just beautiful, and took off over
Zurich and then flew over Basel as the weather cleared. We had a
fabulous flight home. We stopped in Reims to refuel and it was
bright sunshine and blue skies all the way.

'We dropped Large off somewhere and just Barry and I flew
together over London to Biggin Hill. It was wonderful and my great
memory of Barry is that fabulous flight together up the Thames and
over the London Eye. I try not to think about when he was ill, but
of our day together before he had been diagnosed.'

A month earlier Barry had told Maggie about his problems swallowing food and she had also noticed her brother was losing weight.

'When I had been in Australia earlier in the year Barry had been
complaining about food. The first sign to him that something was
wrong after he had the problems with swallowing was that he
started to lose weight. Barry was very conscious of how he looked.
He used to moan about having those little fat bits on his sides that
hung over his jeans. Suddenly they disappeared and he was not
doing anything to actually lose weight. That was the start of it.'

However, it was her son Scott who noticed the biggest difference,
when he met up with his uncle at the British Grand Prix.

'Scott had not seen him for a long time and when he saw Barry at
Donington Park he rang me and asked what was wrong with him. I
told him nothing, but he insisted that he did not look very well.

Scott could see the difference whereas people like me, who had seen Barry regularly, could not.'

Steve Parrish had noticed that Barry was drinking huge quantities of water, but when the news was delivered in a routine morning call from Barry in Australia it came like a bolt out of the blue.

'I just can't imagine how it must be when the doctor tells you you've got cancer. Barry just simply said, "You are not going to bloody believe this but I've been diagnosed with cancer." At first you think they're joking, but you soon realise that somebody does not joke about things like that. Barry often rang in the morning – his evening – for a chat. He had been to my office at Whittingdon Farm in Ashwell many times to pick me up in his helicopter and now I was sitting there being told my best mate had cancer.

'Not so long before this I realised there was something wrong when he was flying us by helicopter to Ireland. He was drinking so much water and kept telling me it was because he lived in Australia that he was dehydrating so quickly and needed lots of water but it was an obscene amount. He drank about two litres of water on just that short trip to Ireland. Something was not right there.'

Despite the gravity of the situation Steve, like all of us, was convinced Barry would find a way of beating the illness. This was Mr Fix-It, and if Barry said he would beat cancer we had to believe him.

'The thing about Barry was he was so positive about everything. At that point he was incredibly positive – as I'm sure everybody is – but he was more so than anybody else: "I'm stronger and tougher than any stupid disease. I've been through my life doing all sorts of silly things and I'm not going to let some stupid disease get me." I suspect that would be the way the majority of people would take it.

'Barry was Mr Fix-It for me and for hundreds of other people. If you had a problem and couldn't sort it, you would phone Barry and he generally could. For him not to be able to fix something was unheard of. He had enough money to research anything and more contacts than anybody could ever believe. Initially, I thought, if anybody in the world is going to fight this, it's going to be Barry.'

Back home in Australia Barry and Stephanie still had to perform the toughest task of them all. While phone calls to friends and loved ones back in England were hard enough, telling their children, Sidonie and Freddie, that their father had been diagnosed with cancer proved the most painful. Stephanie remembers only too well.

'At first we told nobody about the diagnosis. The kids were away at boarding school. We brought them home and told them, which was very upsetting for us both. Barry just told them what the specialist had told us, and it was truly horrible.

'The specialist explained that Barry had a maximum of eighteen months to live unless he had what sounded like an awful operation. It would be a nine-hour operation on his stomach and oesophagus followed by chemotherapy and radiotherapy. He would not be able to lie down or eat properly afterwards and Barry thought, what is the point? However, after we went to every specialist in Brisbane, eventually Barry decided to have the operation.'

Barry was no stranger to long operations with painful periods of recovery following his crashes at Daytona and Silverstone all those years ago. This was different, but after much soul-searching he decided to go ahead. Then a passing comment by a nurse when he arrived at the hospital with Stephanie changed his mind for good.

'We went to the hospital and Barry told the nurse that he hated doctors. She told him he was going to see plenty of them. Barry said, "I'm not. Fuck that – no operation," and went to the local health food shop and bought a book, *How to Beat Cancer*.

'It was a very stressful time but later we found out that the cancer had spread and an operation would have made no difference.'

Barry tackled cancer in the only way he knew. Finding out as much as possible about the subject, then using every contact and following up every lead had been a proven formula for his first fifty-two years. Why not tackle the biggest challenge of a very challenging life applying those same successful principles?

Friends like Steve Parrish were also on the case: 'When you find out what it is, you start asking questions. You realise that you know other people that have got it. Like Barry, I started researching lots of things. I had another friend, not a close friend, who had similar cancer to Barry and he's still alive to this day.

'His name is Stuart Page and he lives in Lincolnshire. He took the opposite route to Barry and had the operation straight away. They took away the whole of his throat and oesophagus and replaced it with a carbon fibre tube. I got Barry to talk to him, but Barry still opted to go the alternative, natural route. In hindsight perhaps Barry should have had the operation. It's impossible to say if it would have fixed him because the odds of recovery are very small because it's one of the most virulent forms of cancer you can get.

'If your mate's in trouble you try to be there. I was talking to everybody about cancer. People from all over the world used to ring me and say they could cure him. I don't know how they got hold of my number and I didn't know if they were crackpots or genuine. I could not take up every single offer. There was one guy who only wanted the payment of the flights to Australia and he could fix him. There were hundreds of people thinking of him at the time and every one of them had a cure.

'Everyone knows someone that can fix you and his phone and fax were non-stop with people offering this and offering that. It must have been hugely confusing for both him and Stephanie. Barry was not a person who took advice from other people. He gave information and advice but he didn't often take a lot. I just can't imagine what was going through his mind. I can only presume that something changes in your mind and your body to keep you going. I was desperate to help and felt he should have had the operation. He knew that.'

After much research Barry decided to go down the Breuss diet route to fight the disease. Austrian Rudolf Breuss believed that starving cancerous cells of protein could cure the disease and that was good enough for the former world champion. For three weeks he survived on a concoction of raw mixed vegetables. What little body fat he had fell away and so did his faith in the treatment, as Stephanie recalls.

'The diet made him so miserable because he lost so much weight – around sixteen pounds in a very short time. One night he had had enough of raw vegetables and was back to the lamb chops.'

Despite the loss of weight Barry flew to England to compete in a Classic race at a very emotional Goodwood weekend in Sussex. Barry had promised his old friend the Earl of March that he would be there to compete in his hugely popular Revival meeting. Barry didn't make the long trip just to compete – he also intended to win.

The Revival meeting is very much a car-orientated event but there was not a dry eye in the house when Barry won the Classic motorcycle race riding the Manx Norton. Four wheels or two wheels, everybody had heard of Barry Sheene.

Barry met up with Steve and Maggie before flying home for more research and, hopefully, treatment. His sister was saddened by what she saw.

'We realised that things were getting pretty bad by October. He came over to Goodwood and you could see then that it was starting to take a hold on him, especially as he had lost so much weight.'

Typically, all Barry wanted to discuss with Steve was that Goodwood victory.

'I met up with him after Goodwood, just a couple of hours before he flew back to Australia. It was still very early on and he had just won the race. Barry was adamant that some stupid cancer was not going to get him: "Cancer is for normal people, it's not for me and anyway, my new lightness made the Norton faster."'

Support for Barry was pouring in from all over the world. Over twenty thousand messages of goodwill were posted on his website and hundreds of letters and faxes arrived at his home. Unfortunately, not one of those heartfelt messages contained what Barry really wanted, a cure.

Like so many others Kenny Roberts continued his search for

anything that would help his old rival. 'Barry asked me to get some drug from Mexico after he had researched it but he never actually came back to me for it.

'I found out about another treatment where you take all your blood out and replace it. It was relatively new and very expensive but when I called Barry to tell him about it I could never get through. I started to put two and two together then, that he was not as well as he had said he was. The wife of a guy I knew was diagnosed with cancer at about the same time as Barry. She had the treatment where they replace the blood but the cancer came back and she didn't make it. She was actually very good for a couple of years. I think that Barry was probably right, that the operation would not have done any more, but you never know.'

Barry knew that the Breuss diet had not worked and was scanning the world for a new solution. As always, Stephanie was at his side during this long, painful journey of discovery.

'After Barry had come home from Goodwood we flew off to Mexico. We ended up at a clinic that looked more like a vet's, in the middle of nowhere, and we just rolled in off the street with no appointment. The sign outside said, "God is our Director". They wanted ten thousand dollars up front so we left.

'When we got home a blood test revealed that things were getting worse. Barry was starting to get desperate and was asking, "Just what am I to do?"'

Barry was scared, very scared. He had never found himself in this situation before: with a problem that neither he nor somebody he knew could solve. Stephanie knew Barry was willing to try anything and take any chance, however bizarre, to find a solution.

'He even tried to find a cure from a witch doctor in the Malaysian jungle. He flew to Kuala Lumpur and then drove right into the middle of the jungle to meet the witch doctor. I don't think he did any good and we returned home with a supply of herbs that were disgusting. Barry even went to a faith healer before deciding to go to Perth for some very special treatment.'

Steve Parrish kept in constant touch with Barry by phone. At first their conversations contained plenty of laughter and determination, but as time elapsed and no cure was forthcoming the mood began to change.

'I guess for the first three months we were all convinced he was going to survive. It was only when it went on and on that doubt crept in, more probably from me than him.

'I used to speak to him regularly and it was around November time that the situation really began to bite with him. He had won the *Motor Cycle News* Lifetime Achievement Award and we got him live on the phone to the ceremony in Birmingham. At that point he was quite chirpy but Barry was also great at putting on an act. I know he wasn't right because I had been speaking to him earlier. By now we were all feeling quite helpless.'

A trip to Perth was really the last throw of the dice for Barry. British specialist Dr John Holt had devised a method that used a microwave-style treatment, bombarding his body once a day, five days a week, with ultra-high-frequency radio waves. Barry and Stephanie then had to wait two months before discovering the outcome.

Hopes of a miracle still prevailed but were shattered when Barry returned home for a blood test in January 2003. It was at that moment both Barry and Stephanie accepted that he was not going to win this battle.

'The blood test showed that the cancer had tripled and we knew that was it. They discovered another cancer in his abdomen. He was a typical man and would never ask the doctor questions but the nurse told me, "You realise that Barry will not see Easter?" The doctor later confirmed it could be about six weeks.'

Stephanie and Barry kept the dreadful news from everybody. Nobody back in Europe realised just how quickly time was running out, although Steve picked up the signs in his phone conversations with Barry.

'The turning point was when he went to Perth and had three

weeks of microwave treatment. It was almost the last resort – a big effort – and he was convinced that it was going to fix him. I was constantly getting phone calls from him and I remember the different tone in his voice when he told me it hadn't worked. I think that was the time he thought, oh fuck, and it was also the point for him to go down the other route, as his chosen path had not worked. However, he didn't give up until a week or two before he died.'

The most successful grand prix rider of all time, Italian Giacomo Agostini, was one of the first to discover that Barry was so very ill. When his old friend and rival turned down the offer to ride one of the Italian's magnificent championship-winning MV Agusta machines in a Classic race, the fifteen-time world champion realised that all was not well.

'We had a Classic meeting on Phillip Island in Australia and I knew that Barry was sick. I asked if he would come and he said, "OK, no problem." I told him that if he came I would let him ride my MV Agusta and he thought that was fantastic. When I arrived at Phillip Island he was not there and I phoned him. He told me he was not so good and it was a long way to fly by helicopter. I said, "OK Barry, and I'm sorry." On the Monday when I arrived at Melbourne airport on the way back in Europe I called him to say hello. He said to me that he was very bad but I told him he was still young. "No," he said, "I don't think I have a long life," and after two months I got the very bad news.'

In many ways the charismatic Agostini paved the way for Barry in grand prix racing and far beyond. Not only did he win those fifteen world titles but he also brought a new dimension to the sport racetrack. His good looks and charm secured a celebrity lifestyle never previously experienced by grand prix riders. Like Barry he commanded adulation long after his retirement.

Both Ago and Barry had seemed content with life after grand prix racing when they met at the British Grand Prix in July 2001. The Italian had no inkling of what was round the corner.

'I saw Barry the year before at Donington and he told me he had bought the new helicopter. He looked even younger and was smiling. He told me he flew every day around Surfers Paradise. He was up and really enjoying life but it was very quickly that he left us.'

Just six short months later all those dreams were shattered and Barry was fading fast. It was so distressing for Stephanie to witness the man she loved just withering away but there was nothing they could do to stop the dreadful disease spreading through his body.

'Barry started walking with a stick and would keep coughing up this dreadful black stuff into a bucket. One day I saw him looking at himself in the mirror in the loo. That moment he knew that death was in the air.

'Barry took to his bed and it was so awful seeing him torture himself. One evening he asked me to cook him a big fish but Barry knew he could only drink watery soup.'

For twenty-seven years Steve had watched Stephanie look after Barry. She was constantly at his beck and call, whether to record a lap time or to clean his visor during his racing days, or just to ensure they had the correct toothpaste in the bathroom. Barry issuing instructions was part and parcel of life with him.

'Stephanie was unbelievable and as strong as hell. She was never a fusser and as always Barry was telling her what to do up till the last few weeks. She was not a person to panic and, not being a doctor or nurse, she knew she was just someone who was there for him. She would ensure he got the right food and would travel with him as he tried to find the cure. It must bond you as a couple even more.

'Although Barry and Stephanie were close you would not call them a close family. The kids were going about as if everything was normal and there he was just withering away. What can you do, because all the sympathy and feelings in the world does not bring anybody back?

'It's bad enough to lose your best mate, but to lose your father and husband; you just can't imagine what it must be like to see him just fading away. You would rather see him run over.'

*

Back in Europe Barry's insistence that he was still winning the fight meant nobody, including his closest friends and family, knew just how ill he really was. It took a visit to Australia by an old friend of Barry's, photographers' agent Julian Seddon, in late January to alert both Steve and Maggie to the gravity of the situation.

'I had a phone call from Julian who said, "Stavros, for God's sake, get yourself down here, because if you don't get down here quickly you are not going to see Barry again." I was really shocked. When you just speak to someone on the phone you obviously don't know what they look like. I was seriously thinking that he had two or three years, but Barry died just six months after diagnosis.

'I literally phoned up, booked a flight and set off the next day. I didn't book a return because I didn't know when I was coming back.

'I took with me a special drinks mixture that Barry had asked for. It was a liquid he could actually swallow despite the problems with his throat. I got five or six of these drinks and put them in my bag. Of course, I tried to sneak them through customs but sure enough the dogs found them and I got such a bollocking. When I told them it was for Barry, though, they let me through with them. Let's be honest, it wasn't something dangerous like a raw steak or a dead stoat.'

Maggie received a similar distressing phone call from Julian: 'After Christmas I got a phone call from Barry's friend telling me to get out there soon. I arrived on 10 February after a horrible couple of weeks following the funerals of two great friends, Rod Quaife and Pat Mahoney. My son Scott flew out a couple of days later and brought a load of stuff out that a doctor had recommended. Scott stayed a couple of weeks and that was nice because he spent time with Barry, but he had to come home to start testing for the new racing season. We drove him to the airport and we knew that he did not want to go home because that was it. I didn't want my daughter to come out because I wanted her to remember Barry as he was. He took her out for her twenty-first birthday and bought her a watch that she never takes off. My daughter really has never forgiven Barry for not going down the conventional route. From day one she felt he should have had the operation which would have given him more of a chance.'

Steve had last seen Barry three months earlier when they met after his Goodwood success. Cancer had left its appalling mark as it continued its unremitting destruction of a body that had for so long seemed indestructible. Steve was totally unprepared.

'As I walked into the house there was this skeletal figure who looked more like his father Franco, to be honest. I hardly recognised him. Everything had dropped off him and there was just this big jaw and teeth. He had lost everything and looked like one of those desperate children in a famine.

'The shock was huge. Barry had changed so much in three months it was unbelievable and it was horrible to see.

'We were both very emotional beneath the surface. We were supposedly tough bike racers and I think we were covering for each other. I was not saying anything horrible or being emotional. I wanted Barry to think that I thought he was all right. Barry was probably thinking that he didn't want me to think that he was not all right. It resulted in a kind of stand-off situation.'

When son Freddie returned home from boarding school to see his bedridden father after a three-and-a-half week gap, he experienced the same shock. He told Stephanie it could not be his father and must be his grandfather Franco lying in the bed.

Barry was fading by the day and there was nothing anyone could do to prevent it. All they could do was make the final chapter of his life as comfortable and pain-free as possible.

If dying of such an appalling disease was not enough, cancer also throws up some ghastly side effects that can make those last few weeks an even bigger nightmare, especially for the sufferer but also for family, and friends such as Steve.

'Barry had this horrible disgusting fluid that was forming inside him. Apparently, if you damage your knee then you get fluid on your knee. If you are damaged in your guts you get fluid in there. They started draining him once every fortnight. He'd go into hospital and they would put a pipe in and drain it off. It got to the stage where every three days he was blown up like he was pregnant and that's when Julian called me. All he could eat were mashed up bits of vegetables, nothing nice. The worst thing was that he would ask me to fire up the barbecue and I would be out in the garden, cooking steaks for everybody while all he could have was a cup of something all mashed up.'

Steve drove Barry to the hospital in Surfers Paradise for the draining sessions. A brief conversation with a very straightforward nurse confirmed what Steve really knew. The end was very near.

'I used to go to hospital with him when he was being drained off. One day a nurse just came out to me sitting outside Barry's room and said, "You know he has not got many days left." I was shocked because she didn't know who I was and I was certainly not a member of the family. It was something I didn't want to hear. I knew it but I didn't want to hear it. Somebody actually saying it. My mate, the great and legendary Barry Sheene, was not going to last much longer. It was so cold and horrible that I found it very hard to take in.'

Time was running out for Barry but he still wanted Steve and his friends to have a good time, even if he could not be there himself. A chance visit by Australian world champion Mick Doohan soon turned into a premature wake.

'Mick came round to see Barry one day. I had been sitting with Barry all week and he told me to get out of the house for the evening. Mick flew me to Morton Island where former grand prix racer Daryl Beattie and a number of mates were staying. Everybody got thoroughly pissed and told stories about Barry. We had a wonderful evening. It was what I needed, the chance to get pissed and wake up feeling like shit the next day.'

Shortly after the wake Steve decided to go back to England. He felt that Barry should have just his close family around him when

he finally passed away. The time was approaching for the final goodbye after twenty-eight years of friendship and trust. It was a
moment that Steve will never forget.

'He was lying on his bed and sat up when I came in. I knew that
I was never going to see Barry again. It was extremely tearful. To
hug someone who was all skin and bone, which was not very nice
anyway, to say goodbye without any chance of seeing him another
time was very emotional. To say goodbye to someone, which you
never normally do without saying, see you another time, was a bit
like that *Fawlty Towers* thing, don't mention the war. What the hell
do you say instead?

'We both broke down and I remember a big hug and walking out
of the room. I walked straight into his sister Maggie who helped
console me. We drove up to the airport and I pretty much cried the
whole twenty-four hour flight home.

'It was the saddest time of my life. I then sat at home in England
waiting for the phone call because I knew it was not going to be
long.'

Barry had been asked by the Australian Grand Prix Corporation
to wave the chequered flag at the forthcoming Formula One grand
prix in Melbourne. Of course, he was never going to be well enough
to fulfil the task and Stephanie knew his own chequered flag
was being prepared. She was relieved that his dreadful suffering
was coming to a close.

'A nurse was coming every day and she was marvellous but Barry
was really bad just before the grand prix in Melbourne. He was
getting worse every day and really torturing himself. Freddie came
home from school on the Tuesday. Barry was throwing up this
dreadful black stuff all Wednesday night and he agreed the next day
that he should go to hospital.'

Barry left his beautiful Gold Coast home for the last time. It was
the penultimate lap of his life but the cockney boy with the glamorous wife still managed to retain his trademark sense of humour.

'Barry was so agitated but he could still be funny. When we

arrived at the hospital the nurse asked him if he was allergic to any-thing. He may have been drifting in and out of consciousness but he still managed to reply, "Yes I am and it's fuckin' cancer."'

On Monday 10 March 2003 Barry lost his final battle, surrounded by Stephanie and his family.

'Barry started breathing strangely and then died at two o'clock, surrounded by those who loved him and whom he loved. It was a great relief to us all after watching him torture himself. We were all there, Freddie, Sidonie, his dad Franco, sister Maggie and her hus-band Paul, my mum and of course me.'

Maggie was also relieved the suffering was finally over for her younger brother.

'His last few weeks were absolutely horrendous but we were all there for him and he died holding my hand.

'I don't want to remember those last few weeks of his life. I want to remember my flamboyant brother. I have a picture in my memory of us flying along the Thames with Barry at the controls of the helicopter. It's much nicer than the memory of him being so very sick.

'He was a larger-than-life character but when all was said and done he was still my little brother and always will be.'

It was a typically cold dark March morning when the phone rang in rural Hertfordshire that Monday. Steve knew who it was before he picked up the receiver. Stephanie told him the suffering was finally over for his best friend. 'In the end I was pleased to get the phone call because the worst part was seeing him going downhill so quickly. You wonder if there really is somebody up there when you see that happening to someone. It happened and I've certainly learnt from it but I certainly could have done without it.

'I had been waiting for the phone call for about two weeks because I knew it was not going to be long. The call from Steph came early on that Monday saying that Barry had slipped away. It was a godsend, to be honest, because I knew it was going to happen. The quicker it was the less embarrassing it was for Barry. He was embarrassed because he didn't like to get beaten. I do believe he's sitting up there thinking, I can't believe this thing that affects other people has got me.

'I remembered that walk down his garden to the helicopter and what he said: "If anybody asked, 'I wonder what that's like', we knew, because we'd done it. We probably did bigger, better and dafter things than most other people. There are not many things I've not done with Barry.'

Less than six months after that first fax another one from Australia arrived. Once again it was stark and straight to the point.

Barry Sheene, Britain's 500cc motorcycle world champion in 1976 and 1977, who has been a resident in Australia for many years, died today after a brave battle against cancer. Sheene, aged fifty-two, passed away in hospital on Queensland's Gold Coast at about two o'clock. Queensland time. He is survived by his wife Stephanie, daughter Sidonie (eighteen) and son Freddie (fourteen). A private family funeral will be held later this week.

Cancer had finally claimed another victim. Barry had so much to look forward to but the dreadful disease makes no concessions, as Stephanie knows.

'Barry was so desperate not to go. He was not ready to go. He had everything he had worked for all his life. His family, the helicopter of his dreams and he need never have worked again if he didn't want to. He was snatched away and it was so grossly unfair.'

THE BEGINNING

The heavy curtains at the Royal Opera House pulled apart with just the faintest hint of a swish. The well-dressed audience hushed expectantly as the orchestra struck up the first chords of a melodrama of love, jealousy and murder. Watching from the wings, a spotty teenager prepared to make his debut. In sharp contrast to the stage upon which he would later become famous, this was the hallowed surroundings of the Royal Opera House in the heart of London.

Halfway through the first scene of Puccini's opera, *Tosca*, Barry Stephen Frank Sheene stepped into the spotlight for the first time in his life. For a week he shared the stage with opera legends Maria Callas and Tito Gobbi. While the location and fellow stars gave little indication of what lay ahead for Barry, he was in many ways perfect for the part.

Barry and his older sister Maggie went to school in Trafalgar Square, at St Martin-in-the-Fields. One day in the playground Barry and another pupil were having a dispute, involving the usual bout of fisticuffs. A woman peering over the wall watched the action with interest. She then approached the two boys to ask if they enjoyed fighting and if they could sing. Barry quickly turned the situation to his advantage, spotting an opportunity to miss some of the lessons he despised with such passion.

Yes to both questions came quickly from the school-hating youngster and, after an audition, the part of a singing and fighting hooligan was secured. Maggie knew the casting director had got it right.

'It was perfect casting and they certainly found the little hooligan they were looking for. The playground of the school was attached to the large St Martin-in-the-Fields church where, as always, Barry was caught fighting – by the lady who then organised the audition. They got permission from the headmaster and Mum and Dad, for Barry to make his first public appearance.'

Barry had been born into a very different community to the Royal Opera House, but both had Royal in the title.

As its resident engineer, the workshop of the Royal College of Surgeons, situated in Queen's Square, just off Gray's Inn Road in central London, was Frank Sheene's kingdom. Full of the equipment needed to keep the surgeons and students up and running, it also seemed to contain a great many bits and pieces from racing motorcycles. Scattered amongst the medical paraphernalia the names of Itom and Bultaco must have seemed more than a little out of place.

It suited Frank and his wife Iris perfectly. A four-bedroom flat and the all-important workshop came with the job. In the daytime Frank would keep the wheels of the hospital turning, while in the evenings and at weekends he kept the wheels turning for his great passion in life – racing motorcycles.

Frank and his brother Arthur were well-known figures on the national motorcycle-racing scene. Arthur was a speedway rider at Coventry at the height of the sport's post-war popularity when massive crowds packed stadiums throughout the country to watch their leather-clad heroes battle it out on dusty shale with the familiar smell of Castrol R oil in the air.

Frank was a road racer, preferring the tarmac to the shale. He had raced around the legendary Brooklands banking before the war and when hostilities ceased he competed with moderate success at circuits throughout the country, including the 37.7-mile mountain circuit on the Isle of Man. Frank loved the thrill of competing, but his great passion was not controlling the throttle but working out how to get the machinery to go faster than that of anybody else.

British-built machines such as Norton, AJS Triumph and BSA bolstered their impressive sales by dominating the racetracks of Britain. Frank's ability to coax that little bit extra out of the single-cylinder engines made him very popular with the young men seeking their fame and fortune on two wheels.

However, it was with the smaller two-stroke machines that Frank was earning a reputation as a master tuner of engines. Meticulous preparation plus a little bit of workshop improvisation made Sheene-tuned engines a must for budding stars. Little 50cc Itom machines, which raced round cycle tracks such as Herne Hill, plus the 125 and 250cc Spanish Bultacos, soon became race winners with Frank's magic touch.

Life in the Sheene household in this little corner of central London was busy to say the least. Frank worked for the hospital in the day, on the bikes during the evening and was away at weekends administering tender loving care to his beloved engines at race circuits throughout the country. Iris worked as a housekeeper at the College. Their daughter Margaret was born in 1945 and was joined by Barry at eight fifty-five in the evening on Monday 11 September 1950. Frank was overjoyed to have a son who he hoped would one day share his passion for motorcycle racing and engineering while Iris was delighted to produce a son for Frank and a brother for Margaret. The five-and-a-half-year-old daughter soon discovered that having a younger brother was no fun at all and, in the case of Barry, was an absolute nightmare.

To the day he died Barry hated authority. Being told what to do by somebody was like a red rag to a bull. His absolute refusal to accept anybody else's point of view started from his very early days in the pram. Living with Barry as he took his first steps in the world was not a pleasant experience for Maggie.

'He was a little shit, actually. I was five-and-a-half years older than him and was the little princess, Daddy's blue-eyed girl. Then suddenly this new baby arrived. He soon became the blue-eyed boy but he was so naughty and he never did get over telling lies. One day he came in and said, "fuck off" to Mum. She asked him where he had learnt such a word and his immediate reply was, "from Margaret".'

In his defence, Barry had a tough time in the first few years of his life. Chronic eczema made days and especially nights a nightmare of itching and calamine lotion. His ability to overcome such adversity was later shown after the accidents at Daytona and Silverstone.

Another one of Barry's great strengths was to turn any form of adversity to his own advantage. This was a skill he had nurtured barely after parting from nappies for the last time.

'Barry was a bit sickly. He developed eczema when he was just a few weeks old and he learned at a very early age how to get things done that he wanted. He never got over that. To the day he died he was getting his own way, although obviously not completely. Barry would say jump to Mum and Dad and they would say, how high? But later on he was very good to them.

'He would hold Mum to ransom. If we were out somewhere and he wanted something but Mum said no, Barry would reply that if he didn't get what he wanted he would say the fuck word. Needless to say he got everything that he wanted.'

To Frank's delight, dungaree-clad Barry took time off from upsetting his sister to walk round the workshop, spanner in hand. The youngster would soon have his hands on anything mechanical, although one such excursion into the unknown almost cost him the ultimate price. Maggie can still remember her brother's screams after an investigation into the workings of a clockwork train went horribly wrong.

'It was one of those wind-up clockwork trains which had the big coil that unwound. Barry had taken it to pieces and was playing with it in the bath. It was wound up and went towards him and caught a certain part of his anatomy well and truly. We had to rush him to the hospital, which, fortunately, was just across the road, but the doctor didn't know what to do. The more they tried to loosen it, the more the spring tightened and in the end my dad snatched a pair of bone-cutters and cut it free. It was a wonder that he had anything left because it was caught right on the end of his little spring carrot. You could have heard him screaming on the other side of London.'

School soon beckoned for the young Sheene but it was not a happy experience for either master or pupil, as Maggie recalls.

'He hated school. It was the authority thing. Barry never liked being told that he could not do something and that was what school was about. You were told you are not allowed to do this and you are not allowed to do that and Barry rebelled. He was wilful. Very naughty, always getting into trouble and being told off.

'I really didn't like him when we were younger. We used to fight. You know, proper fights and I used to throw things at him. I threw a tray once and cut his head open and also knocked his big toenail off after a fight round a door. He kicked me one day and I had to go to hospital after developing a blood clot. I won that one in the end, because I had time off school but he still had to go.'

A rebel at school and a 'little shit' at home, and if that was not bad enough eczema was replaced by chronic asthma. The condition was not helped by the fact that Barry discovered the 'delights' of smoking when just nine years old. A crafty fag behind the bicycle shed became a regular part of school life, as did the regular canings he received from the exasperated headmaster when caught with smoke on his breath.

This was the 1950s and the dire warnings about the dangers of smoking were a long way off. Both Iris and Frank had a very liberal attitude to his smoking at home, which was soon accepted despite worries about his asthma.

Even an alcohol-fuelled prank, which resulted in Barry's school-boy victim needing his stomach pumped after sampling the contents of Franco's drinks cabinet, was followed by little more than a telling-off from his parents. The headmaster, as you can imagine, was not so amused.

Barry soon developed a 'system' in which the threat of an asthma attack enabled him to get his own way. He avoided having to participate in team sports that he hated, such as rugby and football, by organising a string of hospital appointments. The young Sheene 'acquired' doctor's appointment cards from the desk at the asthma clinic at the local hospital. A friend's father filled in some fictitious appointments, confirmed by a typically illegible doctor's signature, and Barry was free to indulge in more pleasurable pastimes than lessons or sport, even when the asthma attacks had long disappeared.

Frank was busy travelling the country to keep his ever-increasing stable of riders and machines fully serviced. He would usually be accompanied by an inquisitive and very pushy young Barry. His constant questions and cheek were regarded more as an irritant by certain riders, including eight-time world champion Phil Read who was riding for Frank and who later became a friend, an opponent and finally a bitter rival of Barry.

'Barry was a nightmare when I first met him in 1961, after his father asked me to ride one of his Bultacos. He was a cheeky cockney kid who always used to be in the garage saying, "What's this? What's that?" We used to give him half a crown to fuck off. I rode Franco's 125cc Bultaco that he thought was the quickest thing.

'I won the 350cc junior race at the TT races in the Isle of Man and went into the finishing enclosure where I met my mum – I didn't know that she was there. I went to have my picture taken with her and Barry, who was about twelve at the time, put his arm round my shoulder to ensure he also got in the pictures. That's how cheeky he was.'

The legendary races on the dangerous, demanding and extremely long TT mountain circuit on the Isle of Man were the highlight of the motorcycle-racing calendar in Britain. The British rounds of the world championship were staged there in the first week of June. Five years before his limelight-pinching picture with Phil Read, Barry had travelled there with the family. This time there had been no photographs for the youngster whose asthma wasn't helped by the damp misty climate of the island.

Maggie was there when her brother was laid low by a particularly painful attack which resulted in a visit to the hospital more famous for treating injured riders and motorcycle riding spectators.

'We went to the Isle of Man for the TT races when he was very young and he ended up in an oxygen tent in Noble's Hospital for three days. The climate really did not suit him.' Neither did the road circuit, but more of that later.

It was only a matter of time before Frank assembled a small motorcycle for his young son to tear around the yard at the back of the College. Two wheels were soon followed by four and driving lessons for Maggie.

'Dad made Barry a little bike when he was six years old. He used to ride in the back yard at Queen's Square. Later he got a little old car, an Austin, I think. It had a crash gearbox and Barry soon learned how to get this thing into gear and drive from one end of the yard to the other and he showed me how to do it as well. He actually taught me how to drive a car.'

Ironically, soon after mastering the art of two wheels with an engine Barry fell off his pushbike and broke his arm, proudly showing off the plaster cast to his classmates.

His weekends consisted of family outings to racetracks throughout Britain. Mum and Maggie made the sandwiches and the tea, Frank fettled the engines and Barry had the time of his life riding round the paddock on a small Triumph motorcycle and getting involved with matters that were usually none of his business. He had his nose in every engine and was already learning his trade of wheeling and dealing to keep one step ahead of authority and the opposition.

When he was fourteen years old he broadened his horizons by travelling to the continent for two grands prix, working as a mechanic and gofer for friend of the family, the American Tony Woodman. Frank duly signed the obligatory letter to the relieved school, stuck fifteen pounds in his son's back pocket and wished him well. Barry was away from home for over a month at the Austrian and German grands prix, sleeping in the back of a van, working on Woodman's Matchless and AJS bikes and having the time of his life.

Returning to England, and especially school, made the young teenager even more rebellious and certainly more determined to leave school as soon as possible. The need for cash to finance weekend outings to the Empire Ballroom in Leicester Square was also becoming a priority. Barry had discovered that dancing was an ideal way to meet and then impress the opposite sex. In the same year he travelled abroad with Tony Woodman, he reported that he had lost his virginity over a snooker table in the crypt of a church.

The problem for his mum and dad was what Barry was going to do when he left school. The clues were in his knowledge of the internal combustion engine that was remarkable for a fifteen-year-old. He was also a very accomplished motorcycle rider who helped his dad run in engines on the Spanish Bultaco racing machines which he had started importing. He had been to Spain to visit the Bultaco factory and already displayed an ability to learn foreign languages very quickly, especially if girls or cigarettes were involved.

Those trips to Spain also brought about his father Frank being called 'Franco' by his son. Franco it has been ever since.

Despite his enjoyment of riding motorcycles Barry wasn't considering a serious racing career at this time. After his friend Woodman crashed at the North West 200 race on a road-based circuit in Ireland and was paralysed from the waist down, racing motorcycles for a living was certainly not on his agenda.

Instead, Barry embarked on a typical jumble of jobs to keep the cash flowing before finally realising that racing motorcycles, rather than just tuning their engines, could be a very lucrative business.

He worked in the spares department of the local Ford dealership and took his life in his hands riding a Franco-tuned 125cc BSA Bantam through the London traffic as a courier for an advertising agency. In search of more cash, Barry worked for a friend valeting cars at his West End garage before convincing the boss of a company that delivered antique furniture that he had an HGV driving licence.

Long-haired Barry was simply freewheeling along, discovering the delights of life as a teenager in the 1960s. Work was seen as a method to obtain the necessary finance for the pleasures of life, which included girls and at least thirty cigarettes a day.

Barry's seventeenth birthday came and went without a wheel of a racing motorcycle being turned in anger although he was still helping Franco run in the Bultacos, often at Brands Hatch, in the well-supported Wednesday afternoon practice sessions.

Word began to filter back to Franco that his son was looking more than useful in these test sessions. He was travelling as fast as or faster than some of the customers.

It was inevitable. In March 1968 Barry Sheene made his racing debut at Brands Hatch, riding one of his father's 125cc Bultacos. It was not a debut with a fairytale ending. The engine seized, throwing Barry over the handlebars. Typically, he refused medical help and against Franco's wishes went back out on the track to finish in third place in the 250cc race.

Just a week later Barry was back, full of confidence after his first podium finish. That confidence was turned into the first two wins of his distinguished career. Maggie remembers his first win well.

'I didn't go to the meeting where he won his first race because Mum was in hospital to have an operation on her feet. She was in Charing Cross hospital and after the race at Brands Barry and Dad came straight there and dumped the winner's laurels on her bed.'

The track beckoned the young Sheene but he initially decided to continue looking after motorcycles rather than racing them himself. Looking back, it appears a strange decision and the forthcoming summer months helped him decide to take up racing.

Three years previously Barry had enjoyed the grand prix lifestyle with Tony Woodman. He now decided to extend the experience with a three-month trip to Scandinavia, Austria, Germany and Holland, working on the Bultacos of racer Lewis Young.

Grand prix racing in the late 1960s was tough. The circuits were dangerous, officials had a very different attitude to safety compared to the present day and money for the riders was only obtained after much wrangling. Barry slept in the van, lost weight and gained plenty of experience that would stand him in such good stead in years to come.

Those months on the road were the turning point. Barry returned home focused on what he wanted to do – race motorcycles.

On his return from Europe Barry resumed his racing career on Franco's Bultacos at club meetings. In 1969 he embarked on a full-time career with a little bit of work parking cars in the Olympia car park to keep the funds rolling in. Barry was determined to pay his way. His father may have had access to some very decent machinery and had passed on his knowledge of how to make them go faster but the family did not have the resources to keep pouring money into the ever-deepening pit of supporting a racing team.

Barry had found a purpose in life. He had three Bultaco machines immaculately prepared by himself and Franco plus, of course, the obligatory transit van that served as transport, caravan and a place to entertain the girls. His performances away from the van and out on the track were also being noticed, especially by the motorcycle press.

Mick Woollett was not only sports editor of *Motorcycling* magazine but also a passenger in the world sidecar championship. He had met Barry the previous year when he was working for Lewis Young.

'Everyone was very pleased to have a gofer because the riders were busy working on their own bikes. While they were doing the serious work it was very handy to have an assistant to do the lesser tasks like collecting the tyres or oil, cleaning the van and cooking the lunch.

'It was what we were used to in those days. Everybody would travel around in vans and nobody would stay in a hotel. Barry was a natural mechanic, up to a point, and had an aptitude for just about everything.

'As soon as Barry began to do well, we signed him up as this charismatic youngster to do a weekly column. I used to walk to the Royal College of Surgeons from Fleet Street to help with the writing. I would give him a few ideas and then ghost the column for him, not that Barry was ever short of something to say. Franco used to set up the bikes and generally look after him and Barry was always up for a laugh and would smoke, drink and obviously chase girls, which he did even more when he was successful.'

Travelling the length and breadth of Britain, often competing at three race meetings over a bank holiday weekend was the norm for the Sheene family. For Franco it was the perfect scenario, preparing race-winning machinery for his son to ride. Iris was happy if Franco and Barry were happy. Maggie often just went along for the ride because after their early disputes she now got on much better with her younger brother.

'I think Mum was all right about Barry going racing. Dad had wanted him to race from the moment he came out of the womb. I met and married somebody that I worked with when I was twenty. I moved out from home and Barry moved into my bigger bedroom and so he was glad to get rid of me. Unfortunately my marriage didn't last very long, but when I came back I was in the smaller bedroom. I didn't have many boyfriends and so there were not too many around for Barry to irritate.'

Sport, and motorcycle racing in particular, has a particularly nasty habit of stopping you in your tracks, just when you think you've got everything sorted. This happened to Barry on Saturday 12 July 1969, when he seriously considered stopping a career that had barely started.

Bill Ivy had been a frequent visitor to Queen's Court long before he became a grand prix star and 125cc world champion. The Kent-based rider cut his teeth on the 50cc Itoms built and prepared by Franco before seeking world championship glory with Yamaha. With his great friend and fellow world champion Mike Hailwood, he partied his way through first the paddocks of Britain and then the world. In every way the pair were the role models for young Barry. On the track they were the toughest professionals you would want to meet but they were also serious partygoers once the leathers were off.

Like Hailwood, Ivy was turning his considerable talent to car racing but was struggling financially. Consequently, he agreed with the Czechoslovakian Jawa factory to race their fast but unreliable 350cc machine at the East German Grand Prix at the Sachsenring road circuit. In practice the Jawa seized and Bill Ivy was killed when his helmet came off in the crash.

News of his death was relayed to Barry in the paddock at Brands Hatch. He was devastated. When he got home Maggie recalls a reminder of his painful childhood returned, brought on by his considerable grief.

'Barry was eighteen when he was told at Brands that Bill had been killed. He was devastated and when he got home he had a really bad asthma attack. It was the last time Barry had an attack, but it was brought on because he was good friends with Bill. I think Barry modelled himself on Bill and Mike Hailwood. They used to have really nice flats in Heston and Barry certainly liked the lifestyle they were leading.'

It was a massive setback to the young Sheene, but it taught him how to deal with death, which was an accepted part of the racing scene in those dangerous days.

Barry decided to continue racing and finished second behind grand prix regular Chas Mortimer in the 125cc British championship. He started the 1970 season with three Bultacos, which he was sure would give him a real chance of going one better and actually winning a British title. His private life had settled down with the arrival of a certain elegant blonde, Lesley Shepherd, who he had met eighteen months earlier.

Life on and off the track was good and the opportunity to purchase a former 125cc Suzuki grand prix machine was an opportunity not to be missed. The former works Suzuki rider Stuart Graham had somehow managed to hang on to the machine and offered it for sale at two thousand pounds. Barry's savings plus a loan from Franco, which was repaid, bought him a bike he knew could open doors way beyond the British stage.

He won the 125cc British championship from Mortimer but, more important, he broadened his horizons by riding on foreign soil for the first time. Ironically, it was a part of the world he knew well that provided Barry with his first taste of the big time. Franco and Barry had been to the Bultaco factory many times and were personal friends of the Bulto family and so it was no great surprise that it was the Spanish Grand Prix that provided the venue for Barry's grand prix debut.

Many years before, Barry had accompanied his father to the 2.355-mile tree-lined Montjuich Park circuit – since replaced by the Olympic Stadium in 1992 – to watch the famous twenty-four-hour race.

Barry warmed up for his grand prix debut by winning an international race in Spain. This was before the family arrived at the demanding and dangerous circuit for the final grand prix of the season and his first big confrontation with Angel Nieto. The Spanish glamour boy was, and still is, enjoying Sheene-style adulation after winning thirteen world titles before his retirement.

Just sixteen days after his twentieth birthday Barry burst on to the world championship scene with a stunning display. It certainly stunned Nieto and the patriotic Spanish crowd. Barry eventually finished second, just eight seconds adrift of the Spanish hero riding the Spanish Derbi machine, after twenty-seven gruelling laps. It was just the prelude to a battle for the ultimate crown that was to follow a year later, in 1971.

That result at the final grand prix of the season convinced Barry and Franco that the way ahead was a full-scale attack on the 125cc world championship even though it would cost a great deal of money to travel to the eleven rounds in Europe. Barry was not yet a big enough name to attract serious cash.

Once again it was back to the transit van, and now also the luxury of a caravan, but instead of Brands Hatch and Oulton Park it was long trips to Anderstorp, Imatra and the Sachsenring that were drinking up the diesel.

Derbi had been so impressed by his performance at Montjuich Park the previous year that they offered Barry a 250cc machine to ride in the grands prix. However, the machine was never reliable so Barry focused on the 125cc championship battle with Nieto. He supplemented his income and retained his popularity at home by returning as often as possible for international meetings.

It really was the classic David-and-Goliath battle for the 125cc world championship: the long-haired English youngster living in a caravan, versus the Spanish superhero who enjoyed all the trappings of a successful racing career, luxurious hotel rooms, mechanics and a different girl on his arm in every country. Although their lives off the track mirrored the gap between a factory rider and a privateer, Barry and Angel became great friends, even at the height of the championship battle. The Spanish legend regards it as a true friendship that lasted until Barry's death.

'Our friendship was forged in those 125cc days. The Derbi was probably a bit quicker than his Suzuki and that's why I was able to beat Barry. I became friendly with Barry's girlfriend and his family. Later I just remember things like his BSR 4 number plate on his Rolls-Royce and the fact he was so open, which was why he became friends with many of my friends back home in Spain.

'We always had a great time off the track. Because the circuits and the races were so dangerous in those days it was such a big relief that we were all still there on the Sunday night. It was like a big explosion of emotion. All the mechanics were just happy to have their riders still there. Barry was always in the middle of it.

'At one time I had a bit of a thing with a girl in the paddock who was the girlfriend of another rider. Barry decided to tell the other rider. When I arrived at the circuit Barry told me he had told him and I spent the whole time at the race crapping my pants thinking that he was going to get me. This really made Barry laugh, who thought it was brilliant.

'The first time I met him was at the Derbi factory when I was riding for the team. He came up to the factory in Barcelona with his dad and I already knew that he was involved with Bultaco. He turned into one of the best friends I ever had in the paddock and a fantastic guy, and a great world champion. He was the Valentino Rossi of his day and did incredible things for motorcycling and, in particular, English motorcycling.'

Barry put up a fantastic fight for the title, which would only be decided at the final grand prix of the season, at the dusty Jarama track on the outskirts of Madrid. He secured the first of his twenty-three grand prix victories with a memorable win at the fastest venue in grand prix racing, the awesome 8.761-mile Spa-Francorchamps road circuit in Belgium. Three weeks later he won again, on the Anderstorp airfield in Sweden, and really put the pressure on Nieto a week later. Over the dangerous tree-lined road circuit at Imatra on the Finnish side of the Russian border Barry was a comfortable winner of the 17-lap race, while Nieto retired with mechanical problems for the second grand prix in a row.

The pressure was on the Spanish hero but for Barry balancing the books was almost as important as winning that world title. To keep the diesel flowing into the transit Barry accepted an offer from the team manager of the Van Veen Kreidler team after a chance meeting in the toilets at Spa. Barry now had a ride in the team chasing the 50cc world championship with Dutch rider Jan de Vries.

Just a week before his 125cc triumph in Sweden Barry rode the tiny bike to victory in the pouring rain in the Czechoslovakian Grand Prix on the Brno road circuit. He is still the only rider to have won both 50 and 500cc grand prix races and, what's more, he went out later to finish third in the 125cc at Brno. That solitary 50cc victory started a sequence of three grand prix wins in the space of just three weeks.

Mick Woollett was there: 'There was probably quite a lot of money, at least to Barry, tied up with the Kreidler deal and so he rode in the 50cc race before the 125 event. He was trying to protect the lead that Jan de Vries had in the world championship. It was a remarkable achievement to win the first time he had ever raced the 50cc Kreidler and was a perfect illustration of his versatility. He had a natural ability and I'm a great believer in talented riders. Untalented riders can improve themselves but the talented ones are just talented from the word go, like Duke, Agostini, Saarinen and Hailwood.'

Chasing the world title they may have been but in addition to those fun and games off the track, Angel Nieto remembers that he and Barry were quite happy to let their antics spill on to the battlefield.

'During the 125cc race at the Dutch TT in Assen, Barry and I were leading by a massive distance and started slowing up, passing each other all the time. Finally, we stopped completely and started hitting each other, trying to make the other go first and Borje Jansson came past to take the lead. We then both set off after him, overtook him and I won the race from Barry.'

Even later in their careers when they were both world champions, the fun and games continued.

'The first time I ever rode a 500cc machine was at an international race at Jarama. Barry knew that all the fans had packed the circuit to watch me in action and that it was a really big story. I'd had trouble adjusting to the 500 in the first practice session, with the back wheel coming up all the time. Barry soon realised this and nodded to me to follow him in the race and then would slow down to allow me to pass to send the crowd wild. Barry would pass me again but every time he started to leave me behind he would slow down and let me pass again just to get the crowd going. He eventually passed me to win the race but I really thanked him at the end for being such a friend.'

Following a third place at Monza in Italy, where Nieto only finished second, the stage was set for the final showdown in Jarama but Barry arrived in Spain bashed and battered for the most important race of his career so far. He had damaged his wrist and ankle in a well-paid non-championship meeting on the roads at Hengelo in Holland and had then taken another pounding when he crashed at the Race of the Year meeting at Mallory Park back in England. Barry was diagnosed with nothing more than severe bruising but the injuries turned out to be far worse.

To honour his contract with Kreidler he rode in the 50cc race at Jarama. It was after that race that a rib popped out of his rib cage as he bent to take a drink of water. Barry knew he was in big trouble before the showdown. Typically he taped up the offending rib, gritted his teeth and went out to finish third with Nieto clinching victory and with it the title. Despite the pain Barry joined his great rival at the celebration party.

A later medical examination revealed that the local hospital for Mallory Park had missed the fact that Barry had suffered compression fractures to three vertebrae and five broken ribs in his accident there. It was probably better that he hadn't known that before the Jarama race. Once again it was something he never forgot. Barry always insisted he received the very best medical treatment and when he was in no fit state to ensure this was happening, those around followed his instructions.

Barry returned home to plan the future and let the injuries heal. He had had a great year including four grand prix wins and that second place in the 125cc world championship. All in all he had won thirty-eight races at home and abroad and was being hailed as a future world champion by the British press and public. Giacomo Agostini had recognised the talent of the young British star on a trip to race in Britain.

'I remember when he started in the 125s and I think the first time I saw him was probably at Brands Hatch. Quickly I realised he was a good rider because he was already winning and he was very smart and very aggressive.'

The lucrative non-championship race meetings in Britain not only brought some much needed cash into the pockets of the riders but gave British fans the opportunity to watch the world championship stars in action. Many of these riders had already turned their back on the British round of the world championship on the Isle of Man but were happy to take on the cream of British racing at the likes of Silverstone, Brands Hatch and Mallory Park.

Heroes of the track at that time included Jarno Saarinen of Finland and the multiple world champion and TT star Giacomo Agostini, who was riding the glorious-sounding MV Agusta in the John Player-sponsored meeting at Silverstone. Despite the excitement of watching Saarinen and Agostini in action, along with nine-time world champion Mike Hailwood, who was making his comeback, it was the black-leathered Barry who stole the show. In a fantastic 250cc race he took the lead on the last corner from the likes of world champion Rodney Gould, brother-in-law to be Paul Smart, and Saarinen. He won the 125cc race on the Suzuki and pushed Ago hard on his underpowered 500cc Suzuki in the two main races. It was a defining day for many British fans. It was the dawning of a new era heralding the end of the 1960s, which had been dominated by the four-strokes of Hailwood and Agostini.

However, not all the British fans took to the new kid on the block quite so quickly. It was not just the long hair, the white leathers and total lack of respect for authority that upset the die-hards but also Barry's refusal to race on the Isle of Man.

During that 125cc campaign Barry had been forced to venture back to the Isle of Man mountain circuit for the third round of the world championship. This time it was not asthma that was his downfall but a crash on the slow Quarter Bridge corner on the second lap. He vowed he would never return to the island, which many enthusiasts considered to be the spiritual home of British motorcycle racing, because the circuit was outdated and too dangerous. He kept the promise and, for some, he was never forgiven. Mick Woollett was not among them.

'Barry could ride anything and still holds the record for the fastest-ever grand prix lap at Spa-Francorchamps but he realised at that early age that the TT was just not worth the danger factor because if you made a mistake there you were likely to be killed. Who could blame him?'

Smart and aggressive Barry may have been, according to Agostini, but perhaps he was just a little bit too cocky for his own good at the start of the 1972 season. He felt he was ready to take on the world after Yamaha paid him to ride their machines in the 250 and 350cc world championships.

Barry had spent the latter part of the winter combining racing with a holiday in South Africa with Maggie and her new husband, racer Paul Smart. Paul had spent the last year travelling around Europe with Barry who fully approved of his sister's romance, as Maggie recalls.

'A friend of mine came to some British races to watch Barry. She thought Agostini was the best thing she had ever seen. She wanted to go to his next race, which was the Dutch TT at Assen. It was quite a big adventure for us then to go to Holland, especially as I only had a little Mini. I don't think she ever met up with Ago but I met Paul. He was riding in three classes that day. He crashed in the 250 and hurt his little finger in addition to plenty of cuts and bruises. I felt a bit sorry for him and the rest is history.

'Barry and Paul got on quite well. Paul and I got married on 31 December 1971. We didn't tell anybody, got married in the morning at Maidstone Registry office and then went to the bike show in the Horticultural Halls in London in the afternoon. We rushed up to London and one of the first people we bumped into was Barry. I told him we had got married and he ran round the bike show telling everybody.

'Barry and Paul had done a year of the grands prix together in

1971. They had a twelve-foot caravan and two transit vans. Needless to say, Barry convinced Paul that his transit was better for pulling the caravan. They had a mechanic each and so off they went, the four of them. By the end of the season the transits were still going, but only just, but the caravan was completely destroyed. Paul would come back to the caravan after a night in the paddock, only to find that Barry would have a couple of birds in his bed. The caravan was so small Barry and Paul had to share a bed. Barry would say, "Jump in Paul, there are two of them."'

Sadly, unreliable machinery plus a badly broken collarbone sustained in a crash at Imola brought Barry back to earth with a massive bump in 1972. He only finished on the grand prix rostrum once that year and his confidence subsided in a season of breakdowns, injuries and wrangles with Yamaha. His first season as a factory rider had proved to be a disaster.

It was back to the drawing board for Barry. He decided to move into the bigger and more dangerous classes of racing. It was a new beginning when he signed for Suzuki in 1973 to compete in the first FIM Formula 750 European Championship, riding one of their 180 mph-plus machines imported from the States. Unfortunately, although the speed was there the bike handled, in Barry's words, 'like an airport luggage trolley' but after fitting the engine into a local-built Seeley frame, a championship-winning campaign was on the cards.

The final race and title decider of the eight-round world championship came at Montjuich Park where three years earlier Barry had made such a sensational 125cc grand prix debut. A calculated second place to Australian John Dodds was enough to give Barry his first international championship title.

Back home he regained all the popularity he had lost the previous year by winning two major British titles and surviving two big crashes at Brands Hatch and Silverstone. His career was back on track and Barry was voted Man of the Year by the readers of *Motor Cycle News*.

Sadly his romance with Lesley had nearly run its course. Long periods apart, punctuated by stories of Barry's exploits while on the road, were to bring about their final separation.

Pastures new beckoned Barry, both on and off the racetrack.

GOOD OLD DAYS?

From the outside looking in, it appeared to be just about the perfect lifestyle. Travelling around Europe in the summer months racing 180 mph motorcycles with your mates in front of massive crowds followed by drinking, the odd fight and chasing the opposite sex seemed a pretty decent way of earning a living.

Rather like the children of the 1960s, who still remind us about their LSD-fuelled parties and the Summer of Love, motorcycle racing in the 1970s was definitely not what it seemed from the outside. Scrape the surface and a very different picture emerges, although it's only the passage of time that makes you realise just what a crazy existence it was.

Coping with the unnecessary waste of so many young lives, the greed and contempt of some of the organisers for both human life and dignity plus the pure adrenaline fix of racing such powerful projectiles on tracks which were public roads for the remaining fifty-one weeks of the year has left permanent scars on many.

This was the world of Barry Sheene. From that very first trip to Europe with Tony Woodman he quickly leant how to shape events to his advantage in a way that had never been witnessed before.

When Barry retired from racing in 1984 so much had changed. Those frighteningly dangerous road circuits had been erased from the world championship calendar, the organisers had seen their gross profits slashed dramatically, having been forced to pay all riders a proper wage, and the risk of death or serious injury had been greatly reduced by proper medical facilities and rider protection.

Without a doubt, Barry's influence on these changes was massive, if not always intentional. He was a vital member of the breakaway World Series movement in the late 1970s which never actually materialised but whose threat stormed through the corridors of power with such effect that riders got an instant pay rise of 300 per cent. He knew his presence at a race meeting could increase the size of the crowd by as many as twenty-five thousand and expected to be paid, often in a brown envelope, accordingly. He brought new sponsors into a sport that had previously only entertained the executives of oil companies and spark plug and tyre manufacturers.

Barry thrived on the wheeling and dealing necessary to achieve the best deal for himself. It was a dog-eat-dog world that suited the cockney scrapper who had honed his skills bunking off school and getting free admission to the local Palais all those years ago. In so many instances it was motorcycle racing which benefited as much as Barry Sheene. Sadly, we will never really discover just how much racing in those turbulent times scarred him. Unwittingly Barry, together with Steve Parrish, had very quickly developed an unwritten code of rules, as Steve recalls.

'More than twenty-five teammates and associates were killed while we were racing and Barry and I may have been the very best of friends but we never actually discussed people being killed. It was like a taboo subject, it happened but you did not discuss it. It was just one person less in the paddock and his place in the team or somebody else would soon take his sponsorship.

'We talked plenty about carburation jetting, gearing, birds and money, all the flash stuff in life, but never death because I suppose it could happen to us. I don't know how we managed to steer round it but we bloody well did.'

Going to funerals would also remind Barry and Steve about the forbidden subject and so they never went.

'Barry and I never went to funerals. When we heard somebody had been killed we would say he was pushing too hard or he was asking for it and that was the end of it. There were some people out there who I was convinced were going to die, like Chris Guy and Paul Lewis, who happily survived while others who you thought it would never happen to did die. You could not have met more sensible and steady guys than Dave Potter and John Newbold but their luck just ran out.

'I know it sounds horrible but we were not tactile, loving people when it came to racing and many other things. You just had to mention kids and the two of us could burst out crying but as my wife, who has since divorced me, said, racing motorcycles in that era made you a hard, horrible bastard. She was probably right but only in certain ways. I suppose when I was racing I imagined that one day I was going to wake up dead and so I was hard on myself. I didn't get too emotional about people dying because I didn't get involved. I just completely blanked it. Life went on and it made me a very hard, callous person. I coped with most things but not deaths and funerals and so they were never discussed.

'Barry was the only really close friend I had in those days but since I stopped racing I have many more friends, including those in racing, because they don't suddenly die. You would socialise with all the other riders, have a beer and a laugh with them, but you never allowed yourself to get too close to them. If you did you could have got hurt in a big way and it would have screwed your head up. Barry was such a pragmatic person. If you can do something about it, do it but if you can't, get on with something that you can. If something was a lost cause he would get on to the next cause.

'Although obviously we were not there, we felt it must have been like living through a war. You set off in a Lancaster with some of your mates and some didn't come back. We were so passionate about our jobs we would not let it get to us. The invisible barrier would come up.

'It was a very shallow existence but everybody looks back on their youth as a period of fun. We were adrenaline junkies and nothing excited us more than scaring ourselves, both on and off the track. We liked getting away with it but I don't know if we actually liked doing it. We would look forward to the race all week, getting incredibly nervous before the off and then be on cloud nine when it was all over, especially if we had done well.

'The buzz was phenomenal, perhaps the same as shooting down a Messerschmitt in a Spitfire during the Battle of Britain. It's that danger that makes people do it and watch it. If it was not there you would find your Aunt Mabel doing it.'

A tragic May weekend in 1979 summed it all up. That year, Barry and Steve had been joined at Suzuki by Tom Herron. The hard-riding Ulsterman had been giving the works riders a tough time and was rewarded with a place in the team at the beginning of the season. In between grand prix races he had returned home to race at the North West 200 event on the 10.1-mile road circuit between Portrush and Coleraine. The lure of big start money meant Steve had joined him although Barry was never tempted to ride at the event, turning down massive offers of cash to put his life on the line.

It was the fiftieth anniversary of the famous road race but it turned into a nightmare with three riders killed in a single day. Even by the standards of the 1970s it was a terrible waste of life. That weekend in Ireland still haunts Steve.

'Tom had a hand injury from crashing at an earlier grand prix and there was a lot of debate over whether he should ride. There was no way they would have stopped Tom from riding, it was his home race and they were paying him a considerable amount of money to compete in front of the crowd which was well over a hundred thousand. Tom used to hate works riders like Barry and myself, but once he became one he wanted to capitalise on it. He was starting to demand serious money because he was going OK in the grands prix.

'Tom had not been having a brilliant day because we were competing against the bigger-capacity Hondas and Yamahas. It was the last lap of the race and we were approaching the penultimate corner, Juniper Hill, and the chequered flag was in sight. It was typically drizzly weather but we were still doing around 120 mph on this narrow band of dry tarmac in the middle of the road. On our right was the seafront and on our left was a kerb three foot wide, a slatted fence and then a bunch of caravans. We were racing for third place and had been battling throughout the last lap.

'I distinctly remember Tom's treaded front tyre come up alongside me on the left side as we went round the right-hand bend. I looked over and thought "What the fuck are you are doing there?" I was on this very narrow dry line and the rest of the road was damp or even wet. I thought, you bloody idiot Tom, because he had no chance of winning the race and sure enough his bike suddenly disappeared. I never looked back because I was too busy keeping safe on that narrow dry line through the corner.

'That was that. Some of us were making the mad dash to Belfast and then Larne to catch the ferry to Stranraer in Scotland and then drive the 450 miles to Brands Hatch in time for practice at the Shellsport meeting the next morning. Even if we got there a bit late they would put on a special practice session for us, they were pretty flexible about things like that.

'We knew Tom's accident was big but we were too busy racing down to Larne to think about it.

'Half the fun those days was the race to the track and the race to the ferry. Honda Britain team manager Neil Tuxworth still barely talks to me now because I took the front bumper off his Mercedes van trying to pass him coming back from the North West 200 when I had to cut in because there was a car coming the other way.

'There would be me and two mechanics in the van, and I was driving because I was the fastest of the three. The radio was on and we heard on the BBC Light Programme that Tom Herron had died following his accident at the North West 200.

'Everybody gasped and there was a big shock across the van, but the next thing was, "Let's see if we can pass that car in front of us on the double white lines." The moment had gone. It was a harsh way of putting up the barriers. A few minutes passed and my mechanic Martin said, "Maybe you'll get the best Suzuki engine at the next grand prix." There was nothing you could do, say or feel that would bring Tom Herron back.

'At Brands the next day people asked about Tom's death and how awful it must have been. "Yes, it was, but what jetting and gearing are you using today?" was my reply as I got on with life as usual, coming second in the race.

'On the Monday morning I got a call from Suzuki. They told me they were too busy to attend Tom's funeral and asked if I could represent them. I don't know if the Troubles over there stopped them from going, though that would have been surprising. Motorcycle racing seemed to bypass the problems and we just met fanatical friendly fans.

'People used to say it must be very dangerous going to Northern Ireland and flying round the world. It didn't even scratch the surface; nothing was dangerous compared to racing motorcycles.

'I flew to Ireland, got a hire car and drove to Tom's funeral. There were thousands of people there but I kept a very low profile. I was only there in body, not in mind. I didn't actually go in the church for the service. I did the respectable thing and said, sorry Tom, hard luck, and got back into the hire car, flew home and got ready for the next race.

'Tom's death was just swept under the table. Somebody else rode Tom's bikes and we got on with the rest of the season. Barry was not close to Tom in any way although they were teammates at Suzuki. He simply said Tom was asking for it and I agreed and said he was fucking stupid trying to pass me round the outside anyway.'

Very occasionally, more personal involvement was unavoidable but once again Steve and Barry kept it to the absolute minimum, as Steve recalls.

'I remember taking my former teammate Mick Patrick's wife Viv home in my van after he had been killed at Cadwell Park in 1977. How ridiculous was that? He was killed early in the afternoon and by five o'clock that evening I was taking her home in my van together with a bag containing his leathers and personal possessions. We stopped and had a pub meal. The poor girl was beside herself but what else could you do? It was surreal. Today she would have been helped with counselling. I helped with a lot of the arrangements but, as always, I didn't go to the funeral.'

Ironically, both Barry and Tom Herron's widow Andrea both grew up in the uncompromising world of the British racing paddock. They first met when he was nine and she was eleven years old as both their fathers were fanatically involved in engine development. It was no great surprise to the pair of them that, over ten years later, they were still living the paddock lifestyle but this time on the world stage, Barry as a star rider and Andrea as the wife of a racer and the mother of two young daughters.

In hindsight, it was not an environment she would recommend for starting a family.

'People talk about the good old days and how we used to have barbecues and great fun but I really think of it as a bad time. It was no way to bring up children because it was no environment for adults, living in vans, travelling around Europe, not being paid, as well as all the dangers. I remember when we were all at the Nürburgring when the organisers were saying, you must go out and practise, even though it was snowing.

'Racing in those days was certainly not a world with money. There were vans in various states of disrepair travelling around Europe from one circuit to another. In a way people had very little respect for their own lives because they were so badly treated by the organisers of the races and I think that had a profound effect on the danger aspect. This gypsy lifestyle also meant that we were not respected by other people. Most motorcycle racers had such tunnel vision they did not notice this but, looking back now, they realise just how others did perceive their lifestyle and treated them with such little respect.

'Riders would have waded through mud every day just to race motorcycles. They would do whatever it took to do it. They had no way of leveraging more money because they would not say, "I will not do this unless you give me more cash" because they would do it anyway. It was a bad cycle.

'All the power was with the organisers who paid out the start money. Riders had to make demands, tell them what I'm worth. Barry had to find out what his own worth was in order to sell himself. But there were a lot of riders who did not know how to negotiate. Barry soon realised that valuing yourself was one of the ways you started to earn money. He then brought sponsorship into the sport. Barry and Kenny Roberts had a very big effect on changing how people viewed motorcycle racers, which gave them more opportunity for both respect and value. Barry valued himself both physically and financially. He was not prepared to ride on dangerous circuits, was not prepared to give his life away and was certainly not prepared to do what he did so well just to put more money in the organisers' pockets.

'It was very dangerous. I do think the danger and the lack of money were very closely linked because if you don't respect people, you don't pay them and you don't take care of their safety. The riders did it because it was what they loved, and those were the circumstances they had to do it in. Riders would go out and race if they had their legs and arms hanging off.'

Kenny Roberts came from America in the mid-1970s to take on the might of Europe, headed by Barry Sheene. The danger he was prepared to accept, but not the way riders were treated.

'It was like being slapped in the face, being told just shut up and ride your fucking motorcycle or go back to America. They made the mistake of running such good non-championship events at Imola in Italy and then we had to go and ride in a world championship round. You were expected to suck everybody's dick just to race in the world championship and it made no sense to me. They would force you to be there and then treat you like shit – it was not right. The safety thing was not a great issue with me but it was how we were treated that was the bigger issue. Getting hurt came with the territory.'

There is no doubt that the ever-present threat of death and the lack of respect from the organisers made the paddock adopt a siege mentality which in turn produced a disregard for normal life and even law and order. Riders expressed their anger in different ways and Andrea was not in any way surprised that they got in so much trouble, both with the law and the opposite sex.

'Riders did behave relatively badly off the track. They did go out drinking and fighting – I'm not speaking just for Tom – and, in Barry's case, chasing lots of women. It was a relief to have been going so dangerously fast and once again getting away with it. They had so many friends killed and they would hear all the time that so-and-so has been killed at the TT or at the Sachsenring. I remember Mike Hailwood telling me it was like living through the Second World War.

'Also, you worried whether you would get any money if your husband was killed. They would have collections in a bucket round the paddock for widows. That was no way to run a sport. It's far better now and I think Barry's contribution to the present-day situation was a very significant one.'

Steve Parrish remembers those paddock parties. They may have been pretty wild but they also had another purpose. On Saturday they helped forget the next day, while on Sunday it was all about sheer relief.

'On the Saturday night before a race you would always have a barbecue, a few drinks and a bit of fun just to prevent you getting too worried about the next day. World champion Kork Ballington always drank a few glasses of wine the night before a race – he said it was the only way he could get a good night's sleep before the big day.

'Then there was a big party on the Sunday night after the race because there was not much to clear away. No articulated trucks or hospitality units. Just the awning on the caravan, check the oil in the transit and it was off to the next race on Monday morning.

'It was the relief of surviving another one and no matter what went on during the race we were all mates. The riders from all the classes got together for a good time. There was a lot of regard for people in different classes. Barry and myself would always wander off together to watch their races from a particular corner.'

Three or four decades later it's very easy to say the riders were their own worst enemies. Why did they race at such dangerous circuits for such poor reward? Why didn't they bond together to work on a united front? There were occasions when the riders did refuse to race, but these were all too rare. However, many had to support a wife and family, or simply had to pay for the diesel to reach the next venue, and simply could not afford to say no.

Even the high-flying works riders such as eight-time world champion Phil Read who survived racing in the 1960s and early 1970s had to accept the situation or not race. There was no other choice.

'Death and injury was an accepted part of racing in those days. You had the choice, you could either race or you could stop. I chose to race and hoped it would never happen to me. You had to trust your ability not to crash, and if you did crash not to hit something solid. It certainly made you appreciate every day and every relationship.

'You felt lucky about just getting a factory ride and never worried about things like back protectors. The racing leathers were so light you could roll them up and put them in a holdall. Today they arrive in a great big suitcase.

'I remember coming back on the ferry from the TT races in the

Isle of Man one year with Mike Hailwood, who said to me, "Thank God I've survived again." If you were a factory rider competing on the Isle of Man you were paid to commit.

'Once, at the road circuit in Brno, I stopped the practice for the Czech Grand Prix because I was not satisfied with the last corners as there were no straw bales protecting a wall. I was called a trouble-maker. We also had to barter for start money with the organisers. We would race in front of crowds of over three hundred thousand at the Sachsenring in East Germany. You would agree a price before you got there and then try to up it when you arrived.

'Usually the pre-event bartering was done by telegram. When you got there you would tell them you were not going to ride for the agreed amount, and they would say, "That's what we're offering, it's up to you." I used to get fifty pounds for riding a factory MV Agusta or Yamaha in the Dutch TT at Assen, which was pathetic. I tried to get the riders united but they wouldn't stick together.

'We were upset and frustrated by the actions of some of the officials. I remember asking an Auto-Cycle Union official for some straw bales at Silverstone in 1973, but I was told they were unnecessary. Kim Newcombe, who was leading the world championship, was later killed at that corner.'

Barry had long accepted the danger. He had been brought up in this environment and had weighed up the pros and cons of racing at certain racetracks. He learnt to use the situation to his financial advantage when competing at the more dangerous venues. Barry, like everybody else scraping a living in the early 1970s, would sometimes allow his judgment to be clouded by the lure of cash, especially at non-world championship events. The difference was that Barry did it better than anybody else.

Barry had also quickly realised that he could do more about his own safety by taking responsibility for it himself. From the very early days he wore a back protector under his leathers, which were padded to offer extra protection when he crashed. He was also very particular about his choice of helmet and for once the money didn't matter. His crusade for more physical protection definitely saved his legs and probably his life in the 1982 Silverstone crash. Steve was the opposite, with the lure of more cash far more important than personal safety.

'Barry was much more aware of the dangers and was very much into wearing high-quality kit. He worked hard with Dianese to produce a good set of leathers. I was the opposite and just used the leathers and helmet from the manufacturer that paid me the most money. Safety was just not something that I thought about.'

Steve Parrish had dreamed about competing in grand prix racing. That dream was realised when he joined Barry in the Suzuki team at the start of 1977. The first race of the year was at San Carlos in Venezuela. Long before the actual racing got underway, Steve realised that perhaps that long-cherished dream was not quite what he had expected, although, like everybody else, he was prepared to put up with it.

'I would not say the track at San Carlos was dangerous because it was on the edge of a desert, but there were just no facilities. If you needed to go to a proper hospital it was a two-hour drive and you could have easily just laid there and died. There was an old police helicopter but absolutely nothing else, not even phones, and certainly no shade. It was just a bloody track in the middle of the desert with a couple of shacks put up.

'I had to drive to the local hospital in San Carlos with my mechanic Martin Brookman because he was suffering from terrible stomach pains. Nobody would believe what we saw there – an old tin shed with chickens running around in the grounds and cats and dogs everywhere. The doctors were smoking cigarettes and they took Martin into a room, examined him and told us he had appendicitis. They wanted five thousand dollars to carry out the operation and we said no. I did not trust the doctors, and the fee was obviously a con.

'I took Martin back to the hotel in San Carlos. That was another good reason for knowing Barry Sheene: we were staying at the only hotel in the town while all the other riders were staying in Valencia, a two-hour drive away. There were only seven or eight rooms and between Barry, myself and the Venezuelan riders Johnny Cecotto and Carlos Lavado we had them all.

'We gave Martin some painkillers and he started to get better. It turned out it was a touch of food poisoning.

'Because of Martin's food poisoning we were behind with the preparation of the bike and so we went back to the circuit at seven o'clock on Saturday morning to get the work done before practice started. There was a guy at the gate with a machine gun who informed us the circuit was not open for another two hours. We told him not to be so bloody stupid and that we needed to get in to start work. With that he pulled off the safety catch of the machine gun and pointed it at Martin. We retreated without any more questions and I'm certain he would have fired if we had tried to get in. Can you imagine a guard cocking a machine gun and pointing it at Valentino Rossi and saying you are not coming in until nine?'

Two years later the situation was exactly the same when Steve returned, partnering Barry at Suzuki once again. Absolutely nothing had changed.

'I rejoined the Suzuki team in 1979 but had a big crash at the opening grand prix of the season at San Carlos. I slapped myself on the ground, knocked myself out and beat myself up big style. I was taken to the medical centre, which was just an old tent and blokes looking over you while smoking fags. They gave me an aspirin and a drink of water and that was about it.

'I really didn't care and I'm sure everybody else was the same as me. Barry was the only one earning big money. I was paid five thousand pounds a year to race all over the world with the most famous rider in the world. Money and danger just did not come into it.'

It's amazing that the riders and the teams allowed the situation to go on for so long. In the 1970s certain tracks did some token work to improve safety while some of the road-based circuits such as Brno and the Sachsenring lost their world championship status. Other tracks simply built more Armco barriers to appease the racing car drivers who had lost just as many numbers as motorcycling in the 1960s and early 1970s. Armco may have been the perfect way to stop a sliding racing car but, unprotected, it was a killer of sliding human, leather-clad motorcycle riders. Many of the organisers only cared about lining their pockets.

Everybody was treated the same and without a united voice the situation was allowed to continue by the sport's governing body, the Fédération Internationale de Motorcyclisme (FIM). As the racing classes from 50 to 500cc and the earning power and bargaining ability of the riders were so diverse it was impossible to act as a single unit. The FIM and the organisers just sat back, counted the money and took full advantage, as Steve remembers.

'The riders were convinced that the FIM and circuits were all in league with one another and certain people were making an enormous amount of money at the expense of young people's lives. The likes of Barry were paid about two hundred pounds to race at each grand prix and he had to race at the world championship events because of his contract with the factory team. Barry made his money by competing at non-world championship events, but to persuade the organisers to pay that decent start money you had to be a good world championship rider to attract the fans.

'It turned into an amazing scenario. Barry Sheene was famous because he was world champion but it actually cost him money to compete at the grands prix. Perversely, it felt better racing at dangerous tracks knowing that you were being paid decent money rather than just risking your life competing for world championship points. Also, you were there because of what you had done in the world championships and so you didn't take too many risks.

'You got paid appearance money and so as long as you turned up for a few laps you got paid. I used to ride at a little track called St Joris in Belgium. The track was really dangerous, surrounded by ditches and dykes, but if I raced there the brown envelope would come out, stuffed with around three thousand pounds. At these places I would race at 75 per cent because I didn't want to hurt myself. Barry was just the same; the only difference was he would get ten thousand pounds.

'It never crossed my mind or Barry's that we were going to die. You always knew it was going to hurt, sliding along at 90 mph preparing your body to hit an Armco barrier, but going to actually die – never. I vividly remember that I was always fearful when sliding down the track because you knew that unless you were incredibly lucky, which I was, it was going to be a big accident and it was going to hurt. These days, thank goodness, riders slide along knowing they are going to be all right because there are huge run-off areas. It was sheer luck, or by the grace of God or whatever you want to call it, that we did not hit a tree, an Armco or even a house. Barry and I never did hit these trackside obstacles but many others did and paid the ultimate price.

'Everybody was sick of people being killed and maimed yet still having to race at places like San Carlos. There was no solidarity among the riders because if you said you would not race at a certain track others would say, "bollocks, it's good enough for us". There was such a large number of riders, with up to forty competing in the separate 50, 125, 250, 350 and 500cc championship races and all being paid different sums by the organisers.

'I remember at the 1977 Austrian Grand Prix, after a big accident in the 350cc race we said we would not ride in the 500cc but they still got a grid out on the track. Riders who were desperate for their start money just to make it to the next race went out despite the danger.'

The token measures by some circuits and the disappearance of others from the world championship schedule did make a difference. The problem was it was a very small difference because, as Steve explains, the bikes were just getting quicker and quicker.

'The bikes had become bloody fast compared to the Manx Nortons that raced on those old circuits. A good Manx Norton had a top speed of about 130 mph, which was still fast enough to kill yourself, which plenty of riders did. The two strokes we were riding reached 180 mph and constantly seized up and threw people off.

'Barry and I came in at the later stages of bloody dangerous circuits. I can still remember racing at Imatra in Finland, which was such a dangerous track, the old Spa-Francorchamps circuit in Belgium, the old long Nürburgring circuit in Germany. I also still raced at the TT in the Isle of Man. We both raced at Chimay in Belgium because they paid good money and Scarborough in England for the very same reason, brown envelopes under the table plus plenty of good fun including *Motor Cycle News* girls.

'We had to come back to England to earn good money and Barry taught me to negotiate a fee at the beginning of the season with Chris Lowe from Motor Circuit Developments, which owned Brands Hatch, Oulton Park and Snetterton. I would get a couple of thousand quid for each event – good money in those days. I earned as much money doing six races in the UK as I did through my contract with Suzuki.

'Fifty per cent of the circuits we went to were now reasonably safe and fifty per cent were unsafe but we were riding bloody fast motorcycles and so the balance was probably the same as the 1960s. Even some of the purpose-built circuits such as the Salzburgring were horrendously dangerous because there were no run-off areas.

'There was not a single person we could complain to because each circuit was so individual. You would arrive at the track, go to the little paddock office and sign on. Then they would scrutinise the bikes and tell you that you had to have your numbers fixed in a particular way, which was different to the week before at another circuit. There was no continuity in anything.

'The most humiliating part of the process was queuing up to collect your money after the race. Imola was a classic: you would stand for two hours and then be told when you reached the desk you were in the wrong queue for the 500cc class. Even world champions such as Kork Ballington and Jon Ekerold would have to queue but,

as you might imagine, Barry never did. He had the money sorted
out long beforehand.

The situation was totally out of control and it just could not go
on and on. Led by Kenny Roberts, the protests against the FIM and
the organisers got louder and more volatile but it was only when a
long-awaited leader emerged that the real battle commenced. Barry
Coleman was a journalist covering grand prix racing for the *Guardian*.
He shared Roberts' contempt for the sport's governing body and
what he saw as its failure to protect riders' lives or pay them a decent
wage. The pair of them decided to do something about it.

On the eve of the 1979 British Grand Prix at Silverstone the revolution against the establishment began. The riders announced the
formation of their own championship, to be called the World Series.
Forty of the leading riders, including Barry, had already signed up
for the championship which proposed a hundred thousand pound
prize fund at each round and was open only to the 250 and 500cc
classes.

As Barry was doing such a good job looking after himself Coleman
was initially nervous about approaching him to join the revolution.
He need not have worried and Barry's enthusiasm was an enormous
morale booster to all involved, much to Coleman's relief.

'Certain riders had signed up with Tom Herron who was fed up
riding at the Isle of Man and, ironically, the North West 200 . . . but
we didn't approach Barry. He had a long history of individual enter-
prise getting him into a position where he needed to be because he
knew nobody would do it for him. He did a truly amazing job getting minority sport coverage throughout the world. He did it totally
single-handed. Nobody helped him or understood it like he did.
Nobody had done it before and nobody has done it since. Because
of his individual approach to everything we were all a little nervous
about asking him to join us.

'We had signed up top riders such as Patrick Pons, Christian
Sarron and Kork Ballington and Barry sort of knew that something
was going on but we still hadn't approached him. Finally I went to

him and asked if he wanted to be in or not and he told me he certainly wanted to be in. When I explained the plans he asked why we had not approached him before. I thought it might not have been his cup of tea but his response was totally the opposite and from that moment he was the most loyal of all the World Series riders.

'He did not resent the fact that Kenny had been one of the instigators and was very forceful in his views and angry with anybody who showed any signs of wavering. Far from being a highly individualistic person, he was capable of being Mr Corporate and being with a group and sticking with it. There was never a moment that you could question Barry's commitment to that movement in any shape or form. He instinctively understood that the moment had come.'

The history books will tell you that the World Series failed and the FIM World Championships continued with the likes of Barry Sheene and Kenny Roberts still competing. Despite the backing of Mark McCormack's International Marketing Group some of the major circuits were frightened off by the FIM's proposed sanctions and would not agree to host the World Series championship rounds.

Sometimes, however, history books don't tell the real story. The World Series may have failed as a championship but the riders won a major battle against the FIM. In 1980 prize money at grands prix was increased by a staggering 500 per cent and the mandatory start money system was scrapped. This meant an average increase in wages of around 300 per cent per annum for the grand prix riders. Of course, the money was vital but equally important were the shock waves the solidarity of the riders sent through the FIM and the race organisers. They knew that from that moment on they could not treat grand prix riders as second-class citizens, with little or no regard for their safety or dignity.

It was the true bloodless coup. Kenny Roberts noticed the difference almost immediately; not only in the prize money but also in the way the riders were treated.

'It was the first time that proved to people we could do some-thing about it. After that it was a joy to come to the circuits. There were times when we had to play that card again and I remember the 1980 Belgian Grand Prix in Zolder. They just had tyres covering the guard rails, not hay bales. I had seen a guy killed when he hit a tyre wall and came back on the track and was hit by another rider. The organisers told me there were no straw bales in Belgium – I told them it was not my fault.

'Dutchman Wil Hartog was the riders' representative and the organisers argued that he had approved the track – once again I told them it was not my fault. No bales and the 500cc guys would not be racing. The next morning there were straw bales, perhaps not enough of them but they had made an effort, and we raced.

'It turned start money into prize money, but the really big thing was we had a voice. We had at last gained some respect and were not being treated like shit.'

The 'good old days' were finally coming to an end. The majority of those actors on that danger-ridden stage were glad it was all over, including the most successful grand prix rider of them all, Giacomo Agostini.

'Having breakfast with a great friend and then never seeing him again was the most dreadful experience you can imagine.'

WORLD CHAMPION

Nick Harris and his mates all agreed the Union flag looked far better fluttering in the Dutch breeze than it did overlooking the dreaming spires on the roof of Oxford Town Hall. It had been 'borrowed' to bear witness to a very special occasion: Saturday 28 June 1975, Barry Sheene's first 500cc grand prix victory.

The sixth round of the world championship was held at Assen in the north of Holland. Still the biggest event in the Dutch sporting calendar, it takes place around a circuit known as the cathedral of grand prix motorcycle racing, just over four-and-a-half miles of pure joy for both riders and the 135,000 spectators who packed the enormous open grandstands that lined the ribbon of tarmac.

Barry knew that he had to outfox the legend, Giacomo Agostini, to secure that first win. The Italian master was chasing his fifteenth world championship and had made a tremendous start to the season, winning three of the opening five rounds riding a 500cc two-stroke Yamaha after his much-publicised switch from the Italian MV Agusta factory a couple of years earlier.

Just three months after a massive crash in practice at Daytona, twenty-four-year-old Barry was ready for the moment. For fifteen

laps he was glued to the back wheel of Agostini's Yamaha. Lap after
lap he had the crowd going crazy by feigning to pass the Italian on
the left side when they came on to the start and finish straight.
The ploy only changed as they came into that final corner on the
very last lap as the chequered flag was unfurled. The fourteen-time
world champion was caught completely by surprise by the young
upstart:

'I felt so stupid and still have a very bad memory of Barry beating
me at Assen, not only on the last lap but at the last corner. I turned
around three corners from the finish and he was not very close and
so I thought, I'm going to win. I let my concentration slip and he
passed me on the very last bend. Afterwards I was happy for him
and I'm very happy for him now.'

Ago was happy for Barry; Nick Harris and friends were ecstatic:

'As they crossed the line – right in front of us – the Suzuki and
Yamaha could not be separated by the timekeepers, but we knew
who had won. Franco was going crazy on the pit wall and couldn't
wait for his boy to return. The celebrations went on long into the
night and I don't think the Union flag ever made it back to Oxford.
It's probably still hanging on the wall in the Banana Bar in
Amsterdam.'

In Daytona it had been a very different story: Barry had crashed
his 750cc Suzuki at 175 mph during a practice session for the two
hundred-miler. The spectacular crash nearly killed him. It also
brought him instant fame.

Coming off the infamous Daytona banking on to the start and
finish straight, Barry's Suzuki suddenly slewed sideways, throwing
him high into the warm Florida sunshine. He slid three hundred
yards along the tarmac before ending up in a heap almost on the
start and finish line. He remained conscious but it would probably
have been better if he hadn't because the local Halifax Hospital
revealed that Barry had suffered a broken right femur, a broken
right arm, compression fractures to several vertebrae, broken ribs
and a considerable loss of skin from his back.

Little did he realise as he was taken down to the operating the-atre to have an eighteen-inch pin inserted to mend the femur that this one afternoon would change his life. Thames Television had commissioned Frank Cvitanovich to film a documentary about Barry at Daytona. The accident meant he would be returning with an amazing programme.

The cameras filmed the crash in startling detail from that first telltale rear-wheel slide to a crumpled Barry trying to undo his helmet with a broken right arm. It was stunning stuff. Barry's brav-ery in recounting the extent of his injuries to the cameras while lying in the casualty department waiting for treatment propelled him to instant hero status with British viewers. The documentary was to change his life in another way as well. A certain blonde model by the name of Stephanie McLean first became aware of the existence of Barry Sheene while watching the programme at home with husband Clive.

The cause of the crash is still a matter of debate, thirty-two years later. For certain the rear wheel of the Suzuki locked, but why? Barry, until his dying day, was convinced it was caused by the rear Dunlop tyre deflating. Other suggestions included that a new chain tensioner had caught in the rear wheel, a design fault had caused the rear tyre to brush the rear suspension and that a new six-speed gearbox had temporarily seized.

The definitive answer will never be known but one thing is for certain, that afternoon in Florida was the turning point of Barry's career.

A mere seven weeks later, Barry's hero status increased as he returned to the track for a national meeting at Cadwell Park, a homely venue in the Lincolnshire wolds that could not have pro-vided a greater contrast to the wide open spaces of Daytona. A far-from-fit Barry put up a tremendous fight in the *Motor Cycle News* Superbike race round the tight, energy-sapping climbs and turns of the track. He initially led his great rival Mick Grant, but once the Yorkshireman got in front Barry's body cried 'enough!' and he was forced to retire. Nonetheless, he had proved that he was back and his swift return to the track had won him more fans.

At the beginning of May, a week after the Cadwell Park meeting, Barry planned to return to grand prix action at the Salzburgring in Austria for the second round of the 500cc world championship. Unfortunately, the organisers were not so keen to write another page in the comeback chapter. Riders had to bump start their machines to begin a race, in other words push the bike hard with the clutch in and jump on – usually side-saddle – while dropping the clutch hoping the engine would fire. It was only when Barry arrived at the start line for the race that the officials decided that Barry's pinned femur was not up to such a test, despite his efforts at Cadwell. He was steaming mad but even Barry could not persuade them to change their minds.

Barry finally returned to action a week later at Hockenheim in Germany but a misfire caused his retirement from the race. It was won by Agostini, who was striving to bring Yamaha their first 500cc world championship and the first-ever 500cc title for a two-stroke machine. Agostini won the next round at Imola in Italy, where Barry once again had to retire, this time with a transmission failure.

All the protagonists missed the fifth round at the TT races in the Isle of Man. Even Agostini had now turned his back on the mountain circuit and the chance of increasing his lead in the championship. The writing was well and truly on the wall for the Isle of Man road circuit as a world championship venue.

Then it was Assen and the start of a new chapter for both Suzuki and Barry. Just eight days after that first 500cc victory he was on course for a repeat around the frighteningly fast and dangerous 8.761-mile Spa-Francorchamps circuit high in the wooded Ardennes of Belgium. Even in its shortened modern-day configuration Spa-Francorchamps is one of the truly great places to watch grand prix racing on two or four wheels. Racing between the trees on a road circuit on which he averaged – yes, averaged – 135.427 mph, Barry took pole position for the 12-lap race. He was battling with Phil

Read on the glorious-sounding MV Agusta four-stroke but on the last lap Barry was forced to retire after a mechanical noise alerted him to an imminent engine seizure.

His second 500cc grand prix victory came at Anderstorp in Sweden, and this time the result wasn't close. At the circuit near Gothenburg, where the main straight doubles up as the runway for the local airport and the paddock is nowhere near the start and finish line, Barry had fifty-one seconds to spare over Phil Read after starting the 28-lap race from pole.

Mechanical problems brought no points in Finland or Czechoslovakia and Barry eventually finished sixth; the championship was won by Agostini and Yamaha. The race in Finland also brought an abrupt end to Barry's friendship with Phil Read, someone who had done much to help him since the early days riding for Franco on the Isle of Man. However, it was not only the race round the incredibly dangerous circuit on the Russian border that brought about the split. The two riders had quite a reputation with the opposite sex which did not help the situation, and Read thought he had reason to be jealous.

'I think that Barry and my wife Madeleine were quite fond of each other. I won't say more than that. I got on really well with his first fiancée Leslie. She used to tell me how mean Barry was, and that one day he looked at her engagement ring and said, "Darling, that wants cleaning," took it away and never gave it back to her.

'Back in 1972 Barry came and asked me how he could start asking for appearance money. I told him, "Throw away that dirty anorak, get yourself a suit and go and meet the organisers and you might earn a few bob." He did that and he was set up.

'I helped him out in races. I would slow down and we would dice a bit and then on the last lap I would gas it and win. The headlines would be that Barry Sheene challenged Phil Read and that was OK. I used to help him get maximum appearance money because I had been around a lot longer than him and knew the organisers.

'Barry and I were very friendly and he would spend a lot of time at my house in Oxshott and Madeleine would look after him and make him food and check out doctors and physios. We even used to go on holidays together.

'The crux of the disagreement was at the 1975 Finnish Grand Prix at Imatra. Barry and I were still good mates. He was riding the factory Suzuki and I was on the MV fighting Ago and Yamaha for the world 500cc championship. I had to win the race if possible. I said to Barry, "You are potentially the fastest in qualifying, so if I'm with you in the race and Ago's around five seconds behind, let me win." He said "No problem mate."

'Just before the race he came to me and said he had been told by Suzuki that he had to win if possible. I said, "OK that's fine," and thought, that's nice. That really sealed the disagreement . . . if I had won that race I would have been world champion again and per-haps upset his plans of being *Motor Cycle News* Man of the Year. I really didn't have much to do with him after that. I was really angry because I'm sure Suzuki had not told him to win and he should have kept his mouth shut and just raced.'

Barry was not the type of person to allow a fall-out with an old friend to spoil his fun or determination to follow in Read's consid-erable footsteps as a British winner of the most coveted prize in motorcycle racing, the 500cc world title.

He completed a good year with a second place in the F750cc championship behind teammate Jack Findlay to add to his two grands prix wins. He might even have won the 750cc title but missed the final round because of a familiar problem – injury. This time it was more self-inflicted, although it was a bang on the knee by a Mallory Park trackside kerb en route to victory at the presti-gious Race of the Year that started the problem. A bit of tomfoolery a week later at Cadwell Park, where he slipped off the back of a trials bike pulling a wheelie, ended his season as he needed to have his kneecap and the top of his shin in his right leg wired together. Nonetheless, he won the *Motor Cycle News* Man of the Year Award.

He then set about having the time of his life with the London jet set before Stephanie and the 500cc world championship just happened to come along together.

Barry had first ridden the new RG500 Suzuki a year before the start of the 1974 season. It was like a rocket ship and the Japanese factory was confident they could meet the two-stroke challenge from Yamaha while also seeing off the ageing four-strokes. The problem was that the bike had some nasty little habits, in particular seizing the engine or gearbox with no prior warning and throwing the rider off at high speed.

Barry tested the bike in Japan with his brother-in-law Paul Smart and the American-based Brit Cliff Carr. Suzuki signed Barry and Paul plus the experienced Australian Jack Findlay to ride the rocket ships, which the riders treated with extreme caution – and who could blame them? It was a tough year for the trio, both physically and mentally.

It started well, with Barry competing in his first 500cc season on a very fast machine, but second place in the opening round behind Read at Clermont-Ferrand in France and a third at the third round at the Salzburgring was just a false dawn. Those sudden seizures started to take their toll, with Barry receiving a tremendous battering, including a broken bone in his foot when the Suzuki threw him off during the Nations Grand Prix at Imola.

However, it was a crash back at the Suzuki test track at Ryuyo in Japan that really put the frighteners on the team. Barry had persuaded Suzuki to let another American, Gary Nixon, have a ride on the bike with a view to joining Barry in the team at a later date. The result of that test saw Barry almost quit the sport. It also confirmed what the three riders had been saying all along, although for Nixon it was a tough way to find out.

'The plan was to go out and do a few laps then come in and change the head angle, but the bottom fell out of the bike when it seized up on a fifth gear left-hander at around 120 mph. I de-barked a tree twelve feet in the air and broke both arms, an ankle, three ribs and hurt my back and pocket book.

'Barry said he would have quit if I had been killed, and he might well have done, but I lived. I would have loved to have been his grand prix teammate because we got on great after we first met at the Race of the Year in 1970. Eight Americans came over the next year for the Transatlantic Trophy and Barry was the only English guy to come over and meet us at the hotel and take us out to dinner.'

Barry was devastated by the crash and his sombre mood was not lightened when he retired at both Assen and Spa before he became the latest victim of the more than playful Suzuki, which tossed him into the catch fencing at Anderstorp when a water pump failed. It was nothing more than a high-speed crash for Barry but for Agostini it was a disaster that cost him the chance of wrestling the world title from Phil Read and his old MV Agusta team.

'Barry was leading and I was following him. It was possible for me to pass him on the straight but I wanted to pass him in front of the big grandstand. I waited until the next lap and, one corner before the grandstand, I got very close and he crashed. I broke my shoulder and was taken to hospital. I was very angry but afterwards I understood that it was not his fault. Some water had come out of his engine onto his wheels.'

Barry finished fourth in the final race of the season at the Brno road circuit, which was enough to put him sixth in the championship won by Read for the second year in succession.

Back home it had been a better and certainly less painful year with championship wins in the Shellsport and *Motor Cycle News* Superbike series. He also brought Suzuki their first-ever RG500 victory when he won the non-championship British Grand Prix at Silverstone but a final test session back at Ryuyo was a blunt reminder of just what a year it had been. Barry crashed the bike while testing a new frame, banged his head and sustained yet another bout of concussion.

*

Two years later the scorching summer of 1976 belonged to two British sportsmen who broke all the rules. Barry Sheene and James Hunt made the majority of people laugh, shake their heads and wonder how they got away with it. They didn't care what they got up to because, where it mattered, they were the best, they were British world champions on two and four wheels and the public loved them.

At last the RG500 Suzuki seemed to have been sorted out as Barry embarked on a memorable season with two new teammates, John Newbold and John Williams. The Texaco Heron Suzuki team was run out of Bedington Lane in Croydon and Barry insisted he got the best factory bikes, leaving his new teammates at first frustrated and, in the end, downright angry. Barry was on a mission: nothing but the best would do and, as always, he would ensure he got what he wanted, whatever the consequences.

He started the season in blistering style but with the usual amount of pain and discomfort. Despite the cold weather biting at the pins and wires in his legs causing him problems pushing the Suzuki to start, Barry won the opening round at Le Mans in France. The next round was in Austria, where Barry gave a typical two fingers to the Salzburgring organisers who had refused him a start on the line the previous year by winning comfortably from pole.

Round three was in the heart of Tuscany at the new Mugello circuit in Italy. Barry took great satisfaction in beating his old friend and bitter rival Phil Read in a last bend shootout. With maximum points from the first three rounds and with just the six best races counting towards the final points tally in the ten-round championship, Barry was well on course.

His missed the next round, on the Isle of Man, which turned into a historic last-ever 500cc world championship race at the TT circuit. Teammate John Williams' mood was not improved when, holding a comfortable lead, he ran out of petrol almost in sight of the chequered flag.

Barry returned to Assen a year after that historic first victory bursting with confidence. This time it was not the cold weather causing problems but searing heat. The conditions suited Barry who made it four wins from four starts but his first disappointment of the year was just eight days away at Spa-Francorchamps.

Barry upset teammates Newbold and Williams by giving Frenchman Michel Rougerie his special RG500 Suzuki to ride. Another Sheene victory would have given him the title and he just wanted to pile up the odds against the opposition that no longer included Phil Read, who had announced his retirement from grand prix racing, driving back to England before the start of the race. For once Barry's plans misfired because John Williams was so furious with Barry he was determined to show him who was the master of the road circuit.

Williams opened up a big lead over the first nine laps. He planned to slow on lap ten and then very obviously let Barry pass to win the title but it all fell apart when Barry slowed dramatically thanks to a misfire. Williams kept looking over his shoulder waiting for his 'teammate' to appear but he never did, so in the end he almost reluctantly rolled over the line to claim his one and only grand prix victory. Barry finally limped home in second place. The championship celebrations were put on hold.

A third place in the Swedish Grand Prix at Anderstorp would be enough to give Barry the title but third was never going to be good enough for him.

A super-confident Barry made a dreadful start in the 28-lap race but while some of the Japanese Suzuki personnel panicked as he finished the first lap in thirteenth place Barry simply put his head down and picked his way through the field. With six laps to go he eased by the slowing Teppi Lansivuori to take the lead and, barring accidents, the world title was his.

This was not the time to think about where he had left the car keys or what was for dinner, as Barry often claimed were his thoughts when leading a race. His concentration was perfect as he crossed the line thirty-four seconds in front of Findlay and, more important, as the 1976 500cc world champion.

Motorcycle racing in England had never seen anything like it. Sheene's triumph was the lead item on news broadcasts, front- and back-page news in all the newspapers and the nation celebrated with the cockney boy who had struck it rich. The whole weekend in Anderstorp was so typically Barry. The confident race win despite a bad start was sandwiched between two incidents. In the Saturday practice session John Williams had crashed and was lying unconscious on the side of the track. Barry stopped and removed Williams' helmet before sticking his fingers down his throat to clear his airways, which were blocked with dirt. Barry's prompt action probably saved his life.

On the Sunday after clinching the title Barry calmly announced he would not ride in the three final grands prix of the season. He claimed competing in grands prix was actually costing him money and his time could be spent much more profitably elsewhere. Anyway, he had other fish to fry, particularly the ten-round *Motor Cycle News* British Superbike Championship.

Racing in Britain was not only very lucrative for Barry but also made him accessible to the British fans that flocked to the tracks whenever Barry was on the entry list. It was a big part of his success and of course he milked it. The *Motor Cycle News* Superbike Championship was the biggest non-world championship series in the world.

Barry won the second-round race at Cadwell Park from Mick Grant and afterwards Nick Harris went with him to Cadwell boss Charlie Wilkinson's office. 'Barry wanted to show me just how the system worked. A line of riders queued like schoolboys outside the dreaded headmaster's office. Barry went straight to the front and was immediately summoned by Wilkinson, who had a giant ledger open in front of him. "Ah Sheene, not a bad day," he said. "Now what did we agree?" Whatever they had originally settled was never going to be enough for Barry but a figure around the ten-thousand-pounds mark was duly agreed by both parties and we left while the other riders prepared to haggle for a share of what was left. I never actually saw the brown envelope being handed over but I'm sure it was before the end of the day.

'I returned to my car and thirty minutes later was driving out of the paddock but Barry's day was far from over. He was sitting on the steps of the motorhome with the queue for an autograph – and probably a bit of flirting – still fifty yards long.'

Barry duly won the *Motor Cycle News* Superbike Championship after a last-round showdown with Grant at Brands Hatch. He also won the Shellsport 500 Championship and had a decent Easter weekend against the American in the Transatlantic Trophy series with a first, two seconds and three thirds. His forays abroad on the 750cc Suzuki were not so successful but he did win the financially rewarding Chimay meeting in Belgium on the RG500.

It was a fabulous time for British motorsport, although James Hunt had to wait until October before joining Barry as a world champion.

The public adored both of them. Hunt's mentor and Sheene's great friend Lord Hesketh recalls that glorious summer of (for Barry and Hunt, at least) sex, drugs, rock and roll and, in case we forget, world championships.

'James and Barry were far and away the leading British stars on two wheels and four. They also exuded a heroic attraction that went far beyond cars and bikes. They were both rebels marked with brilliant, intuitive natural talent. It was clear to me that in sponsorship marketing terms they were a nearly unique pairing as was later shown by Texaco. Our outlook on life was very similar. We were surrounded by some pretty wild individuals, some of whom could party and race better than others. In those days loving and living whilst staying at the front of the grid was definitely for the under-thirties.'

Barry could certainly never be accused of resting on his laurels and changes were afoot at the start of 1977 for the defence of the title. Williams and Newbold were replaced by two new teammates, Steve Parrish and another American, Pat Hennen. Rex White was back as team manager, replacing Merv Wright, and Newbold's former top man Martyn Ogbourne joined the team as chief mechanic. Most of the moves had been instigated by Barry, especially his old mate Stavros joining the team for the eleven-round championship where every race now counted towards the final points tally. The Isle of Man TT had gone, with Silverstone replacing the infamous circuit to stage the final round of the championship in August.

The previous year Ogbourne had watched the trials and tribulations of Barry's championship-winning team from the Newbold side of the garage. He had pitched in to help when needed and had earned an impressive reputation with the Japanese for getting the Suzukis to work well. He realised halfway through 1976 that there were going to be changes at the top.

'Merv had come over from America to replace Rex in 1976 after helping Barry when he had the big testing accident in Japan, but then he insisted that John Williams rode one of Barry's bikes at the TT which was still a round of the world championship.

'They took one of Barry's spare bikes and that's where it all began. It was not a personal thing with John, but rather to do with Barry's bike. Barry said at the end of 1976, "either Merv goes or I go". Rex, who had been pushed sideways, came back.'

Ogbourne joined Franco and long-serving mechanic Don Mackay in what turned into an interesting season for all parties.

'In those early days it was me, Franco and Don, who sadly died of cancer before Barry. The fact that Don was gay bothered Iris and Franco but never bothered me. Sometimes they would come back and find the motorhome full of boys and Iris in particular was very unhappy.

'Barry always had us, and me in particular, working on the edge. At Brands Hatch they would all be on the line and Barry turned up on his minibike and started talking to everybody while I was back in the pits changing to intermediate tyres and adjusting the gear ratios. Without the others riders realising, he was delaying the start of the race. He would talk to the starter and keep holding up the start until I screamed up to the start with his bike, ready for the rain with changed gear ratios and intermediate tyres. Some of the times it was so close, and I was frightened I would get it wrong because one mistake with a nut or a spacer and it was all over. He always had the belief it could be done.'

The removal of Merv Wright, the reappointment of affable Rex White plus the technical knowledge of Ogbourne were just what the world champion had ordered. The arrival of Pat Hennen certainly wasn't. Barry still felt bad about Gary Nixon's accident the previous year and believed that Hennen was taking advantage. The mind games started right at the beginning of the year and got more intense as Hennen proved not only a serious teammate but also a dangerous opponent.

Barry also still had that unwelcome friend, the eighteen-inch pin that was holding his femur together following his Daytona crash. It was removed in a televised operation and Barry started the season in the heat and dust of San Carlos. He eventually won a superb battle with American Steve Baker's Yamaha to start the campaign in great style. Hennen was third and Parrish ninth.

They returned home in great spirits but had to wait six weeks for the next round, at the Salzburgring. Barry took pole but then led all the other riders in a boycott of the race following an appalling crash in the 350cc event, in which Swiss rider Hans Stadelman was killed. The seeds of discontent about safety and money were being sown although the World Series was still three years away.

Campaigning was put to one side a week later at Hockenheim, where Barry picked up another maximum after starting from pole with Hennen second and Parrish fourth.

Barry was on a charge and wins at Imola, where Hennen crashed, and at the Paul Ricard circuit in the south of France put him very much in the driving seat and odds-on favourite to retain the title. Even a slight blip, a second place to local hero Wil Hartog in Assen, could not stop the Sheene bandwagon which produced a one-man show of pure skill, bravery and confidence on the daunting roads of Spa-Francorchamps just eight days later.

Barry annihilated the opposition to win at an average speed of 135.067 mph, still the fastest-ever average recorded in a motorcycle race. Barry just kept on winning, completing his third consecutive victory at Anderstorp.

He arrived at Imatra not having to push his luck or judgment at the tree-lined, lakeside venue. In fact, second place behind his nearest rival Baker would mean the title remained in Britain with two rounds remaining but it didn't even come to that.

Baker was out of the points fighting mechanical problems in twelfth place with Barry coasting in second behind his great friend Johnny Cecotto when the temperature gauge indicated the Suzuki was overheating. Barry had been kept well informed of Baker's problems and gently nursed the Suzuki home in sixth place to retain the title. He even had the audacity to wave teammate Parrish through to fifth on the last lap, helping him move up the championship table.

With the big picture already painted Barry pulled out of the penultimate round on the Brno road circuit in order to prepare for a triumphant homecoming at the first world championship British Grand Prix outside the Isle of Man. Barry was desperate to celebrate his second world title by winning the last round of the championship at Silverstone.

Unfortunately, the weekend turned into a nightmare for Barry, for Steve Parrish and the fans that packed the Northamptonshire circuit to celebrate another great year with their hero.

Barry started the historic 28-lap race from pole, riding Parrish's machine because his own bike was plagued by head gasket problems. Even so, he was forced to retire, but all was not lost because with just one lap remaining Stavros led the way and the party was about to kick off. It's a lap Steve will never forget.

'I just could not believe it, I was leading the very first British Grand Prix at Silverstone and if I won the race I would finish third in the world championship. I came over the start and finish line to begin the last lap leading John Williams by three seconds, with Pat

Hennen third. Coming round Woodcote on to that start and finish straight the place was going crazy, the crowd cheering and waving me on to my first-ever grand prix victory at my home race. I glanced at the pit wall and Barry was hanging right over it with my pit board on which he had chalked the message, "Gas it Wanker".

'It had just started to drizzle and as I went into the first corner at Copse I lost the front end of the Suzuki and crashed. John Williams was caught out by the rain at the next corner and also crashed and Pat Hennen went on to win the race. I was mortified not only because I had lost the chance of a lifetime to win my first grand prix but because Hennen took over my third place in the championship and got the Suzuki ride with Barry next year.'

Barry was none too pleased either because his relationship with Californian Hennen got worse and worse as his teammate's performances got better and better. It was the first-ever American victory in a grand prix motorcycle race. Little did Barry or anybody else involved in racing realise on that August afternoon that this was just the beginning of the flood of American riders which was to swamp the Europeans who had dominated grand prix racing since its beginnings twenty-eight years previously.

Earlier in the year Kenny Roberts had given Barry a taste of what to expect the following season in the annual Transatlantic Trophy battle over the Easter weekend. Riding the 750cc Yamaha, Roberts won the opening four races at Brands Hatch and Mallory Park with only an engine failure and crash preventing him from completing a clean sweep. To add further insult to injury Barry's new teammate Hennen was top scorer in the six-race series with Barry third behind Steve Baker.

The end of the domestic season brought better news for the world champion's legion of fans, although the name Hennen just would not go away. The last round of the *Motor Cycle News* Superbike Championship, sponsored by Brut, was a double points-scoring affair at Brands Hatch but Barry hit major mechanical problems. He limped home in eighth place in the race won by Mick

Grant with Hennen's fourth dropping him to third behind Barry and Grant in the championship.

Barry's retention of the Shellsport title was not so clear-cut, with Steve Parrish once again on the wrong end of fate while the intervention of the type of crass officialdom that Barry hated so much worked in his favour for once. Parrish only had to finish one place behind Barry to win the title in the final round at Brands. He looked very comfortable in second place behind Hennen when his Suzuki broke down and Barry's third place gave him a title that could easily have been on its way back to the States with Hennen.

The American scored more points than both Barry and Steve. However, because he was not riding with a British licence he had been disqualified from second place at an earlier Brands meeting, not allowed to start at Mallory, but welcomed to ride and scored points at all the other rounds. That second place at Brands would have given Hennen the title but this was 1977 and officials and circuit owners still ruled the roost and held the purse strings.

THE SQUADRON

The squadron flew in over the Cotswold stone walls and neatly planted fields for a reunion. The grass surrounding the long runway glistened in the spring sunshine as first a light aircraft and then a helicopter landed. As the squadron reassembled for probably the very last time at RAF Kemble the only man missing was the Wing Commander.

The surviving members of the group nicknamed 'the squadron' by Barry shook hands in front of the control tower. The three flight lieutenants, Raj, Fols and Stavros, were Barry Sheene's three closest friends.

Julian Seddon, a photographer and, to his surprise, Barry's agent, had known both Barry and Stephanie before they met and fell in love. Barry called him Raj because of his 'plummy' accent and dark complexion.

Jeremy Paxton met the Wing Commander through their joint interest in water-skiing. He later became Barry's brother-in-law when he married Stephanie's sister Susan. He earned the name Fols when Barry watched a programme about some disgraced aristocrat who arrived in Australia with no money but with his two most prized possessions, his Aston Martin and his butler Fols.

Steve Parrish had been friends with Barry since the mid-1970s. They had become teammates at Suzuki and lived life on the edge together, both on and off the racetrack. Steve's thick curly hair had earned him the nickname Stavros, after the character in the *Kojak* television series.

All active combat squadrons need support from the outside and Barry's was no different, with Andrew Marriott providing the Wing Commander with advice and support throughout his career. A founder member and partner in the very successful London-based CSS Marketing Company, he was nicknamed Count Jim Moriarty because of Barry's love of the British radio classic *The Goon Show* and the character played by Spike Milligan.

The squadron concept was complete *Goon Show*, dreamed up and acted by Barry in true Milligan style. The butler, Fols, remembers being the last man to be admitted into the Officers' Mess.

'The four of us were the squadron. Barry was the Wing Commander and Raj, Stavros and I were the flight lieutenants, although we were promoted and demoted at various times. Barry had blagged some notepaper from an RAF squadron who flew Jaguars and wrote to me saying I was up for promotion because the Wing Commander was impressed at the way I had dressed up in a schoolboy uniform for him one Tuesday evening. It was pure comic invention. I was definitely the Wingco's batman. Barry would always take his Gitanes out, bite the end of the filter off and say, "Step on that Fols."

'People would come up to him in an airport and say, "Do you mind not smoking," and he would reply, "Yes, when I've finished it."

'Barry could not stand being told what to do and he just did not get on with people who tried to. Barry was the only person I knew who not only got out of receiving a parking ticket in the King's Road but also managed to persuade the traffic warden to get her tits out which he signed with a marker pen. Barry also used some great phrases. He wouldn't say, "I would not leave that on the seat of your car, it may get stolen." Barry would say, "Why don't you leave that phone on the roof? It will save them smashing the windows."

'The La Famiglia restaurant in Chelsea was really the squadron's headquarters. Gigi, the Maitre d', was a very warm, engaging character and always made a big fuss of Barry who always insisted – at least ten times – that he did not want garlic on his food. It was ritual whenever you ate out with Barry, yet he would get at me for forgetting to say please to Gigi for a glass of water.

'If we were a proper squadron in a proper war, Barry would have been the Wing Commander and we would have laid our life on the line for him.'

Raj was the first officer to be admitted, probably because of that accent.

'It came to be when I was talking to him about Douglas Bader and Barry told me that if he had ever wanted to be anything else it would have been a fighter pilot in the Second World War. I think he really did because he was always talking about it. He said he would have been killed though I would have probably lived through it.'

Julian first met Barry when he was sampling the considerable delights of London in the mid-1970s. Barry was spending more and more time in the capital and less and less at home in Wisbech. Really, who could blame him when he had the world at his feet?

'Back in 1975 I met Barry at Piers Forester's house in Chelsea. He had just come through the whole Daytona crash thing and was looking for advertising contacts. Next day I rang Dan Cromer at his agency, which handled the Brut account. They were looking for somebody to support Henry Cooper and later Kevin Keegan. I told him all about this young guy Barry Sheene and Dan Cromer was very interested to meet him. I brought Barry in and, as always, he did the rest. He did his own management and the chat up. His great thing at the time was that he knew after five minutes if it was going to work or not by the body language of the person he was

Family portrait: Maggie and Franco at the back, Barry and Iris at the front

A smart but apprehensive Barry with a friend from the circus

Getting it sorted: Barry 'helping' Franco prepare the 50cc Itom before a race

Best forgotten: Barry starts his short battle with the Isle of Man mountain circuit in the 1971 125cc TT race

Barry celebrates his first grand prix victory

© Mick Woollett

Barry's look says it all as he tries to push the 250cc Derbi into life at the Salzburgring in 1971

Barry at home with mum and the cats

World at his feet: the
grand prix winner
© Hulton-Deutsch Collection/Corbis

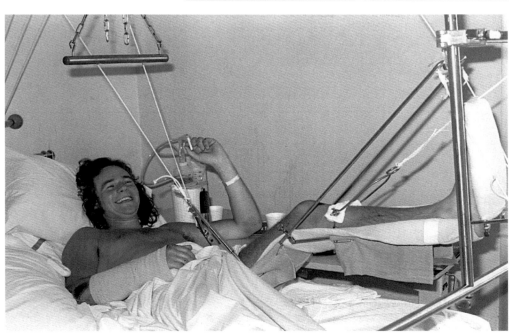

Barry's trademarks: a cigarette, a smile and a broken left femur. Convalescing at
Daytona in 1975 © Mick Woollett

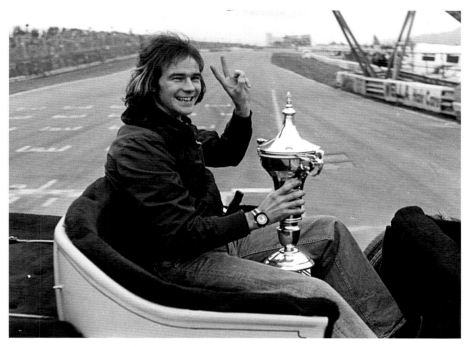

A warm welcome for Barry at Brands Hatch after the Daytona crash © Mick Woollett

World champion © Rex Features

Hitting the headlines in 1976: Barry, Stephanie and James Hunt © Action Images/Mirrorpix

Raising money for the 1978 Gunnar Nilsson Cancer Fund by driving Porsche 911s round Silverstone with Kenny Lynch, George Harrison, Rodney March and Steve Parrish

Above: Defending that world championship from Giacomo Agostini, as well as team mates Pat Hennen and Steve Parrish, at Hockenheim in 1977 © Henk Keulemans

Left: A suitably suited and booted Barry shows off his MBE, flanked by his proud parents

Below: The days of racing over the railway lines at Imatra were about to end © Henk Keulemans

The Family Sheene at home in Wisbech. Left to right: Uncle Arthur, Franco, Iris, Stephanie, Barry and Roman © Camera Press

Barry Sheene, MBE, 1950–2003
© Mick Woollett

talking to. He would talk like hell if he knew it was going to happen or keep pretty quiet if he knew it wasn't. This one did and it worked very well for quite a time.

'I was always hunting around in the advertising business, representing photographers and I was always in and out of the agencies. I was looking for stuff for Barry to do because the photography side was routine for me by then. We didn't really come to any formal agreement and I was paid in bikes or whatever. I was supposedly his agent but I only discovered it when I read it in his book. You would always get rewarded for setting something up for him with a bike or an introduction. Something would always come back.'

Although Julian and Barry were as different as the proverbial chalk and cheese they gelled immediately. To a man used to the London jet set, Barry's upfront approach to life in general, and females in particular, was a pleasant change for the celebrity photographer. Barry loved the London life that Julian epitomised and of course the social contacts were not bad either.

'When I first met him, my studio was near Ringo Starr's place at Vauxhall Bridge and later Steph and Barry wanted to have their wedding reception there but they put that off until he had nearly finished racing.

'I moved my business to Chelsea afterwards and Barry used to love coming to my office because there was a model agency upstairs. I had a sunbed in my office and he would hang around there just for a laugh. One day he had left his car outside on the double yellow line. A traffic warden duly arrived and was told it was Barry Sheene's car and would she like to meet him. She came into the office and Barry said, "You look sweet, would you like to show me your knickers?" which she did. The ticket never appeared on his windscreen.

'The agency upstairs was called Bobtons and we used to spend a lot of time socialising up there, or just gazing at the girls.

'Charismatically, Barry was different to other celebrities because he would talk to anybody. Most of the celebrities I've met really look to people above them and they usually have an eye on the main chance. Barry was already there and didn't need to prove himself to anyone. He would have just as good a conversation with the milkman as he would with the chairman of British Airways or Suzuki. He could talk high finance or empty milk bottles.'

Barry and Steve met for the first time in 1975. This was no London social gathering but the workplace, at Brands Hatch where Barry was one of the judges in the Stars of Tomorrow Competition that Steve had entered. Barry was impressed but unfortunately some of the other judges were not and Steve didn't win.

'Barry was there with girlfriend Lesley. I won both the 250cc and 350cc races on my Yamaha and was certain I was going to win the competition. I ended up second and Barry told me he had voted for me and thought I should have won.

'We started chatting and my girlfriend Linda got on with Lesley. We went out to dinner with them that night on the way back and we hit it off. He invited me over to Wisbech when he realised I lived near Cambridge, which was not far away. By the time I visited Wisbech Lesley had gone and Stephanie was on the scene.'

They were great friends from the start, but typically the Wingco had already pencilled in a task for Flight Lieutenant Stavros.

'Barry was in the middle of a six-month drink-driving ban and so I was shipped in to do some of the driving. You can imagine just how excited I was, driving Barry Sheene around in a Rolls-Royce. I used to go down for the weekend and we would do all sorts of stupid things like trials riding and racing around. We just hit it off from the word go and it never waned from then until he died.'

The formation of the squadron was a long way off but already three members were in place. There was no doubt who the fourth should be.

Piers Weld-Forester was a playboy in the true sense of the word. The grandson of the Marquess of Ormonde and a former boyfriend of Princess Anne, he decided to add motorcycle racing to his considerable list of conquests after meeting Barry Sheene.

Piers' obsession with living his life to the absolute limit had been brought about by tragedy, and his own life was to end in a similar way. In 1973 he married the model Georgina Youens, the daughter of the Queen's chaplain, but just nine months later, in March 1974, she was among the 345 killed in the Paris air disaster when a Turkish DC10 crashed.

Barry loved being around Piers and the London set and was soon spending a great deal of time at his house just off the King's Road, enjoying the delights of London, some of which were legal and others which were not. Barry was only too happy for Steve to share in the fun.

'Barry was spending a lot of time in room seven at Piers Forester's house in Waterford Road. Room seven was just a shagging shop really. Barry would go out and pull them and bring one back for Piers and one for me too.

'It was great to be in London, where it was as wild as you could imagine. Piers lived in a massive three- or four-storey house with rooms off everywhere. It would be worth around five million pounds now. It had a huge double garage underneath, where Piers' mechanic could work on the Yamaha TZ750 and also keep the transit van.'

Barry and Steve suddenly found themselves mixing with the high fliers of London whose sole aim was to have a good time. 'Piers could get anything he ever wanted. There were always lots of people in and out of the house, that we would call "waffa waffas" because they were rather posh. There were always lawyers and bankers around and Barry enjoyed mixing with them because he was always on the lookout for sponsorship. He had an angle with all of them and would talk to them all about backing him. Sometimes we would indulge in a few potions to keep in with them. A bit of the white powder plus a bit of dope, although we were not so keen on the dope because it made you dopey and that was the last thing we wanted.

'We were never worried about getting addicted. We would take something and have some fun with it but there was no way we were going to get hooked on it because we had a focus in life. Mine was to keep up with Barry and his was winning lots of world championships.

'A lot of the time we took stuff just for the giggle. I remember one night taking some amyl nitrite. No one else would take it but me, being the joker, did and – bloody hell – I was out of it. I never took it again. Our motto was, "we'll never die wondering" and so things had to be taken, if only once, but we weren't stupid.'

Barry and Steve eased into a very simple schedule. In the winter it was sex, drugs and rock and roll. In the summer it was all about racing motorcycles.

'When the racing season ended in October the fun and games started but once we got near to starting racing again it all stopped. I honestly don't know anybody in our close circle who ever took anything before racing. I remember one rider, Guido Paci, always used to have a tot of whisky before the start of a race because he reckoned it made him a bit braver. Tragically, he was killed at Imola. Very few of the riders we knew would think of taking anything because we were scared stiff it would make you go too fast or be too brave.'

The American racer Gary Nixon was no stranger to 'potions' and was also a frequent visitor to Waterford Road. On one occasion he obtained some laughing gas from a dentist and proceeded to inhale it after putting a black bin liner over his head. When he started to convulse it was Barry who pulled the bag off his head. Gary was a great admirer of Barry, both on and especially off the track before Stephanie burst onto the scene.

'One of the main reasons he was my hero was he reckoned he had 186 women in one year plus Lesley who I also thought was a damn knockout. I remember early in his career when he was racing at Talladega in America. We were walking down the stairs and this eighteen-year-old was coming up. He just said, "Nixon, see you in five minutes." He could pick up anything you could point at. I was always hoping to get the throwaways, but I only got a couple of them. Then he met Stephanie. I remember the first time I saw her – this killer chick got off the plane in France.'

The heartbeat of the Waterford Road scene was Piers Forester, who was beginning to take more than a casual interest in following Barry and Steve on to the racetrack. For him it was just another challenge to master while getting the biggest thrill imaginable. Steve understood.

'Piers was an incredible character. He was a typical aristocrat and loved life to the full. He might have taken cocaine and other drugs but nothing gave him the same high as racing motorcycles. Racing motorcycles gives you such a buzz you just want to go out there and do it again.'

Steve, like many others, discovered he could charm his way through life, opening doors that would have been shut to the majority of people. With his connections this also included royalty.

'At the end of the 1976 season Piers called me to see if I wanted a free winter holiday in Austria. I jumped at the chance, even though I had no idea just what it entailed. It transpired he had told Prince Michael of Kent, manager of the British Olympic bobsleigh team, that I was a top-class bobsleigher and should be invited to their training camp in Igls.

'I was designated driver and Piers was going to be the brakeman. I had never even seen a bobsleigh but Piers had found a dilapidated old one in a chicken shed in Switzerland. We borrowed it, cleaned it up and made our debut against the professionals from the armed forces.

'Initially Piers would not turn up at the designated training times until he had drunk enough whisky to make him brave – and he needed to be because we crashed on every run. We finally got expelled but we had already collected our expenses by then. The following year, the Prince was a guest at the TT races on the Isle of

Man and, minutes before the race started, he enquired if I was more competent at this than bobsleigh. Luckily I was.'

Tragically, Piers was killed at Brands Hatch on a grey autumn afternoon on 30 October 1977 when he fell from his TZ750 Yamaha and slid into the Armco barrier at Clearways corner, right in front of Julian Seddon.

'Piers crashed and was heading towards me with the bike on top of him. He lay on the ground in front of me; by the time we got to the hospital he had died. Just an hour before Piers had come into Barry's caravan and told him he had taken pole position for his race. Barry congratulated him and went out to compete in the next race. That was the last he saw of Piers.'

Barry was devastated and for once did discuss his great friend's death with Steve.

'You never expected Piers to die racing a motorcycle. He turned into a reasonable rider and was certainly no slouch. He was a club racer and his goal in life was to win a race at Brands Hatch. He certainly wasn't chasing world championships. Barry was very upset when he was killed because we just did not think it would happen to him. It was very close to home for all of us when he was killed.'

Piers Weld-Forester was killed before the squadron was formed but there is no doubt he would have been made a senior member.

Jeremy Paxton was the last member to be enlisted after he got to know Barry through a pretty familiar route: Barry wanting something for nothing but in the end repaying a hundred times over. Of course, as Jeremy recalls, this was not with hard cash.

'Baz was a very keen and very good water-skier. I was a full-time skier and met him at Thorpe Park. We just hit it off. He also thought I was good for a load of equipment. He used to invite me over to his place for the weekend and always asked me to bring wet suits and skis. In the end he had 150 unused ski gloves because, according to him, he was always running a little low. He could never run out of anything: if there was a world famine Barry would be the guy with five hundred cans of food.'

Cans of food or not, Barry paid for every one of those pairs of gloves in his own way.

'When Barry wanted to help you he did a great deal. I started up a water-skiing magazine, which you would normally expect to sell six or seven thousand copies. I put a photo of Barry water-skiing on the front page for the first issue and we sold out the print run of twenty thousand copies. He really got the ball rolling for me.'

Of course, you can't have a squadron without aircraft but that was no problem because Barry had long ago caught the flying bug. He already owned a Piper Aztec twin-engine aircraft when he decided that a helicopter would be the perfect way to augment trips round the country in the Roller. He gained his helicopter pilot's licence in record time at the end of 1981, which came as no great surprise to Flight Lieutenant Raj.

'Barry became a manic helicopter pilot. Once he started on something he became obsessed. When he began to learn to fly helicopters he was surrounded by papers, files and books. He did the course in about three-and-a-half weeks and passed. He was a very good pilot and was very funny with his voice contact over the radio. He was always best friends with everybody, including Heathrow. He never used formal radio procedure.

'"Hi, this is Barry Sheene, I'm in my Enstrom just going into Reading to the Ski Centre." Even Heathrow would say "Hi Barry" and in the end everybody would know his voice. Despite all this he was a very diligent pilot.'

After passing his exams Barry proudly parked his new Enstrom 280 Turbo three-seater helicopter on the back lawn at Charlwood. It was the squadron's first aircraft and his love of helicopters stayed with the Wingco until his death. Raj was one of the last people to fly with the Wingco in his much-loved Agusta 109C before he died.

'The last flight I did with him was when he had already told me he had cancer. He had just bought the Agusta that he had taken an enormous amount of trouble in selecting and been everywhere to find it. He had it at Melbourne airport and was on his own. I think he was feeling a bit dodgy and needed another pilot to sit with him. We flew it all the way from Melbourne to his back garden on the Gold Coast. It was one of the best flights I've had. We flew at between five hundred and a thousand feet along the coast. We stayed in Sydney, in a hotel that always gave him the same suite overlooking the Harbour Bridge. When we got to dinner he was feeling very sad and ill. We flew on next morning and landed in his garden after about four hours. I think he only flew it once after that.'

The flight lieutenants were encouraged, perhaps badgered, to take to the air. Both Raj and Fols became helicopter pilots while Stavros stuck to the fixed winged variety of air transport. Naturally, the *Goon Show* humour continued with plenty of jolly japes from the chaps back in the mess, especially at the expense of the newest recruit, Fols.

'I'd just got my helicopter licence and flew my Robinson R22 to Barry's place. We mucked about for the day then, when it was time for me to go, Barry suggested that the weather was not too clever. I thought it was OK to go. I got a bit fogged in and it was all a bit hairy. Gatwick control gave me radar vectors to get back to Barry's.

'When I arrived back at Charlwood, Barry was waiting and told me I was in so much shit I would want to kill myself. He told me I had strayed over the centre line of Gatwick's main runway causing an Air India jumbo jet to abort its landing and go round again which cost more in fuel than my helicopter was worth. He said, "All you can do is ring this bloke up and just grovel and hope they don't do you for it."

'He got me to call one Sid Miggins, supposedly head of Gatwick control. He told me it was a very serious matter, that I had stopped all the arrivals into Gatwick and caused the Air India jet to go round again. Barry briefed me to say I was really sorry and I explained I had only just passed my flying test. I was peeing myself. Nine years later, after this story had been told and retold by Barry, he just dropped into conversation one day, "Oh, by the way, Air India have never flown into Gatwick."

'I remember him and Raj sending me to Nottingham to meet

somebody who wanted to put two million pounds into sponsoring a water-skiing championship. Of course, when I got there I found out he didn't exist. Barry and Stavros used to sit in Barry's office and work out whom they could stitch up. I think they were bored.

'I only got him back once. We were going water-skiing and he came to pick me up in the helicopter from middle of Sonning-on-Thames. I told him to look out for a house with a great big lawn and the only swimming pool in the area. He landed at four different houses before he found the right one, which I suppose is probably illegal. I got my friend to ring up and tell Barry his landings had caused problems at the nearby White Waltham aerodrome and that he would have to make a statement under caution to the CAA. He made all sorts of excuses when he phoned them up and we taped it all and played it back to him six months later.'

Members of the squadron's families also had to endure the schoolboy humour. Raj's ex-wife was caught when returning to Gatwick after a holiday.

'I went to pick up my wife Patsy and her friend Lorna. Barry had asked two customs guys he knew to stop them. We were hiding in the customs office when they arrived. They were both very good looking. The officers told them they had a tip-off and needed to talk to them privately. My wife said, "That sounds like fun", and off they went. The customs guys literally pulled them apart and got very serious about it. Barry and I were watching through the one-way glass before appearing after a few minutes.'

George Harrison was also a close friend of Barry's. The ex-Beatle first met Barry at the 1977 Formula One car grand prix at Long Beach in California. When the squadron was sent on overseas duties, to defend the name of the British Empire in Australia at the 1994 Formula One car grand prix in Adelaide, George was with the chaps, although reputations meant nothing to Barry. George's dress sense, punctuality and music did not always please the Wingco, who was a stickler for discipline, as Fols can attest.

'We all went out to dinner at an Italian restaurant the night before the race. There was George, Barry, Damon Hill, Gerhard Berger, Raj and myself, as well as a couple of other people. George had got his hair in a ponytail and Barry told him that he had not washed his hair and that he had to go back to the hotel and smarten himself up. Incredibly George duly went back and washed and blow-dried his hair then returned wearing a white shirt and black blazer. Earlier in the week George had turned up fifteen minutes late for dinner and Barry went without him.'

This was a big weekend for the squadron because one of their dinner guests was upholding the honour of the country the next day. Damon Hill was taking on enemy number one, German Michael Schumacher, in the final round of the Formula One world championship. The Wingco was determined that nothing was going to distract him from the task ahead, especially not George Harrison. Barry put Fols in charge of the seating plan.

'Barry insisted that Damon did not sit next to George during the meal. He told me all George would do was get Damon chanting Hare Krishna next day, which would do him no good at all racing into the hairpin.

'So of course my mission then was to ensure that Damon and George sat together at all costs to annoy Barry who was so deadly serious. He kept telling Damon to take no notice of George when a courier arrived at the table wearing a turban. He had brought a package all the way from Bangladesh and it contained an elephant god.

'Meanwhile, George was still sitting next to Damon and burning incense under the table. Barry, who was of course smoking a Gitane at the time, kept complaining, "What is that shit smell? You will kill Damon even before the start of the race."

'They unpacked the elephant god and George told Damon it was a gift from him to put in the car during the race to bring him good luck. Barry said, "Fuck off George, it's ridiculous. It will fall down and jam the gear shift or something. He does not want an elephant god in the car." It was just pure pantomime. I think Barry's piss-taking was a great, fun-loving side. He just loved creating events and making an ordinary situation a memorable one.'

A year later the squadron was again on overseas duty in Adelaide, although the late arrival of both Fols and Raj led to an official reprimand from the Wingco. However, he relented on hearing the reasons for the delay, which included visa applications, army officers, Singapore hotel-room sheets soaked in red wine, a complete electrical blackout at the same hotel and, of course, girls. George and Barry were waiting for the flight lieutenants when they finally arrived for duty, as Fols recalls.

'We went out eating and drinking before the grand prix and then ended up in George's hotel room. The legendary Beatle gets his ukulele out and starts playing songs, George Formby, bits of the Beatles. It was amazing and for me it was a magical moment of my life. Barry, after about two minutes, said, "I'm off to bed."

'In the morning over breakfast we were recounting what had happened and what a truly great night it had been. We couldn't believe that Barry had left. He told us he just hated it when George got his "banjo" out. "It's so rude when we are talking. It would be like me getting my motorbike out and riding it round the room." He was not trying to be funny but he genuinely thought it was rude of George to start playing his "banjo" while everybody was having a chat. The great thing was that Barry was in no way overawed or intimidated by George. Everybody was equal to Barry.'

Certainly, Barry's choice of music would not have overawed George as an appearance on *Desert Island Discs* revealed. Barry certainly had the pop star image but definitely not pop star ability, as Raj soon discovered.

'He stands out as representing that period from a sporting point of view. There was not an awful lot happening in music and so in a way he did step over the boundaries. He became great friends with George and sort of eyeballed the music celebrities. In many ways he was a pop star although he had no musical aspirations at all. He certainly did not have an ear for music.'

'His taste in music was absolutely desperate. He loved Glenn Miller, later he liked Simply Red. In fact, he tended to meet people and like their music. He met Elton John in Australia and then played his records non-stop for three months or so.'

Occasionally, the squadron's communications became a little confused, especially while on overseas assignments. Once again the location was Australia and once again it involved mess visitor Damon Hill. This time the Wingco had only himself to blame although, as always, it was portrayed as Raj's fault.

'Damon was water-skiing with Barry on the river behind his house on the Gold Coast before the Australian Formula One Grand Prix. Damon fell in the water and Barry just pulled him out. I think it was as simple as that, but they then concocted this story that there was another boat heading towards Damon and Barry had dived in, rescued him, saved his life and in doing so had damaged his wrist. In fact, he thought he might have broken it.

'Barry then announced that he had broken a bone in his hand, but only because Damon and I decided we wanted to go to a nightclub. The "injury" suddenly became an issue because Barry did not like going out locally. He checked into the A & E department of the local hospital to avoid going to the club. We picked him up from the hospital when we came out of the club quite a bit later and the next morning at Brisbane Airport Barry started telling his rescue story to the press.

'Suddenly it became headlines in the Australian papers and then throughout the world because it was just before the grand prix when Damon could have won the world championship but instead got knocked into the wall by Michael Schumacher.'

Mercy missions were also a speciality of the squadron, especially if the Wing Commander felt that somebody was getting a raw deal. In the very early days he took Flight Lieutenant Stavros on a daring commando raid.

'It was a Friday evening in February 1978. Steph had cooked dinner at Charlwood; we had had a few gin and tonics and as always went to Barry's office to talk about girls and motorbikes when he announced we had a job on.

'He told me that the girl who helped Stephanie with the house-work had lent a load of money to a bloke and he hadn't paid her back. "He lives in Redhill and we are going to break into his house and steal a load of stuff to sell and get the money back. We'll take your car – no great surprise there – and break in," were the official orders from the Wingco.

'I'd got myself a Rolls-Royce because Barry had one, and it was another way of people thinking you were successful. I taped over the number plates and we set off. Once we'd found the address I backed down the side of this semi-detached house in the Roller, Barry had a key from the girlfriend and in we went with torches. I had done some pretty stupid things in my life, but breaking into a house in the dark with world champion Barry Sheene using a Rolls-Royce as a getaway car seemed pretty high up the list.

'We looked the part in our balaclavas and really were full-on burglars. He unplugged the Bang & Olufsen stereo system and television, and also found a shotgun that he decided to take as well. The stereo was huge and barely fitted in the boot. We had to put the television and shotgun on the back seat. I was giggling most of the time, but was a bit "poopy" when we were inside. Just imagine if the police had caught us not only stealing but also with the shotgun.

'Once we reckoned we had got the 250 quid's worth he owed, we drove back to Charlwood and unloaded the stuff in the workshop. We then had to sell it. I bought the stereo and I've still got it. Barry sold the rest and gave the money to the girl. To this day the arsehole boyfriend has no idea where his stereo, telly and shotgun went. Mission accomplished, in true Robin Hood style. For weeks after-wards we kept singing, "Robin Royce, Robin Royce, riding through the Redhill Glen".'

The Wing Commander also had some official duties. In 1984 Stavros asked Barry to be the best man at his forthcoming wedding to Ruth. On reflection, it may not have been the best of choices, especially as far as the bride's family was concerned.

'It was the first time I had seen Barry in a suit and Stephanie was pregnant with Sidonie. We had both crashed at the Swedish Grand Prix: Barry was on crutches and I had a walking stick. We were a couple of old cripples wobbling along.

'The wedding went really well until the best man's speech came along. He hadn't done a lot of research but the upper class Lincolnshire farming folk I was marrying into was looking forward to a speech from "former world champion Barry Sheene".

'I had met my wife at the TT races and Barry's speech basically consisted of him telling her family that most people come back from the Isle of Man with something they have to visit a clinic to get rid of but Stavros did much better and came back with the beautiful Ruth. There was a sharp intake of breath, nervous giggles and then silence from Ruth's side of the room.'

Andrew Marriott, or Moriarty, was not a member of the squadron but, with his own loyal lieutenant Linda Patterson, offered logistical support. His CSS management company opened doors for Barry. Andrew found that once the door had been opened slightly Barry would quickly go through, exploring the possibilities and making swift decisions.

'He was a fantastic person, the cockney kid with so many attributes, including speaking different languages and an interest in wine. He learnt to live the high life the proper way. He earned his place up there, not like some of the modern-day footballers. He could speak Spanish, French, Italian and a smattering of Japanese.

'We were looking after the driver management of James Hunt and he recommended us to Barry Sheene. The two of them had huge personalities and characters. In 1976 they were both world champions and we presented the pair of them together to Texaco, which was Barry's springboard to success. He loved the scent of a deal.

'Barry really didn't need a manager and he could have been the greatest manager himself. He was so smart. I was just the person who picked up the detail and made sure things happened to generate as much publicity for him as possible.

'I handled the logistics for him to do the Fabergé television adverts with Henry Cooper, who was also a delight to work with. He always dealt directly with the factories over his contracts but I helped him with Fabergé, Akai, John Player and Marlboro. He was a damn sight easier to deal with than anybody else. At times he could be a prima donna but he always knew what was required.'

As George Harrison discovered, and loved, nobody overawed Barry. Of course he knew how to court captains of industry but he also had the wonderful ability to make everybody feel important. Suddenly, everyone knew and loved Barry Sheene. His high-profile 'splash it all over' Brut television ads with Henry Cooper were beamed into every British home.

It was the perfect scenario for the British public. Brave, with a beautiful girlfriend, the cheeky cockney completed the deal by being a world champion. A package made in heaven for Moriarty and CSS, but it was the man himself who always produced the goods. Whatever the occasion, whoever the clients, Barry never let Andrew down.

'Once I got him to endorse the Co-op Society footwear division and he had to host two girls from Wolverhampton at the British Grand Prix. They didn't know much about racing but he looked after them brilliantly. He could talk to kids or kings. He had a good memory for names but if he could not remember somebody's name he would just call them "Ace", which of course they loved.'

Wolverhampton girls from the Co-op one day and chat show host Michael Parkinson the next, the Sheene approach was always the same and always just on the edge.

'CSS arranged for him to appear on *Parkinson*. Tobacco advertising was taboo but Barry had a big sponsorship deal with Marlboro.

He couldn't wear a branded shirt and so he wore a white shirt with a packet of Marlboros stuffed in the top pocket. When the bright lights went on for the start of the show the Marlboro logo appeared through the pocket of the shirt. The BBC didn't twig until it was too late. It was typical Barry, bright, clever and naughty. He was one of the most commercially astute sportsmen Britain has ever seen and he broke the Fleet Street barrier from back page to front page.

'He would always speak to the press and would make journalists feel important. He understood how to play them perfectly. I remember one Transatlantic Trophy press conference near Tower Bridge. The captain of the American team was Dale Singleton, who was supposed to be a pig farmer from Georgia. I organised for a piglet called Elma to be there for the photographs but Dale missed his flight connection and so we were stuck with Elma and some grumpy photographers. After much persuasion Barry agreed to hold the pig and seconds later it crapped all over him but the next morning he was in the papers holding Elma.'

So the perfect client – well, almost. Barry would sit in his office at Charlwood with the answerphone on. Important calls or friends never reached the end of the message as Barry picked up the phone. Others would have to wait and some never got a reply. There were also special codes for some callers. The codes would not have caused the Bletchley Second World War code breakers any lost sleep. In fact, for Moriarty's able lieutenant Linda, breaking the Sheene code was easy, rather predictable and certainly embarrassing.

'The only way Barry would pick up the phone to me was if I talked dirty for a couple of minutes on the answering machine. You can imagine what the other people in the office thought when I had to suggest certain things to our top client and world champion before he would even pick up the phone. Damon Hill asked us to help with his personal PR. I told him and his wife Georgie to take a leaf out of Barry Sheene's book, although without the special code: have two phones, one with an answer machine and one for private use. Barry understood how important it was to be available to the press through his line with the answer machine. They talked to him because he talked to them. He never turned anybody down and his opinions were always meaningful and made the headlines.'

Moriarty also had to put up with the usual Officers' Mess japes and was also called up to organise crumpet for the chaps.

'I often worked as the pit lane reporter for the ITV *World of Sport* Championship and more than once he grabbed hold of my testicles when I was talking, which of course he thought was highly amusing. He certainly knew how hard to squeeze them. I would also ghost-write his motoring column in the *Sun* because Barry was not really interested in testing Morris Marinas.

'He would have his picture taken with the car and then make me drive it. He would say, "Why drive a Marina when I have a Rolls-Royce?" Once I brought down a rear-engine Renault turbo to Charlwood for the photograph. He decided he would test that one and scared the life out of me.

'Barry phoned me one day to tell me he had a lunch date with newsreader Selina Scott. He asked me to come with him because he told me he wanted to pull her and wanted some help. He never got anywhere close.'

Flirting was regarded very much as a recreational must by the squadron's officers, even if it happened to be with members of the support staff, as Linda already knew from those code-breaking phone calls.

'Once I went to Hockenheim to report on the German Grand Prix for the *Sun*. We all had a great dinner and Stephanie went to bed. Barry kept asking me which room I was in. I went to my room and didn't know what to do. Do I take off my make-up and do I let him in if he knocks on the door? He never came and next morning I was cool with him. He was always flirting, but I knew if anything had happened our relationship would have changed and it would have been the beginning of the end.

'I suppose it was appropriate that even the last time I ever saw

Barry, at Goodwood after he had been diagnosed with cancer, noth-ing had changed, thank God. I came up behind him and put my hands of his shoulders and said, "How are you?" Without looking round he said, "Get down on your knees because I've got some-thing to show you." I went bright red and once again he had caught me out.'

Wing Commander Barry Sheene stands at the top of the squadron's roll of honour, the driving force behind a concept built on humour, respect, fantasy and plenty of love. The Wingco was not killed in action but his flight lieutenants knew he would have laid down his life for any of them in time of real conflict. However, as Stephanie points out, it would not have been without demanding something in return.

'If the squadron had been stuck on a desert island Barry would have had Fols digging a hole for him to have a crap, Raj up a tree picking a coconut but it would have to be the right coconut and Stavros swimming out to sea to catch him a fish for supper.'

KENNY

Little has changed in nearly thirty years for Kenny Roberts, the constant thorn in Barry Sheene's side. He's still small, incredibly quick on two wheels, loud and takes no shit from anybody. The former dirt-track champion from America came to Europe to take on the very best in grand prix motorcycle racing, headed by world champion Sheene, and won.

Just winning was not enough, though. Kenny won three successive 500cc world championships, caused Barry to leave Suzuki and then produced a son who also became a world champion. That's not a bad CV for a dirt-tracking lad from Modesto in California who was not that worried if he never came to Europe.

Kenny may have come out on top in the end but it was a classic head-to-head confrontation in the same mould as Ali–Frazier, McEnroe–Borg and Schumacher–Hill. It was a battle between two very different characters with opposing riding styles that produced some mighty confrontations both on and off the track.

Barry had been the master of unsettling both opponents and teammates by clever manipulation of the media, but it just did not work with Kenny. He was quite happy for Barry to sound off while concentrating on the job in hand – pinching his world title.

'We both enjoyed the jousting in the press and it certainly made us better racers. What I used to enjoy was reading what Barry had said about me this week and I would just lay low. People would say, "Have you seen what Barry says about you?" And I would say, "I don't care, it doesn't make any difference to me and has nothing to do with my salary or my job. He can say what he wants and I just race." I just did not get involved which made the whole thing a lot bigger.'

However, Kenny did understand just how big a name Barry was in Europe and how difficult it would be to shift him from the top of the podium.

'In America grand prix racing would receive no coverage. Sheene was 500cc world champion and Giacomo Agostini was fifteen times world champion but we never saw them ride the Ascot mile on the dirt. When I first came to Europe, Sheene was bloody famous. There were billboards in London advertising Texaco and I would think, what the fuck is this all about? In America I was known in the racing business but certainly not outside. This is a very small industry with little outside coverage, but when Barry was around outside coverage was not a problem. They all liked the flamboyant character that drove to the races in his Rolls-Royce or flew in by helicopter. I would drive to the grands prix in the motorhome with my wife and kids. It was two completely different people.'

It was not as if Barry had not been warned about the Americans. Pat Hennen took no nonsense from his teammate and had pushed him to the limit both in the world 500 and domestic championships in 1977. Barry had also witnessed the style and determination of Roberts on home soil in the Transatlantic Trophy races, in some of the classic European races such as the Imola 200 and when Barry raced in the States. Despite all the warning signs Barry did not take the Roberts threat seriously until it was far too late to do anything about it.

Roberts had learnt his trade in the rough, tough world of dirt and sliding, the AMA Grand National Championship staged on mile and half-mile dirt track ovals often situated in state fairgrounds throughout America. He had won the title twice for Yamaha against the all-conquering Harley Davidsons before dabbling in road racing. His ability to control a motorcycle with both wheels sliding transferred from the dirt to the grippy tarmac with startling success, which stunned the cream of Europe.

On the racetrack Roberts knew all about Barry and what to expect long before he arrived for that first grand prix of the 1978 season at the sweltering, dirty San Carlos circuit in Venezuela. Kenny remembers they were good friends until he had the audacity to challenge Barry in Europe.

'We were actually pretty good buds until I started racing against him. I first knew Barry when he came to America to race at Daytona, where of course he got hurt, and Ontario. We had plenty of fun together and I almost drowned when we crashed a hire car into the canal at Imola in 1974. Barry was operating the handbrake, I was steering and Gene Romero was working the pedals. We flipped over into the canal and I was trapped. I couldn't get out because the door was jammed against the wall of the canal. Eventually Barry and Gene got me out.'

In order to learn the European circuits, Kenny started the season also riding a Yamaha in the 250cc world championship but, as the season progressed and the 500cc title became a real possibility, he concentrated his efforts on dethroning Barry.

In their first confrontation of the season it was Barry who came out on top. Everything looked on track when he produced his customary win in the heat of San Carlos while Roberts, who had won the earlier 250cc race, retired with mechanical problems. Barry then flew home in seemingly great spirits for the start of the European season.

On the flight from Venezuela he became sick and once home began vomiting and losing energy. Barry started to worry when the symptoms just would not go away. Four weeks later, at the second grand prix of the season held in Jarama on the outskirts of Madrid, Barry felt even worse and this was reflected in his performance.

Hennen won comfortably from Roberts to take the lead in the championship with Barry a distant fifth and still complaining about a total lack of energy. When Barry complained, he complained long and hard and often through the press. Sympathy waned when he continued to moan, although results suggested he had a legitimate gripe. Any number of specialists failed to come up with a diagnosis as the Americans began to pile on the pressure.

Roberts was buzzing and won three on the trot, at Nogaro, the Salzburgring and Mugello. Barry had previously won at all three venues but two thirds and a fifth was the best he could muster as the championship started to slip from his grasp.

Roberts was starting to enjoy life in Europe. He led the world championship and didn't have to travel anything like the same distances as when he raced at home. Even the weather was not as bad as they had predicted back home but the toilets were another matter!

'I was just enjoying putting on road-racing leathers because the dirt-track leathers were oily and dirty and I had to eat up all that shit that the Harleys had been throwing up when I was racing in the States. It was perfect for me. The one thing I had been told before I came to Europe was that I would not like the travelling involved, but Europe was no travel compared to America. We would get in the car to drive to Daytona and it would take three days. No hotels, you would drive for three bloody days. So driving, for example, from England to Sweden, was nothing and you also get on a boat for a party. People had told me it rains all the time in Europe and really painted a bad picture about the 500cc world championship. From what I saw at Imola and the transatlantic series I had mixed feelings before I actually came.

'It was former 250cc world champion and Yamaha race manager Kel Carruthers who convinced me that I had to get over there because at the time the only thing I was interested in was beating those Harley Davidsons and had no ambition to come to Europe. However, what Kel didn't warn me about were those Imola shit houses.

'I remember coming out of the bathroom at Imola and asking him, "Where's the toilet?" He told me, "You see those footprints on the floor either side of that big hole, that's it." I told him, "I wondered what they were for but you must be kidding." He replied, "Just be careful that the shit does not hit your shoes." I saw my wife at the time going in there and thinking what the . . . It was unreal.'

It was also unreal for the Europeans to find the Americans way out in front as the summer break approached. The gap in the calendar left by the exclusion of the TT races from the championship had tragic consequences. Hennen, lured by a big payday, decided to race on the Isle of Man mountain circuit. It was a decision that cost him his racing career and very nearly his life. He crashed and was in a coma for three long months. He never raced again.

Barry was also chasing the cash during the break, on the roads at the Chimay circuit in Belgium. He won both the 500 and 750cc races at his annual payday but had a nasty scare when Franco was hit by a crashing bike in the pit lane and broke his ankle.

Before returning to grand prix action Barry relaxed on Heron boss Gerald Ronson's yacht, where he started to feel better. There were six races left and he trailed Kenny by ten points as the battle recommenced at Assen. Now it was just a two-horse race with Hennen ruled out for good.

Although he was now feeling better, Barry could finish only third at Assen and, a week later, at Spa-Francorchamps while Roberts increased his lead with two second places. Barry had to fight back, and he did at the bumpy two-mile Karlskoga circuit in Sweden. Having won his second grand prix of the season with Roberts down in seventh place the stage was set for a showdown. Kenny held a three-point advantage as they caught the ferry to Finland and the dreaded Imatra circuit. There were three rounds remaining.

Although the race was won by Dutchman Wil Hartog, with both Barry and Kenny failing to finish, the race was significant because it was the beginning of the end of Barry's relationship with Suzuki.

Barry broke down in the race when the crankshaft bearings failed. This was after he had warned the team, and the Japanese mechanics in particular, that he had heard a rumbling in the crankshaft during practice. However, they insisted it was OK and so the fifteen world championship points that a win would have given Barry went up in smoke.

Chief mechanic Martyn Ogbourne watched Barry and the Japanese get more and more involved in a war of words as the weekend progressed.

'I think the Japanese had lost all hope of winning the title and they had given up on him, although there are two sides to everything. Suzuki had always built a special bike by halfway through the season. Barry had just the one: it was light and it was trick. He was meant to save it but Barry practised on it at Imatra and had hardly gone out on the spare. It forced an issue to get more bits but I never realised at the time just how tight the budget was.

'It became a battle of wills. Japan said you will just do this number of laps on the special bike and Barry said he would do more than they wanted. Barry kept saying there was something wrong with the cranks, the Japanese would check and say they were OK. They couldn't have done anything anyway because there were no more bits to go in. Then the bike went *phut* in the race. Barry was convinced the breakdown cost him the World Championship.'

Barry was absolutely furious and the let the team have it with both barrels, especially through the press. His temper had not abated a week later when the circus arrived at Silverstone for the British Grand Prix with Britain's number one still in with a chance of retaining the title. Unfortunately, the weekend turned into a farce which not only left Barry out of the reckoning, but the time-keepers and tyre companies with a considerable amount of egg on their faces.

The rain started to pour down after the 28-lap race had started. Some riders came into the pits to change tyres. It was a long process on a motorcycle and Barry was in for over seven minutes while others stayed out, bravely skipping across the puddles on slick tyres. The spray and the unscheduled pit stops caused mayhem in the timekeepers' box and when the chequered flag was finally shown nobody was quite sure who had actually won. In the end a rather bemused but extremely grateful Kenny Roberts was awarded victory and, more importantly, fifteen World Championship points. Barry had ridden quite brilliantly after the enforced tyre change and thought he had won, but the timekeepers disagreed and third place was his reward.

Barry trailed Kenny going into the final round at a circuit that neither liked. The 14.189-mile Nürburgring high in the German Eiffel Mountains was a throwback to a bygone age. It was a road circuit and dangerous, bloody dangerous, with little run-off. Four years earlier the leading riders had refused to race there because the organisers wouldn't put down enough straw bales to protect the Armco barriers that lined the track. Two years previously Barry had given 'The Ring' a miss as he had already clinched the title.

Kenny had never set eyes on a circuit like it before but he led the championship by eight points. Barry needed to win and Kenny to finish no higher than fifth to take the title.

Kenny learnt the circuit by riding round on a road bike when the track was open to the public. Barry and Steve Parrish had been there earlier in the year, not on two wheels but on some rather exclusive four wheels that, as Steve explains, were not exactly suited to the task.

'Between the Dutch and Belgian Grands Prix we decided to go and have a learning session. Of course, Barry did not want to use his own car so he told Rolls-Royce there was something wrong with his car, asked them to look at it and requested one on loan in the meantime.

'They gave us a brand spanking new Rolls-Royce Shadow. It

smelt so new, had a lovely walnut dashboard and probably even in those days was worth around forty thousand pounds. We arrived at the Nürburgring where you could pay three deutschmarks for a lap of the circuit. We did a deal to do ten at a time but then found out this Rolls-Royce was only doing about seventy miles on a tankful. As we drove in the bloke giving the tickets out looked at us a bit strange because I don't think he'd ever seen a Rolls-Royce go round there before; plenty of Ferraris, BMWs and Porsches but not a Rolls-Royce.

'We just ripped the arse out of this car for two days. Barry would do three laps and I would do three laps and then we would refill with petrol. It was hilarious because we were passing people in sports cars with the Roller on two wheels and the tyres screeching. The brake and warning lights were constantly flashing because this car hated every minute of it and was certainly not designed to be raced round the Nürburgring. More and more spectators came to watch at places like the Carousel as we raced round.

'The poor old car was completely fucked at the end of it, all the warning lights were flashing, there were no brake pads left and the tyres were virtually bald.

'We stayed at the hotel at the circuit and I pulled this girl and took her back to my room which I was sharing with Barry. Things were just about to get underway between us when she farted. Barry, who was there to watch, started laughing so much she left.

'After two days of "testing" we headed back to Spa for the Belgian Grand Prix. We were bombing along the autobahn at 120 mph, which Rolls-Royces would do up and downhill all day long. Suddenly there was such a bang and the front tyre burst.

'We both thought we were going to die and I've never been so scared in my life. This car was more like a boat, veering across the three lanes completely out of control. I had my feet on the dashboard and Barry was grappling with the wheel. It finally spun at 40 mph and we slid to the side of the road and stopped. Both of us shit ourselves. We may have been racing all season and had just completed two crazy days of testing at the Nürburgring but that was the scariest thing that had happened to us.

'To this day I don't really know how Rolls-Royce took it back. Barry somehow managed to give it back to one of the Rolls-Royce dealers in London rather than taking it back to their headquarters in Crewe. I think he also persuaded the dealer to put on a new set of tyres and brake pads. We never heard any more about it.

'We certainly learnt the Nürburgring in style but it didn't do us much good. Barry finished fourth and I broke down although I was lucky to race at all. For a bit of fun, which on reflection was a bit silly, I cut some swastika shapes in my tyres when I went to have the bike scrutineered which did not go down too well with the organisers.'

The learning session courtesy of Rolls-Royce had helped but it was not enough. Roberts and Yamaha were cautious, mindful that any mistake could hand Barry the championship. Kenny finished third, just over two seconds in front of Barry, and was duly crowned the first-ever American world champion on two wheels. The transatlantic avalanche had begun.

It had been an incredible contest, which Kenny had won hands down despite Barry's enormous efforts to unsettle him, both on and off the track. The press had a field day, but beneath the headlines and innuendos both riders had enormous respect for each other. Kenny had always been happy to play along with the game to keep the pot boiling.

'We never hated each other and I never said that Barry couldn't ride a motorcycle. I respected what he did because if I smoked that much and never trained I couldn't have raced in a grand prix for that long. His specialty was in the heat and he won the race at Caracas in Venezuela every year. In my opinion, I don't think he had the natural ability that I had because he had not had the same upbringing as me on the dirt tracks and other stuff. I think I spent more time worrying about what I did on the racetrack than he did. I don't think that he was always so concerned about what actually happened on the bike.

'I don't care what you do but if you don't have a rival you are just beating your head against a wall. You have got to have a rival and you have got to have a good guy–bad guy scenario.

'I certainly made it more interesting for him because once you have achieved your goal there is only one way to go. The media would eventually have destroyed Barry. I just came along and heated it up. It was lucky for me that I had talent and nothing else.'

It was a tough time for Barry, who was riding as well as ever but at the wrong end of the season. However, he kept a firm grip on the British scene where he retained the *Motor Cycle News* Superbike and Shellsport titles, but all that really mattered was winning back the 500cc world championship from Roberts in 1979.

The year started well when Barry persuaded Heron Suzuki to re-employ Steve Parrish. They were joined by Tom Herron for the twelve-round championship, which started with Barry's customary win in Venezuela. With Kenny missing the race following a crash in pre-season testing it was the perfect start for Barry, who returned home with fifteen points.

The good mood did not last. At the Austrian Grand Prix Barry limped home in twelfth place with Kenny fighting back from injury to win. It was a bad weekend for the Sheene family. Franco, who was still working on the bikes, left a washer under the disc that caused Barry major brake vibration. It was a situation that Martyn Ogbourne had seen coming for a long time but that did not make it any easier to resolve.

'Mistakes were being made. At Snetterton the year before Franco forgot to fit a retaining clip and the brake pads fell out. He fitted the wrong brake discs in the rain at Silverstone and then left the washer under the disc in Austria.

'After Snetterton I went in to see Barry and told him that Franco would fucking kill him but he told me he could do nothing because it was his dad. I asked him what would happen if I ended up having a big argument with Franco, whose side would he be on? I was on the losing side because he was Barry's dad. I really was caught between the devil and the deep blue sea.

'Franco would say one hundred things and 95 per cent of them would be bollocks but 5 per cent would be right. That's what age and experience is all about and that's how you learn because people like Franco had been there and done it. I had to make allowances for when he was wrong. You must filter out the 5 per cent.'

After Austria, Barry did take due notice of his chief mechanic's concerns and made the difficult but correct decision to stop Franco working on the bikes. It was a tough call for Barry but he could not continue to put his life on the line out of family loyalty.

Although he started from pole the bad luck continued when Barry retired with big end problems in the German Grand Prix at Hockenheim where Kenny finished second. Another pole a week later at Imola only brought fourth place and Kenny began to pile on the pressure with victories in Italy and Spain where Barry could not start the bike after a crash in practice.

A new 2.590-mile purpose-built circuit had replaced the old rock-lined road circuit at Rijeka in Yugoslavia but, ironically, it was a small rock that caused Barry more agony at the sixth round. Barry retired when a stone flew up and hit one of the screws in the right knee he had damaged falling off his trials bike four years earlier.

To make matters worse it was a young Italian, Virginio Ferrari, on a Suzuki who was challenging Yamaha and Roberts for the title. It was a nightmare for the proud former world champion but he did as he was told and finished second by just one tenth of a second in order to protect Ferrari, the winner at Assen who now led the championship as Roberts had finished only eighth.

It was time for Barry to start reasserting his authority, both in the championship and with Suzuki, by getting back to the front. The leading riders boycotted the shortened Spa-Francorchamps circuit when the surface started to break up so it was on to Sweden and that outpost of Scandinavian road racing, Karlskoga.

Barry was a comfortable winner, completing five successive

victories in Sweden, but Kenny was fourth and regained the championship lead as Ferrari failed to finish. He increased his lead in Finland with a sixth place, three behind Barry in a race won by Dutchman Boet van Dulmen.

Barry realised the championship was beyond him with just two rounds remaining, but he still had the chance of restoring some pride by winning the British Grand Prix at Silverstone. He certainly tried.

A race where many different riders challenge for the lead can generate great excitement and is the hallmark of grand prix racing. However, sometimes a duel between just two riders absolutely on the limit of their skill, bravery and sheer determination in a game of high-speed chess can stir the blood even more.

It's the ultimate contest and rarely has there been one to match the Roberts–Sheene confrontation at Silverstone on Sunday 12 August 1979. It's still talked about today and was the one motorcycle race that had the nation on its feet as it was televised live by the BBC.

For Barry it was the chance to grab something from a disastrous season. For Kenny it meant fifteen world championship points and keeping Ferrari at bay. The weekend did not start well for the Englishman. In fact, it was a tough time for everybody involved in the team, as Martyn Ogbourne recalls.

'It was the only time I saw Barry have a go at Stephanie, when she picked up his helmet during qualifying. Barry had never shouted at Stephanie before and I realised just how big the pressure was on him to win the race. We had gone wrong with the setting and Barry didn't quite come in and throw the bike against the wall but he was in a state and just could offer no more input.

'We were just going slower and slower. I realised how much trouble we were in because the whole of Silverstone expected him to win. It dawned on me he was carrying that weight around like a great big millstone. I sent him away and went back to a setting we had used before.'

Barry qualified in fifth place with Kenny in pole but after an evening with Stephanie at Lord Hesketh's place he returned the next morning ready to do battle. His mood improved dramatically after the warm-up session.

'Barry came in the next morning and it was a like a weight had been lifted off his shoulders. I told him the bike was nothing like he had seen last night and I had taken off all the stuff he had wanted. I had gone back to a bike I knew he could go fast on. He came in after the warm-up and said, "I can win."'

Barry failed by just three hundredths of a second. Victory was imperative if he was to have any chance of taking the world crown but for once finishing second was almost as good. Barry was again the darling of the British public after showing just how good a grand prix rider he was.

After some early sparring with Hartog and Ferrari, Kenny and Barry upped the pace. This was a gladiatorial contest between two men at the very top of their game. At the height of the battle they even had time for a little fun. Barry famously put two fingers up behind his back as he passed Kenny whose Yamaha just seemed to have the edge on top speed down the 180 mph Hangar Straight.

The battle continued unabated until they raced through Woodcote Corner coming on to the start and finish straight to begin the last lap where they were confronted by a back marker on the racing line. It was George Fogarty, father of four-time World Superbike champion Carl. Kenny went up the inside and Barry took the long route round the outside.

The result was a 150-yard lead for the American with one lap to go. The Silverstone crowd willed their hero along in a dramatic last lap. At first slowly, and then not so slowly, Barry started to claw back Kenny's advantage, inch by inch and then yard by yard.

This time there was no back marker at Woodcote as Barry closed to within a couple of feet of Kenny's Yamaha. The American drifted wide coming on to the start and finish line and Barry was forced even wider, just clipping the Northamptonshire grass on the outside of the fast right-hand bend. The crowd rose as one to salute Barry's last bend and last lap effort that came so close to giving him victory.

When the dust finally settled Barry took the plaudits and Kenny the fifteen points. With Ferrari finishing only fourth behind Hartog, Roberts looked certain to retain his title going into the final race, at Le Mans in France.

Barry finished the season winning in France, but with Ferrari crashing out Kenny's third place was enough to give him the title. Barry was down in third place, just two points behind the young Italian.

Despite the problems abroad Barry had a good year at home, especially at Donington Park. It had been a tough year, with Tom Herron killed at the North West 200, but it had been good to have Steve back in the team. A proper teammate, this was never more clearly illustrated than in the Race of the Year at Mallory Park where Steve recalls going beyond the usual call of duty.

'Barry had bad knees because of his accidents and sometimes his knee would lock up when a tendon or a ligament got trapped. He had been out on the bike for the first untimed session in the morning at Mallory, went to get off the bike and couldn't straighten his leg.

'Qualifying was in an hour and a half and they had to get Barry to an osteopath to sort it out. We organised to take him to the guy he usually saw down Wisbech way and so of course there was no chance of him riding in the qualifying session.

'Barry could not be seen leaving the track and so we laid him in the back of the Rolls covered with blankets and coats with Franco at the wheel. The problem with Mallory was you had to go across the track to get out and so Barry rang race control and asked for the 125cc practice session to be stopped because Franco needed to drive out because he was not feeling so well.

'Before they zoomed off Barry asked me just to do a couple of laps for him on his bike in order to qualify for the race. On the back row would be fine, just as long as I got him qualified.

'Sure enough at eleven o'clock the announcement went out for

all Race of the Year bikes to paddock exit for qualifying. We let
them all go for a couple of laps and then "Barry Sheene" emerged
from the awning. I was wearing his helmet with a dark visor, his
leathers, his boots and of course riding his factory RG500 Suzuki
with the famous number seven. Barry was in the back of the Roller
on the way to Wisbech.

'I had arranged with Martyn Ogbourne just to do four laps, out lap,
warm-up lap, two fast laps and in. I did the four laps and raced straight
back into the awning where they started ripping Barry's bike apart,
claiming they had a major mechanical problem. I used to park right
next to Barry and went straight out of his awning into mine.

'In the back of my truck I ripped his leathers and boots off, put
mine on, changed helmets and ran to the holding bay where my
bike was being warmed up. There were thirty minutes left of the
qualifying session and so there were no problems. I even managed
to call in and change the suspension setting.

'When the time sheets came out I had put him on the front row
by qualifying third fastest on his bike while I was down on the
second row after qualifying in sixth place. He got back an hour later
and could not believe he had qualified on the front row. The Auto-
Cycle Union would have gone mad if it had found out. We had to
wear dog tags with our blood group and so if I had crashed they
would have put the wrong blood in me.

'He went on to finish second in the race and I finished fourth or
fifth. I always told him I was a better rider and he just had better
bikes.'

Despite the good form the writing was on the wall for Barry's
relationship with Suzuki. Little did he realise when he crossed the
line to take the chequered flag at Le Mans that their love affair had
finally run its course. He had won eighteen 500cc grands prix and
two world titles for the Japanese manufacturer but, as with many a
true love affair, it was time to move on. Yamaha beckoned.

MY WAY OR THE HIGHWAY

He may have had a funny way of showing it but Barry Sheene was madly in love with Stephanie for every single minute of the twenty-seven years they spent together. It's no good pretending it was the standard glamorous-model-runs-off-into-the-sunset-with-sporting-hero relationship, because it wasn't.

It was a complex love affair that was hard for some people to understand. Barry relied totally on Stephanie for support but his enormous insecurity meant that he still sought extra reassurance.

Stephanie stood by Barry through good, bad and desperate times. They cherished the good times when Barry was world champion and as a couple they were the talk of the town. She helped nurse him back to fitness after his Silverstone crash and then supported him in retirement and their subsequent move to Australia. Together with Freddie and Sidonie she fought with him against the cancer.

She also turned a deaf ear to stories of her husband's infidelity. She put up with his intolerance and obsessive attention to detail. Barry demanded 100 per cent commitment and loyalty from people around him, and that included Stephanie, but he could not live without her. She knew that, but Stephanie also felt exactly the same way about him. It may not have been love at first sight but once it blossomed it never died.

They met in 1975, got together as a couple six months later and finally married in 1984. The world they lived in was so unlike anyone else's. Celebrity status and domestic drudgery ran side by side with the threat of constant danger and pain. No wonder the actual marriage proposal from Barry to his intended was far removed from getting down on bended knee.

It came on an August morning in 1982, in the lavatory of his private suite at the Three Shires Hospital on the outskirts of Northampton. It was not the most romantic of locations and nor was it the most romantic of proposal speeches from the bridegroom, as Stephanie recalls.

'After the operation following his Silverstone crash in 1982 Barry had not opened his bowels for a long time and, despite enemas and medicine, nothing was happening. He was getting really stressed and one day told the nurses to leave us alone in the loo at the hospital.

'He was so desperate to go that he stuck a teaspoon up his backside. I was shocked and told him that I could not believe what he was doing and that he could perforate his bowel. His reply was not what I expected. He simply said, "Steph, you've seen everything now so I suppose I'll have to marry you," and that was that.

'Five years earlier, when we lived in Putney, we thought about getting married but didn't want anybody to know until we told them. Barry hated a fuss and was not one for birthdays or anniversaries and so when Franco and Iris started preparing a list of relatives Barry said "fuck this" and called it off.

'We got married on 16 February 1984 in England, just before we left for the South African Grand Prix. We went to Epsom Registry Office without telling anybody. When we came out there was a load of builders on the scaffolding opposite shouting "Good old Bazzer". Iris took it as a personal slight that we had not told her and did not talk to us for a few days.'

It was not only Iris who was miffed that she had not been told about their big day. Linda Patterson, who looked after all Barry's personal PR, wasn't happy that it was the press who told her that her client had finally tied the knot.

'I got a call from the *Sun* saying they had heard that Barry had been married that afternoon. I told them no chance; if Barry had got married he would have told me. Then the *Express* and *Mail* rang and I started to worry. I rang Barry and asked him if he got married today and he replied no, of course not, I got married yesterday. He did not tell anybody because he did not want to make a bun fight out of it. I was so pissed off.'

Stephanie and Barry first met by chance in London, outside the fashionable Tramp nightclub, in 1975. Stephanie remembers that no words were exchanged.

'I had never heard of Barry Sheene and didn't even know that grand prix motorcycle racing even existed when my husband Clive got me to watch the ITV documentary about Barry's crash at Daytona.

'In September of that year I went with Clive to the Fashion Models' Ball and afterwards ended up at Tramp. As we were going in I saw Barry outside on a pair of crutches. Once inside I told Clive that I had seen that bloke from the television documentary. He sent me outside to find him and ask him in for a drink, but when I got there Barry had disappeared.'

While Stephanie knew very little about the bloke from the television documentary apart from the fact he was back on crutches, Barry had certainly seen pictures of Stephanie. A beautiful slim blonde, she was at the height of her modelling career, featuring on the front covers of all the right magazines and starring in the Old Spice television adverts. The only problem was that she was married with a young son, Roman.

'I met Clive at the BBC Television *Top of the Pops* studios. The big hit at the time was Gary Puckett and the Union Gap, singing

"Young Girl". I was the young girl with both still photographs and images of me dancing on the stage, all false eyelashes and showing my knickers, flashing on the screen when they were singing.

'Clive was the manager of Paul and Barry Ryan who had a big hit, "Eloise", and was also a photographer. We got married and it was a pretty big ceremony with the likes of Cat Stevens attending but we were both too young. I was eighteen, and by the time I was twenty-four it was all over. We had Roman, but it was a rocky road.'

Stephanie came to London when she was just seventeen years old. With three friends from Manchester she began life down south as a bunny girl at the world-famous Playboy Club in Park Lane.

'My father was a Warrant Officer in the Military Police and my mother was from East Prussia and had fled in the war from Russia to Germany where she met my dad.

'We spent a great deal of my early life in Malaysia before coming to England and settling down in Chester. I moved to Manchester when I was seventeen to work for the Lucie Clayton Modelling Agency. I was living with three other girls and a gay guy called Peter when we applied to work at the Playboy Club in London.

'You had to be eighteen but I forged my date of birth on the papers and got the job as a bunny girl. The three girls, Marie, Lynne and Judy, also came and we shared a tiny little room off Baker Street. We were all down-to-earth girls and would pee in the sink to save the long climb up the dark stairs to the loo.'

Down to earth or not, they certainly made a lasting impression on the London scene.

'Lynne was going out with DJ Tony Blackburn, while Judy was seeing Peter Morton who set up the Hard Rock Café chain and Lynne eventually married Ritchie Barrie, who was the boss of Fabergé.

'I was modelling for *Vogue* and *Cosmopolitan* and also appeared in a film as an extra. I was a vestal virgin and had to rub oil on to Charlton Heston's shoulders.'

It was not exactly a match made in heaven. Barry was a scruffy cockney boy racer on crutches after falling off the back of a trials bike with a reputation of dating the ladies and then not returning their calls. Stephanie was a beautiful model with a circle of high-society friends and perhaps, most important, a husband and young son. However, it was Stephanie who made the first move.

'A few days after seeing Barry outside Tramp my modelling agency was preparing some new promotional cards for me and I remembered the colourful leathers that Barry had been wearing in the documentary. Our agency was in the same building as IMG who did some work for Barry. I got his number from them and rang him to ask if I could borrow a set of leathers.

'Barry asked me round to pick them up and it was the first time we met. I honestly did not think anything about it at the time and the only thing I really remember about him are the weird shoes he was wearing. I took the leathers home and tried them on. Barry rang later and asked how they looked.'

Barry was hooked but realised the situation with Stephanie was very different to his many conquests back in room seven at Piers Forester's Chelsea home. Barry knew he had to tread carefully.

'Barry rang again the next day and invited Clive and me to lunch. Clive couldn't make it because he was working but I went after I had been out riding in the morning. I had lunch with Barry in London. One thing led to another and it all happened so quickly.

'I remember he had seafood salad and steak at that very first lunch and he wanted me to have the same. He just liked me to eat the same as him and could not understand why I wouldn't.

'It started to get very serious and we both decided we would tell Clive at Easter in 1976 but he found out just before and there was a huge upset.'

Huge upset there certainly was. Barry Sheene was now making headlines on the front pages as the British media had a field day. The love story was all over the popular press, especially after Barry and Stephanie really went public with their romance at the second round of the 1976 500cc world championship at the Salzburgring.

'We stayed in the beautiful Kobenzl Hotel overlooking Salzburg. Ted McCauley from the *Daily Mirror* tracked us down and also stayed at the hotel. Little did he know, but Marianne Hartzog, the owner of the hotel, let us both listen on the other telephone to Ted phoning over his copy. I was annoyed because he said I was a Playboy model and conveniently forgot to mention *Vogue* or *Cosmopolitan* but I couldn't butt into his call.'

The story was out and Stephanie set about getting Barry a little bit more up to scratch on the clothes and style front while he just went on winning races to celebrate his new romance.

'My first job with Barry was to trendy him up and in particular do something about that dreadful hair that he never used to wash. I soon got him to my hairdresser and even Barry was pleased with the outcome. The first time I stayed at Wisbech I was going through his drawers and found hundreds of pairs of white socks. Apparently he would go to Marks and Spencer in London to buy them. It was only many years later, at a Formula One race in Barcelona, that the paddock fashion police nabbed him about wearing those socks. I was always told never to trust a man with white socks. I should have listened.'

Barry's eating habits also caused Stephanie more than a little embarrassment.

'When I first met him I thought he must have come from a big family because he ate so much. We would go to the Heskeths' for dinner with twenty others when they raced at Silverstone. There would just be enough Yorkshire puddings to go round but when they arrived at Barry's plate he took eight, leaving the rest of the guests without. Barry just did not understand.'

Stephanie had already discovered just how cosseted Barry was by Iris and Franco. He could do no wrong in their eyes, even if it meant upsetting his sister.

'Early on I was amazed when Maggie told me that Iris just blanked her own daughter because her husband Paul had beaten Barry in a race. She ignored Maggie because Paul had the audacity to beat her son.'

Barry finally moved out of Queen's Court in Holborn at the end of 1971. His new home, where he was of course joined by Iris and Franco, could not have been a greater contrast. Ashwood Hall, on the edge of the windswept fens, was a six-bedroom farmhouse at Walton Highway near Wisbech in Cambridgeshire.

Soon after Barry and Stephanie started living together they moved back to their beloved London, buying a house in fashionable Putney. The house was in Deodar Road, which Barry soon nick-named Armpit Avenue.

So what was the attraction? Why did Stephanie give up that life of glamour and glitz to travel the world spending hours in smelly garages with the threat of tragedy never far away?

'He was so cheeky and I had never met anybody who could get away with so much. The first time we went to meet my parents in Chester was after Barry had been racing at Oulton Park. I told him not to do anything silly or embarrassing when we got there, like grabbing my boobs. One of the first things he did when we arrived was tell my parents exactly what I had said about my boobs. I was gobsmacked, while my parents just laughed nervously. Barry just had so much front.

'I was such a little goody two shoes and Barry was so outrageous. He was sometimes surprised that things he said upset people so much.'

Steve Parrish watched his friend fall head over heels in love. Like Barry, he realised this was not the usual conquest and then cut and run. This was for life.

'He was madly in love with her and I've never met such a tactile couple. Even at home they would always sit in the same chair together and cuddle. I think it started for Barry with his family.

'Steph did have a big influence on Barry when she came along and, as she said, she trendied him up. She smoothed off the rough edges because Barry was still a London biker. The timing was per-fect because it was just at the time he was becoming the face and the personality people wanted. He was getting sponsorship from clothing companies such as Mashe jeans and Fruit of the Loom. The cockney kid made good with the beautiful blonde model on his arm. He just loved all that.'

True love can circumnavigate most problems and doubts but there were times in those early days of passion when even Stephanie wondered if she was doing the right thing.

'I went to my first race that year and it was so very unromantic. It was a very different life and I did think in those early days, just what have I got myself into? I remember sitting on an empty petrol can and drinking vegetable soup in a windswept, smelly garage with Barry's teammate John Newbold and his wife Allison thinking just that. I had to get involved in the racing as quickly as I could, so I started to learn timekeeping by operating the stopwatches. I used to sit in Andrea Herron's caravan at places like Scarborough and she would give me lessons.'

Although they were a well-known couple, being a celebrity in the 1970s was very different to how it is today, as Stephanie explains.

'They were very happy days because Barry was winning races and we were in love but we were not really the Posh and Becks of the 1970s. The press didn't pursue you like they do these days and Barry was just an ordinary bloke whereas David Beckham likes to dress up and wear diamonds. However, Barry was brilliant at keeping up his profile, which he did even when he had stopped racing, but I still had to come back from the races to do all the drudge things at home, like cooking and washing.'

In between those days of bliss and domestic drudgery the new celebrity couple did move among the higher echelons of society. Stephanie recalls a special weekend in France in particular.

'One year, when Barry was racing at Paul Ricard, we stayed down on the coast at Bandol with George Harrison and Libby, Ringo Starr and Nancy, Paul Simon and Eric Idle. We were well down the pecking order in terms of who was the most famous. Sadly all the real sports personalities from that time, George Best, James Hunt and

Barry, are now dead. Franco used to say, "Not good for the sport, all this publicity."'

Their mode of transport was the Rolls-Royce Silver Shadow with the obligatory BSR 4 number plate. Despite Franco's misgivings the sport thrived on all the publicity and the media just could not get enough of Barry and Stephanie.

The legendary Eamonn Andrews appeared with the famous red book in the Horticultural Halls at the Sporting Motorcycle Show in London on 25 January1978 to 'surprise' Barry with a *This is Your Life* invitation. Unfortunately, it was not the surprise it was meant to be for either Barry or Stephanie.

'Of course Barry was not meant to know but Gary Nixon let it slip. Barry knew it was going to happen but didn't know when. Barry rang Steve Parrish asking him to check out the name of a researcher who had rung Gary. Steve discovered she worked for *This is Your Life* and so the cat was out of the bag.'

Later that year Barry appeared on Michael Parkinson's chat show with Shakespearean actor and motorcyclist Sir Ralph Richardson. In between those television appearances he popped in to Buckingham Palace to receive the MBE awarded to him in the 1978 New Year honours list. Only two people were allowed to accompany him to the Palace and Stephanie insisted that he took Franco and Iris and wore a suit. For once he followed her instructions.

In that same year Barry confirmed his celebrity status when he bought his very own manor house at Charlwood on the Sussex–Surrey borders near Gatwick airport. The thirty-four-room mansion came with duck pond, workshops from which he ran the Sheene team from 1980 until his retirement and plenty of lawns to land a helicopter. He sold both his Putney and Wisbech properties to finance the purchase of a house which was home for Barry, Stephanie, Iris, Franco, Uncle Arthur and later Sidonie as well as an Alsatian named Nixon (after Gary Nixon) and various cats and ducks until they moved lock, stock and barrel to Australia in 1987.

As the likes of David and Victoria Beckham have discovered, the road to fame and fortune is not always smooth and you can be reminded of that fact at the most inconvenient times.

'I was in hospital in Australia about to give birth to Freddie and was crying out for an epidural. The anaesthetist came in to administer it, saw Barry and that was that. He was telling Barry how he had watched him race at Mallory Park in England while I just carried on screaming and got on with the birth. It was so typical.'

Stephanie could have carried on her highly lucrative and successful career as a model but there was one big problem, Barry did not want her to and for one particular reason.

'I could have carried on working but Barry could not handle the fact I would be working with male models. He was very jealous and I could never look sideways at another man, not that I ever did. I gave up my career to be with Barry. I was happy to and it was never an issue. Once, when we were out dancing in those early days, I got tapped on the shoulder and it was Omar Sharif, who I had once worked with. Barry was amazed that I knew him, but when Omar sent me a picture of us together he would not let me hang it on the wall.'

Julian Seddon became great friends with both Barry and Stephanie. He realised very early in their relationship that they were very much in love. Julian also knew that Barry wanted, as always, to have things very much his own way.

'The first time I met Barry at Piers' he was not with Steph, but the second time he was and they were an item very soon after that. She was very pretty and I knew because she worked on a calendar with me. I met her before I met Barry, when my friend Francis Giacobetti was doing a feature for *Lui* magazine. They were down at Runnymede, near Windsor, and I turned up at lunchtime and there was Giacobetti with a camera stuck up Stephanie's skirt.

'We also did some work together on some British Leyland calendars and she looked great. I had put up a lot of these calendars in my office and early on when Barry came in he took every single nude picture of Steph off the wall. He took all the calendars and all the pictures I had of her, he took everything. Mr Control coming in.'

Julian also noticed a change in Stephanie as the relationship blossomed.

'I watched Steph improve in every way during the course of her relationship with Barry. She had a great sense of humour, but very different to Barry's when I first met her. She acquired about 80 per cent of his wit, humour and repartee and she still has it. She is fantastic and everybody looks up to her. She always stuck with Barry and really looked after him right from those early days when she would clean his helmet visor with washing-up liquid.'

To say Barry was not an easy person to live with is a vast understatement. He knew what he wanted and usually got it. From his childhood at Queen's Court, Iris and Franco moved heaven and earth to ensure their only son's wishes and demands were always met. He was obsessive about detail and genuinely could not understand why this irritated people so much. It was never going to be easy for Stephanie, but she soon learnt to adapt to his ways.

'He really was two people. Barry himself and Barry the racer. He was obsessed with bowels and every day would write down when he had been, together with his blood pressure, what he had eaten for breakfast, lunch and dinner and if we had had sex the night before. He had a code for everything.

'He would know if the gravy had an extra few granules from the day before and if the Mars bar he ate every day had not been in the fridge long enough.'

Barry required all aspects of his life to be organised in their own little boxes and woe betide anybody, and Stephanie in particular, who tried to shake them about.

'In later years, once Barry had eaten he would go to bed and he never thought of entertaining. We went for Christmas lunch with some friends at the Sheraton Hotel in Australia. We were early, as always, and they were half-an-hour late because they had been caught in a traffic jam. Barry ordered and had started his Christmas dinner before they arrived. When they were halfway through their meal he went to get the car ready to leave.

'Another time, he convinced Mick Doohan to fly all the way to Ireland to the Belfast Motorcycle Show because he would have such a great time. Mick went but Barry was in bed by half-past nine.'

Stephanie also knew that Barry was a great stickler for order. 'We always followed the same routine when we flew to England. I would be glad we were travelling first class because Barry would be sitting in front of me in seat 4K and not alongside me when we flew British Airways. He would have a glass of Chardonnay when we boarded and if they did not have his favourite he would send one of the crew out to the duty free to buy a bottle. Then of course it would not be cold enough. He would also complain if there was no redcurrant jelly for the lamb because that's how it was at home. We had twenty-five jars of the stuff as back-up.

'He would always have to be first off the plane, even if we then had to wait forty minutes for the luggage. Movie choice was a night-mare and he would always ask for what people were watching down the back rather than choose from the massive selection in first class. The great thing was that Barry dealt with all the details of tickets and passports. It was always all sorted.

'Barry would always want to stay at the same hotel and in the same room. It always had to add up to seven. If it did not he would get really upset. We always stayed in the same hotel in Belgium and Barry would always steal the towels. They were thin blue ones and we've still got some at home. In a restaurant Barry would always ask for the same table and sit in the same chair.'

The same was true at home: 'Every night he was home we would have to have our dinner with the news on, which for the kids must have been the most boring part of the day. At half-past six we would kick him out so that we could watch *Neighbours* and he would go to the office and start phoning people in England who had just woken up.

*

There was also some fun and games, usually at the expense of authority. He had been involved in a long-running feud with Vernon Cooper, who was chairman of the Road Race Committee of the Auto-Cycle Union, the sport's governing body in Great Britain. They had long argued over rider safety, the TT races on the Isle of Man and, of course, money. One night before a race meeting at Donington Park and after more than a few glasses of red wine, Barry sent Stephanie and Steve's girlfriend Linda on a mission to exact some revenge.

'We were staying at the Donington Manor Hotel and the night before the race the boys persuaded us to go out into the car park and let down the tyres on Vernon Cooper's Jaguar. Linda and I crept out into the car park and let down all four tyres by sticking matchsticks into the valves, although we had to keep hiding because Linda was laughing like a startled hyena. She was worse in the morning when we saw the four flat tyres while eating our breakfast. Luckily we left for the circuit before him.'

There was also the famous incident when a television set suddenly found itself unplugged and descending rapidly from a French hotel window into a wedding reception below.

'We were staying at a hotel in Le Mans and the night before the race there was a noisy wedding reception in the atrium below our room. Barry rang reception and asked them to ask the people at the party to quieten down. Nothing happened so Barry ripped the television off the wall and threw it out of the window into the middle of the reception. It more than did the trick. The next morning Roman and Adam, his friend who had come to the race with us, remarked about all the broken glass outside. The hotel never said a word. Barry won the race the next day and there was a new television in the room.'

Barry had a fearsome reputation with the girls long before he met Stephanie. His exploits with the likes of Piers Forester, Stavros and Gary Nixon were the stuff of legend. After he met Stephanie he calmed down. The wit and the cheek remained, but genuine exploits were few and far between, and certainly never serious.

Amazingly, Stephanie never tried to find out if her man was being unfaithful. It really was a case of what the heart does not know, the heart does not grieve.

'He probably screwed around because of his insecurity but it was not an issue. I never really suspected him and had no proof. Barry was very clever like that and what I didn't know I didn't try to find out. Barry always had an answer but I always knew when he was lying because he had that look on his face and put his finger up to his tooth.

'I honestly never found anything out and I always believed it was better not to dwell on what I didn't know. Nobody ever phoned up to say he was messing around with their wife. Often Barry was all mouth and trousers.'

However, on one rare occasion Stephanie did do a little detective work, together with Linda. It hardly required the assistance of Sherlock Holmes to work out what was going on when they followed Barry and Stavros to Gatwick airport after dinner at Charlwood. The result certainly surprised the boys when they returned home after a 'quiet' drink.

'Linda and I followed Barry and Steve to the Gatwick Penta one night. We looked through the blinds and saw them chatting up a couple of Air Florida hostesses. We went back to Charlwood and I burnt my wedding dress. Linda collected all Steve's clothes together and threw them out of the window on to the lawn.'

It was not the first time Steve had found his clothes thrown out of a bedroom window. Flirting and whatever followed was part of the challenge of life. A bit of clothes-throwing just spiced it up a little more and added to the fun, as Steve remembers.

'It was all a bit of a game when we went out, making sure that "her indoors" never found out. Barry did flirt a hell of a lot although his bark was worse than his bite. He loved to be seen flirting because it was all part of his image. Showing off when he was out was certainly a way of hiding his insecurity.

'Going out and getting girls was almost the same challenge as going out and setting a new lap record.'

Even an alleged incident involving Formula One star Gerhard Berger and Barry just a week before the 1996 Melbourne motor racing grand prix did little to faze Stephanie. A girl claimed she had been sexually assaulted by Barry and Berger in a shopping centre near Barry's Gold Coast home. The girl eventually withdrew the allegations but it had not made good reading for the two stars. Stephanie told Barry that he had completely misjudged the situation and almost paid the price.

'It was Barry being stupid. I thought he would slow up when he got older. He didn't realise something like that could blow into something so big. Barry could not understand how things he said sometimes could upset people so much.'

Barry had announced his retirement from racing at the beginning of 1985. Racing-wise it was absolutely the correct decision, but for Barry it was a very tough one to make. As always, Stephanie was there to help him as he sought fresh pastures to feed his insatiable appetite while not dwelling too much on past glories. It was the moment great sportsmen dread but Stephanie understood.

'When you are a big name in sport the time comes when one day you are knocked out of the tree. Some people can't handle it but you have to get on with new areas of your life.

'You may be a famous person but people forget you are just the same. Barry always made an effort to be special but he had to begin a totally new era and it was hard to accept. He was looking for new things to do and once said he would rather suffer a frontal lobotomy than race a motorcycle again, but of course he did. He also had his weekends commentating on the V8 Supercars and on the RPM television programme for Channel Ten.

'Whenever he walked into a room women would turn their heads but that was not happening as much. It was the same for everybody. When we first used to fly into Heathrow all the taxi drivers would know him and say, "Hi Baz, we saw you racing last weekend," but as he got older they would say, "Hi Baz, my mum was your biggest fan."

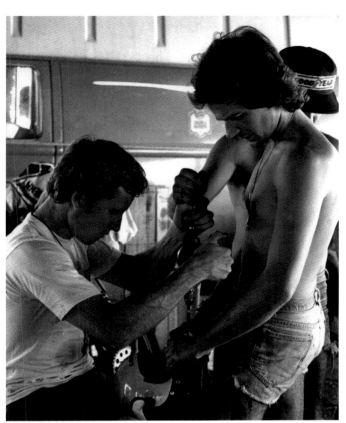

Helping hand: Barry helps Kenny Roberts drill a hole in his helmet to combat the heat in San Carlos, Venezuela © Mick Woollett

Cheer up: Barry and Kenny reflect on their epic battle at Silverstone in 1979

A classic Roberts/Sheene encounter at the 1979 Dutch TT in Assen

Second he may have been, but Barry won all the plaudits and champagne at the 1979 British Grand Prix © PA Photos

Still at it: Kenny and Barry fighting it out at Spa-Francorchamps in 1981 © Henk Keulemans

Marco Lucchinelli and Barry celebrate that double victory at the 1981 Swedish Grand Prix

The remains of Barry's Yamaha are cleared from the scorched tarmac on that August afternoon in 1982

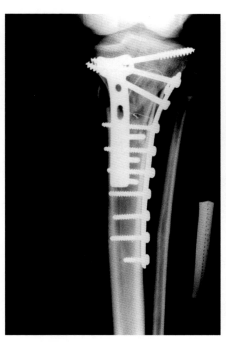

Jigsaw completed: the result of Nigel Cobb's seven-and-a-half hours at the operating table

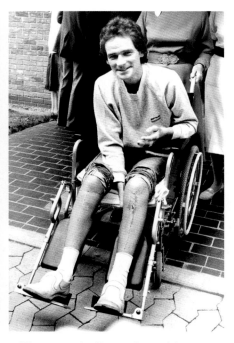

War wounds: Barry shows his scars as he leaves the Three Shires for the last time

Steve had the audacity to lead Barry in the 1983 Gold Cup at Scarborough –
but not for long

Barry and Steve,
the best of friends
until the very end

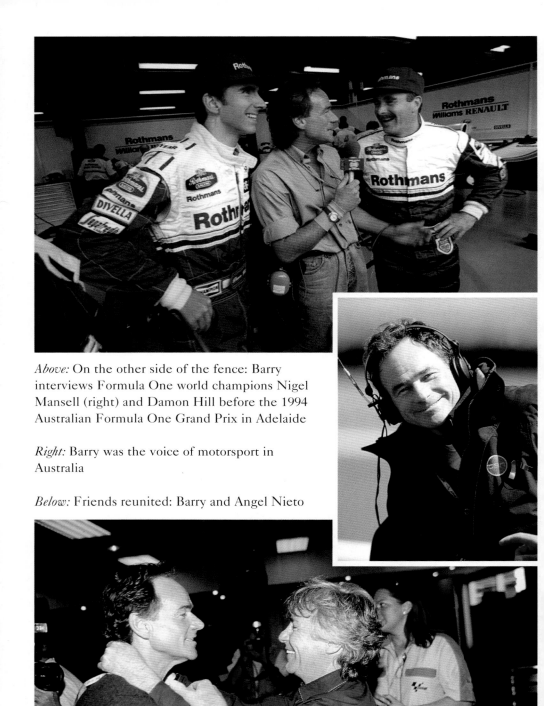

Above: On the other side of the fence: Barry interviews Formula One world champions Nigel Mansell (right) and Damon Hill before the 1994 Australian Formula One Grand Prix in Adelaide

Right: Barry was the voice of motorsport in Australia

Below: Friends reunited: Barry and Angel Nieto

The packed trophy cabinet in Barry's office at Manor House © Camera Press

Family man: Barry at home in Australia with Freddie, Stephanie and Sidonie

The final tribute: Valentino Rossi flies the number 7 flag after winning the 2003 Australian Grand Prix at Phillip Island © Getty Images

'Barry also hated having to pay for anything but all of a sudden had to start. Before then he had always taken it for granted but had always offered something in return.'

Part of Barry's regeneration programme was a move to Australia. Out of the blue, after a trip to Hamilton Island with George Harrison in 1986, Barry announced he was leaving Britain. It took everybody by surprise, including Stephanie.

'Manor House, Riverbend Avenue, Surfers Paradise, Queensland, Australia was our new home but I could never fathom out exactly why we came to live in Australia. Barry had come out here for a holiday. Then he bought some land. The next thing we were talking to some architects and he told me we were moving to Australia.

'Sometimes I wondered why we came to live over here because he always wanted to go back. Franco and Iris really did not want to come but, as always, they wouldn't upset Barry. I don't know what was in his head. It's a great lifestyle but sometimes you can feel cut off from everything. I didn't go back to England for six years. I don't think I was allowed to.

'Barry did a deal with Pickfords to move us to Australia. He starred in a video for them and they moved us all the way to Australia for free. Barry insisted in bringing over all the old furniture that looked OK in the old house at Charlwood, including his horrible oval bed.

'When we arrived I asked for a new sofa but was told I would have to pay for it myself. I thought a new home in a new country would require new furniture but of course I was wrong. He liked the old furniture because he was not ready to let go of all his memories of Britain.'

Son Freddie duly arrived soon after they moved to Australia and life seemed good for the young family in the sunshine.

However, it was not long after the Gold Coast incident with Gerhard Berger that Barry and Stephanie separated. They both needed a break from each other although, predictably, Barry only wanted to be apart for a couple of weeks. Stephanie made him wait quite a bit longer.

'Our separation had nothing to do with other women. We had just had enough of each other. When this happens to other couples they can't afford to split up. I moved away to see what it was like. I had a house built just two kilometres away and nobody else was involved. When we split up Barry got drunk, did outrageous blokey things and probably screwed around.

'I didn't go out with anybody else when we separated. If I had Barry would never have been able to handle it. He soon realised he could not live without me and used to invite me round for dinner. His cooking was dreadful but nonetheless he was soon telling me to peel the onions his way rather than the way I had been doing it for over thirty years. We both knew we were always meant for each other. The separation had to happen and our marriage was much better after it. Barry started to realise he couldn't push me around too much.'

It was a tough, tense time for family and friends, but like Stephanie everybody always believed they would get back together. Barry, however, was not finding life in Australia easy and nor did he enjoy getting older.

His brother-in-law Jeremy Paxton had watched the tension simmer between Barry and Stephanie. He thought that he might be able to help.

'I moved out there for five weeks to be with him.

Barry had ME, a debilitating illness. I don't how bad it was physically, but I would say now that it was a form of depression. I think he was down and very demotivated. It's not uncommon with human beings that have achieved so much in their lives. Barry had that huge lift into that arena of public awareness and his comedowns must have been massive.

'Stephanie was so supportive on every level. In the early days she would listen to Barry, she would be the shoulder to cry on and would be there to wipe his arse when he was incapacitated. She did everything for him. She loved his character but it was that very character that then became the beast that started to turn on her. In a way that is what she fought against. That's when the sparks flew and neither would compromise. Of course you can't get through life with no compromises.'

Stephanie moved back in and, to everybody's relief, resumed the cooking duties. After an incredible twenty-five years they faced the second instalment of their life together with a little more patience.

Stephanie was Barry's rock. He knew it. Even when he was back in Europe the phone would never stop ringing on the Gold Coast.

'Barry could only be himself with people he knew really well. Plenty of people try to get to know you when you are famous but he was no good in situations like cocktail parties. He once rang from England to check the name of Adrian Newey, who was the designer for the Williams Formula One team at the time.

'Before we went out Barry would always say to me, "Be nice to me this evening." I always was.'

JUST ONE OF THOSE DAYS

The silence was broken only by the singing of birds from distant trees. An ominous column of black smoke spiralled lazily into the cloudy sky, high above the flat Northamptonshire countryside. Slowly the silence was punctuated by sounds of human concern. Then, ambulance sirens, screaming minibike engines and the babble of distressed voices drowned out the birdsong.

Scattered over an area the size of a football pitch were pieces of debris, large and small. Among the wreckage lay two leather-clad bodies, one of them smoking like the hundreds of pieces of burning motorcycles that surrounded him. Neither body moved but both were breathing so there was still a chance of survival.

The time was half-past four on Wednesday 28 July 1982, a warm but cloudy summer afternoon, the location a strip of scorched tarmac crossing the Silverstone race circuit. Neither Barry Sheene nor Jack Middelburg would remember very much about what happened that day.

It had already been a big week for Barry. He had finally persuaded Yamaha to give him one of their factory V-4 motorcycles that might not only give him the chance to win his first British

Grand Prix but also the opportunity to regain the 500cc world championship that meant so much to him. He had lost the title to Kenny Roberts back in 1978 after reigning as champion for two glorious years. The lippy but talented American had then held the title for the next two years despite a fierce battle with Barry but, as Silverstone approached, both were chasing a new man at the front.

Sheene and Roberts shared second place in the world championship but both were twenty points adrift of Italian Franco Uncini, riding a Suzuki. There were four rounds to go, including Silverstone, and with fifteen points awarded to the winner, twelve to second place and ten to third there was a realistic chance of catching the Italian. Nothing less than victory at Silverstone would suffice, however.

Barry's last grand prix win had come almost a year before, at Anderstorp, but Yamaha had at last given him a glimmer of hope. All season Barry had been riding the older square-four machine while Roberts had been given the fastest 500cc racing machine Yamaha had ever produced. The V-4 OW61 Yamaha had a top speed approaching 190 mph but handled badly. Roberts' difficulty in getting the rocket ship to steer round corners both amused and frustrated Barry, who really fancied his chances of solving the handling problems, but time was running out.

Stephanie did not need reminding that Barry wasn't happy about the situation.

'There was a lot of aggro going on at the time, especially about the bike. Barry was pretty wound up as he was before any practice session, especially if things were not going his way, and I don't think it was about Franco Uncini leading the championship. I think Barry was almost resigned to the fact he was not going to be world champion again but he was going to have a bloody good go because he was still a bloody good rider. In every sport, every dog has its day until somebody new comes along and it is hard for everybody when this happens. I never used to get involved in all that. Barry would come into the motorhome saying, "fuckin' Kenny" and "fuckin' somebody else" but I would keep well out of it. I never had a problem with Kenny and we got on really well.

'Things were not going Barry's way and the year was not turning out how he thought it would. He felt he could get something happening with the new bike but he obviously didn't have enough time. Once something happened he would try his utmost to sort it out. If it wasn't going to happen it wasn't going to happen, but Barry would harp on and on about it, always saying what if, I should have done this or he should have pulled his finger out. He was always like that. I would tell him to leave it alone, it's finished, it's over, and when he went on and on I would do this action, like winding up an old-fashioned gramophone, saying here we go again and he would get mad.'

Despite competing on the older Yamaha, Barry was riding as well as at any time in his career. He had already finished second in Argentina, Austria, Spain and Belgium that year and was constantly nagging Yamaha for the chance to take on Roberts on equal machinery. The phone calls and complaining increased a hundredfold when Yamaha gave New Zealander Graeme Crosby the second V-4 by Yamaha ahead of Barry. However, once Crosby confirmed what Roberts had been saying all year about the handling of the machine Yamaha at last relented, but they left it very, very late.

Barry got his hands on the ill-handling monster on the Monday morning of the week of the British Grand Prix. After a special practice day for 500cc factory riders on the Monday, there was an open practice session for all classes on Wednesday with official practice starting on Friday morning and the race on Sunday. Barry had very little time to sort out the problems that had already caused Roberts more than a few heart-stopping moments.

A few runs on the V-4 confirmed Barry's worst fears. Drastic surgery was required if the bike was going to be OK for the practice on Wednesday, let alone the grand prix. It was rapidly dispatched up the M1 to Spondon Engineering in Derby where big changes were made to the steering head angle. The Yamaha was returned ready for action on Tuesday evening.

Steve Parrish, as always, was in the next garage. Like Barry, he had also somehow forgotten to pay the twenty-two pound fee to the Silverstone circuit to take part in the unofficial practice session.

'I hadn't paid to practise and just went straight out on the track. Barry would always arrange that I had the next garage to him and with my caravan nearby his team would get a steady supply of tea from my girlfriend Linda. I remember poor old Ken Fletcher, his chief mechanic, working all night before the practice, rebuilding the modified frame and altering the geometry.'

Stephanie recalls: 'For me, it was just a normal practice day and I just went about my business. First of all I got all his racing gear together, leathers, boots, gloves and especially his crash helmet. Barry would sort out all his other gear, but I would always look after his crash helmet. I would wash all the flies off, which he had collected from a previous race, and clean the visor with Fairy Liquid, which would stop it fogging up if the conditions were damp.'

Under his leathers, the clothing never changed. As always, he wore his lucky blue underpants and the Gary Nixon T-shirt given to him by his American racing friend a few years previously, which had started a winning run. Round his neck hung the 1973 FIM 750cc European championship medal and a Brazilian 'fica', a good-luck charm that was supposedly a symbol of virility.

A foam back protector, which guards the back from the waist to the back of the neck, is a vital part of safety equipment for modern-day grand prix riders. Barry had long recognised its importance and had made his own from three-quarter-inch foam. Later in the day that home-made piece of equipment was given the ultimate test and passed with flying colours.

Computerised timing was also a thing of the future and it was down to Stephanie and garlands of stopwatches round her neck to keep a check on her man and the others.

'I was the only person that Barry would let do his timing and so

I had to check the stopwatches were working, have plenty of batteries and also prepare the time sheets – generally gearing up for those timed practices. Once he checked his times on my watch he would go round everybody else to check the times were the same. I would always stand next to Linda on the pit wall while she was timing Steve. Barry really depended on me and told me who to keep an eye on. He had asked me to time about twelve other riders that day, so he could compare their times at the end of the session.'

Of course, it was not only Stephanie who provided support for Barry at the racetrack.

'Iris and Franco were there in the motorhome. Barry, as always, would have been kicking everybody round the garage, telling them what to do while Iris, as always, would be making sandwiches and tea for everybody. I made Barry the usual cheese and tomato sandwich for his lunch. He always wanted things to be the way he liked them. It always had to be cheese and tomato and you could not put cucumber in there because he would ask, "What's this, why are we having cucumber today?" He was like that until the day he died: the same thing at breakfast, the same thing for lunch. If we were out for dinner he would have what he fancied but if we were at home he always wanted the same thing all the time.

'He was weird like that. He never changed his make of toothpaste and if the shaving cream he was using ran out or they stopped making it there was hell to pay. He always had to have Close Up toothpaste and we used to buy around a hundred tubes at a time. We are still using now.

'Apart from a KitKat, he would not want any other food during the day and so he was choosy but pretty predictable. The first thing I always had to do at a grand prix was make sure I had the tickets. I was in charge of our tickets for guests, sponsors and friends and he used to get me in such a state about it. I also had packets of cigarettes coming out of my backside. He was chain-smoking at the time and I always had to have a huge bag, not a dainty little handbag but a huge haversack. As well as the tickets and cigarettes, I kept his asthma inhaler in the bag. He used to have a nervous puff on his inhaler before going out on the bike; he always thought he needed some medication. He was smoking cigarettes right until he got on the bike. They would even let them do it on the start line.'

Official grand prix practice sessions were split into classes. The British Grand Prix actually consisted of five races, starting with the tiny 125cc machines and then going up through the 250 and 350cc categories before the main race of the day, the 500cc. There was also a sidecar grand prix and a non-championship Formula One four-stroke race for mainly British riders, but the 500cc race was the big one, equivalent to the Formula One race at a car-racing event. However, the Wednesday practice at Silverstone was unofficial and so all the classes went out on the track at the same time, apart from the sidecars. It was a recipe for disaster but time was not on Barry's side as he tried to get to grips with a racing motorcycle that had almost conquered the considerable talents of Roberts and Crosby.

It was certainly not the ideal scenario for testing. The screaming 500cc thoroughbreds had to bob, weave and sometimes even duck between the 125cc also-rans in a scary game of high-speed tag. The 2.927-mile Silverstone circuit was fast even by grand prix motorcycle racing standards, the 500cc machines reaching speeds of around 180 mph with the slower 125s travelling at just over 120 mph. It created an unacceptable speed difference of around 60 mph between the fastest machines in each category, a lap time differential of nearly ten seconds. Throw in the 250cc, 350cc and the lumbering Formula One machines, all fighting for the same inch of tarmac and perhaps the only surprising thing about the whole day was that the accident only came on the very last lap of the afternoon. Sadly, when it arrived it was big, very big.

On any other day Barry would have complained to the organisers about the practice arrangements but he had other things on his mind. Progress was slow but he was getting there, and Barry knew he was in with a real chance in Sunday's 28-lap race. The changes that had been made to the bike were working better than he had anticipated and, despite the pit lane marshal checking his watch, he managed to sneak out for a final couple of laps before proceedings were halted for the day.

The first of these laps was good: his lap time would have put him near the front row of the grid and it was only Wednesday afternoon. The second and last laps were very different. The folly of letting all the classes practise at the same time was finally exposed in the most dramatic way.

As Barry raced down the 180 mph Hangar Straight, head and helmet tucked behind the screen of the Yamaha, before braking for the fast right-hand Stowe Corner, a sequence of events that would change his life began to unfold near the start and finish line.

Stephanie was ready to pack up for the day. 'I was on the pit lane wall in front of the garage, stopwatch in hand as usual, waiting for the session to finish and thinking, that's it for the day and we can get back to the Heskeths' for a shower, come down for drinkies at seven and have a civilised dinner for a change. Barry had been getting in a state all day about the bike. He had come into the motorhome and had a good moan about whatever. Everybody was a "cunt" or a "fucking idiot", and he would have a good rant and rave.'

Less than a mile from the finish, West German Alfred Waibel was also pushing hard for the final time on his 125cc MBA machine. He had finished twelfth in the Yugoslav Grand Prix just ten days earlier and was looking for a top-ten finish this time. He approached the fast left-hand Abbey Curve flat out in fifth gear at around 120 mph before straightening up in order to dive under the famous *Daily Express* Bridge and line up the approach to the very fast Woodcote Corner.

The Frenchman Patrick Igoa was right behind him on a 250cc Yamaha and, despite nearing the end of the practice, felt he had both the pace and confidence to ride round the outside of the smaller-capacity machine. After all, it had been happening through-out the day with the more powerful bikes that were hogging the racing line. The track was dry and so despite having to ride off the racing line and on to the 'marbles', the area of slippery discarded rubber and dirt either side of the racing line, it had caused no more problems than a few two-fingered salutes from the faster men once their manoeuvres had been successfully completed.

Igoa may have had the confidence but just lacked the pace to squeeze past Waibel's MBA. The young Frenchman just nudged Waibel on the way out of the corner. The contact was minimal but just enough to rip Waibel's leathers on his right side and break the footrest of his bike, as well as causing Igoa to fall from the Yamaha on the outside of the bend. Nine times out of ten, perhaps even ninety-nine times out of one hundred, both the Frenchman and his machine would have slid on to the grass and out of danger. A bruised bottom and a broken fairing would have been the worst damage but this time it was different. Inexplicably, both bike and rider slid into the middle of the track and stopped dead. A broken collarbone was the very least of Igoa's problems.

The stricken Yamaha lay just a few yards in front of the terrified rider, with both on the racing line at a very fast corner. At this bend, the oncoming rider approaches blind over the brow of a hill. Time stood still for the Frenchman as the bikes arrived like a pack of snarling greyhounds chasing the hare.

Barry was enjoying himself for the first time in a very long while. As his right hand and left foot smoothly combined to brake for Stowe Corner, Barry spotted the Suzuki of Jack Middelburg in front of him. The previous year the Dutchman had really upset Roberts, beating the American by just three tenths of one second to win the British Grand Prix. It was a major surprise for Roberts, who consequently lost his world title to Marco Lucchinelli.

It would be the perfect end to a difficult day. Confident in the ability of the new Yamaha against the proven handling and top speed of the Suzuki, Barry took his chance at Stowe to pass Middelburg before setting himself up for Club Corner. He twisted the throttle with his right hand and, changing up through the gearbox with his right foot, he accelerated up the slight uphill straight towards Abbey Curve. It is not an easy corner because the approach over the brow of the hill is completely blind, and the rider is already thinking about keeping the throttle open for the very fast Woodcote right-hand bend that leads to the start and finish line.

As they approached Abbey, Barry kept in front of Middelburg, who was quite content to stay behind and check out the handling of the revitalised Sheene Yamaha. Barry took a quick glance over his shoulder as they both accelerated up to 160 mph out of Abbey and towards the *Daily Express* Bridge.

Igoa and his stricken Yamaha were still lying in the middle of the track. With safety arrangements for the unofficial practice day at a minimum, there was nobody at the exit of the Abbey Curve, let alone a yellow flag to be waved to warn riders of impending danger. Former 350cc world champion Jon Ekerold, crossing the *Daily Express* Bridge on his return from a shopping trip, saw Igoa crash and ran down the side of the track, hoping to pull the Frenchman to safety or at least warn the oncoming riders. Like Sheene and Middelburg, he ran out of time.

Miraculously, around twenty bikes of all shapes, sizes and capacities had somehow circumnavigated Igoa and his Yamaha before Barry and Jack Middelburg arrived at real speed. They were not so lucky.

Barry's machine missed Igoa but his front wheel hit the engine of the stricken Yamaha head-on at 160 mph. The fuel tanks of both Barry's and Igoa's Yamaha exploded in a fireball as they cartwheeled. Barry's smoking body was flung into the air like a rag doll before coming to a grinding halt three hundred yards up the track. Middelburg had no chance. The Dutchman ploughed into the wreckage, scattering debris even higher into the air. Parts of smouldering motorcycles rained down while the acrid stench of fire and smoke suffocated the afternoon air.

Barry's body lay motionless on the racing line while Middelburg lay on the freshly mown grass on the left side of the track. The Yamaha that Barry had craved all season lay like the carcass of a dead animal in the centre of the scorched tarmac while Middelburg's now-unrecognisable Suzuki came to rest against a wall.

Stephanie did not immediately realise the implications of the ominous cloud of black smoke.

'Roman, my twelve-year-old son from my first marriage, pointed to a column of smoke that was coming up in the distance. He also remarked how quiet it had become and that there must have been an accident. I told him not to be so stupid, that it was just a bonfire. The smoke was going up just like the smoke from a bonfire and I wasn't worried.

'Then somebody on the pit wall said there had been an accident. I waited quite a while; Barry had not come back to the finish on the bike and after a few minutes I did start to worry a little and wonder just what was going on. Riders were slowly drifting back to the pits and it was soon very obvious it was Barry. I didn't panic because I had been here before.

'Roman later told me he knew it was an accident as soon as he saw the smoke and went on a minibike to see what had happened. It took him quite a long time to get there. When he did he saw Barry lying on the ground and bits of bike everywhere, but what he really noticed was blood dripping from Barry's finger seeping through his glove. That has always stuck in his mind.

'As soon as I knew it was Barry I went straight back to the motorhome to get all his stuff. Cigarettes, asthma inhaler, money, wallet, the clothes he had been wearing earlier in the day and my handbag. I just gathered up everything I thought we would need because I knew we were going to hospital. I got a lift on the back of Roberto Pietri's minibike to the scene of the crash.'

Kenny Roberts was one of the first riders to arrive on the scene. 'It was just like a plane crash. I didn't know anything about what had happened but I knew Barry was involved when I saw him lying on the racetrack. We took his helmet off to stabilise him because as sure as hell he was not breathing properly, it was very tortured. I knew it was important to get that helmet off and not let people grab or jerk him about. It was obvious that his legs were broken but our main concern was to keep him alive. I just made sure he was not choking and hadn't swallowed his tongue but I didn't know what else I could do until the people who knew what they were doing arrived.'

Also quickly on to the scene was Marie Armes, the wife of Auto-Cycle Union official Colin Armes and, far more importantly, a trained nurse. Her immediate actions almost certainly saved Barry's life.

Marie was with her husband in their caravan, parked close to the plush British Racing Drivers' Club suite at Woodcote Corner, as the practice session came to an end. Despite both being off duty, they still tuned in to the Silverstone circuit radio.

'Suddenly the circuit radio was alive. I looked out of the caravan window and saw a ball of flame just by the *Daily Express* Bridge. I then saw a marshal with a red flag over his shoulder running across the bridge. We jumped into the car and drove to the track. The first person we reached was Alfred Waibel. He was very distressed and just kept saying, "It's Barry, it's Barry."

'Then we reached a circle of people surrounding a prone figure on the track. In the centre, bending over, was the familiar sight of black and red leathers with "Roberts" emblazoned on the back. I bent down beside Kenny and realised it was Barry lying there.'

For the one and only time on that cloudy Wednesday afternoon, luck was on Barry's side. The nurse knew exactly how to help save his life.

'Kenny asked me if I knew what to do and I told him to take Barry's helmet off, which he did. I was anxious to make sure Barry's airway was clear and once his helmet was off I managed to hold his chin in a reasonable position.

'The Silverstone Rescue Unit then arrived and I asked for a breathing tube that I could put down Barry's throat. I was just about to insert it when the doctor arrived and so I gave it to him. I will never forget looking up at that sea of distressed faces surrounding us.'

Arriving at the scene, Stephanie Sheene was amazingly calm. 'There he was, laid out on the track. It looked pretty bad. A lot of people thought Barry was dead and were looking on in disbelief. Barry looked pretty dead to me, too, but he was still breathing and drifting in and out of consciousness. I didn't think he was going to die by the time we got to the hospital – I remember I was not too panicked about it. I'm funny like that: if someone drops crumbs on my floor I have a fit, but if something major happens, it's happened and if there is nothing I can physically do, I just have to let others take over.

'I just let people get on with what they were doing. They were not trying to resuscitate him or anything like that and I just thought he was going to be OK. I was pretty good when he had an accident. I remember some of the wives would be chewing their fingernails all through the practice, but I would only worry that he would not get off the start line properly, pushing the bike with those skinny legs of his.'

The sheer impact of hitting another machine at 160 mph would have killed most people. Barry survived but his body took a terrible pounding. His legs and wrists took the full force of the terrifying collision. His left wrist snapped and his knuckles were broken after becoming trapped between his knees and the handlebars of his Yamaha as he hit Patrick Igoa's machine, but it was his legs that took the full force of the crash. Both legs had smashed into the handle-bars, shattering below the knee joints, and were hanging like a child's discarded puppet. The exploding fireball had momentarily engulfed Barry before he was thrown into the air. When he finally came to a halt, not only were his leathers smouldering but also his eyebrows had been replaced by two patches of raw skin.

Steve Parrish was fearful of what he might find at the scene: 'I was in my caravan when news came through about the crash. There were a lot of people looking really concerned coming back from the scene. I went to Barry's garage just as Roberto Pietri was taking Steph to the scene on a minibike. I didn't go; quite frankly, I did not want to see if it was as bad as it sounded. I made my way across to the medical centre and waited for the ambulance to arrive. When Barry was brought in he was not really conscious and was in a real mess, with singed eyebrows and looking really pale.'

As both Barry and Jack Middelburg lay unconscious amongst the debris, arguments ensued as to whether they should be taken to the Silverstone Medical Centre or to Northampton General Hospital ten miles away.

Stephanie recalls the scene. 'Franco was already there, jumping around like Popeye the sailor man, huffing and puffing, trying to get things organised. Martyn Ogbourne kept telling me he was going to be all right. There was a bit of an argument, with somebody saying he should go to the medical centre to be checked out and others wanting to take him to hospital. It seemed stupid to take him to the medical centre because what could they do? Luckily there was a nurse there, who intervened and told us to forget the medical centre and get him straight to hospital.'

In the end Barry was taken by ambulance to the medical centre, but after some frantic prompting he was at last en route to Northampton General, accompanied by Stephanie, Roberto Pietri and Marie Armes. Stephanie remembers that the journey wasn't helped by the rush-hour traffic.

'I remember looking into his eyes in the ambulance on the way to hospital. I wondered just how that fire had got to him. It took for ever to get to the hospital and seemed such a long way. He kept opening and closing his eyes but I can't remember him saying anything or being aware of anybody around him. I didn't say anything to him because I thought he was totally out of it.'

Marie, however, recalls a typical request: 'Barry mumbled something about wanting a cigarette before lapsing back into unconsciousness.'

News of the crash, meanwhile, was spreading like a forest fire in the media, first in Britain then, very quickly, throughout the world. With official practice for the British Grand Prix starting on Friday hardly any journalists or photographers had been at Silverstone for the unofficial practice, which was really just a prelude to the weekend of action. Once that column of black smoke appeared on the horizon those who were there quickly realised they had a big story on their hands.

Nick Harris, who compiled Barry's weekly media column, was one of the few journalists at Silverstone that fateful day.

'I remember that total silence, apart from the birds singing, seconds after the crash. When that column of smoke appeared we all knew that something was very wrong. I was in the pit lane when Ken Fletcher, Barry's chief mechanic, went racing past on a scooter. It was then that I realised it was probably a crash involving Barry. By the time I reached the scene of the accident both Barry and Jack Middelburg had been taken to the medical centre but the total devastation was frightening. What was left of Barry's Yamaha was lying in the middle of the track, covered in foam, while people, including the American grand prix rider Randy Mamola, still in his leathers, were just milling about in silence. Kenny Roberts rode past with tears streaming down his face.

'I took a few surreptitious photos of Barry's bike being hoisted on to the back of a pickup truck, then made my way back to the paddock. It seemed to me that John Brown, the editor of *Motorcycle Racing*, and I were the only journalists there. We located two phone boxes, gathered up as much loose change as we could muster and got phoning, splitting a list of national newspapers, news agencies and broadcasters between us. The crash was already making big news, with reporters and film crews en route to Northampton General.'

The Accident and Emergency Department at Northampton General was close to the busy M1 motorway and had seen plenty of serious crash victims. They quickly assessed Barry's appalling injuries and called consultant orthopaedic surgeon Nigel Cobb. He arrived from another hospital, checked the X-rays and the condition of the unconscious patient and made plans for an operation the next day, which was to catapult him into the national headlines. However, it was not quite as simple as that, as Steve Parrish explains.

'Barry and I had an agreement that, whichever one of us was busted, the other would make sure the best possible treatment would be found. The hospital kept insisting that the local orthopaedic surgeon was the best available. However, we had all previously heard stories of cock-ups at small hospitals.

'There were no mobile phones in those days and so I got on the hospital payphone and set about finding the best orthopaedic surgeon money could buy. Franco had contacts and I had a doctor friend at the Orpington Hospital who had fixed up me and other riders over the years. After about two hours on the phone all reports said that Nigel Cobb knew his stuff and he certainly did.'

Stephanie was also on the phone, asking the same questions and coming up with exactly the same answer.

Next door, Barry was totally unaware of all the activity on his behalf. Mercifully strong medication kept the pain from his shattered legs and wrist at bay, but as he drifted in and out of consciousness his brain reminded him of two of his favourite subjects.

'Barry started to mumble a few things. He was totally out of it but was on about his favourite food, roast beef and Yorkshire pudding, and then he said, "She's a beautiful bird." I don't know who he was talking about, I still don't – as always he denied everything,' admits Stephanie.

'By this time it was getting on to six or seven o'clock and Stavros and a few other riders sat with me in the waiting room. I remember thinking, thank God I won't have to go to the practice tomorrow. We'll have the weekend off. I didn't need the tickets any more and so I gave them to Stavros.'

Parrish confirmed the delivery. 'I will never forget. In those days a rider entering a grand prix was given just four passes from the organisers and that was that. Typically, Steph handed me an envelope with at least fifty paddock passes that Barry had managed to get. She rightly said that they would not be needing them over the weekend. No, I didn't sell them. I just phoned up everyone I knew that wanted to come to the grand prix and handed them out – don't waste anything, whatever the situation.'

Despite the gravity of the situation, Barry's mum relieved the tension in her typical practical way, as Stephanie explains.

'Iris was also in the waiting room. She had thought to make sandwiches, bunged them in a Tupperware container and brought them to the hospital. She was handing them round like it was a picnic. I don't think any of us thought Barry's life was threatened. He hadn't banged his head or anything and he didn't seem to have any internal injuries. It was just his legs. We didn't realise at that stage just how bad it was.'

Once inside the Accident and Emergency unit Barry was quickly examined and Marie found herself involved in both a tough and rather delicate operation with a pair of scissors.

'Sister asked me to cut off his leathers. They only provided me with a small pair of surgical scissors and it was hard going. Suddenly Barry came to and told me to mind where I was cutting and also not to damage his lucky blue pants.'

Unbeknown to Barry the other two riders involved in the crash were alongside him in A&E.

'There were two riders in the cubicles alongside and the Sister, who knew it was Barry Sheene, had no idea who the other two were. I recognised Jack Middelburg's white leathers but had no idea who was next door. I had to ask him his name, and discovered it was Patrick Igoa.

'Barry never spoke to me about that day, but whenever I saw him he always gave me a very special hug.'

It was the end of a dramatic and emotional day for Stephanie:

'They had given something to Barry and he was completely out of it. I stayed on at the hospital for a couple of hours then went back to the Heskeths' with Stavros and had a few drinks. I certainly needed them. It had started as just another day, but ended as one of those days. Already I was thinking, where do we go from here?'

NIGEL COBB

They may have had the same Christian name, but they had little else in common. On hearing of Barry's brush with the tarmac just up the road at Silverstone, consultant orthopaedic surgeon Nigel Cobb was convinced it was somebody from a very different walk of life who was about to receive his undivided attention. Perhaps it was the phone line or the pressure of work that convinced the surgeon that comedian and writer Barry Took had fallen off a motorbike.

'I was at a meeting planning the new Three Shires Hospital, surrounded by paperwork when someone came in and told me I was wanted at the General Hospital because Barry Sheene had had a crash.

'My immediate thought was, what the hell is he doing on a motorbike? It somehow came into my mind that it was Barry Took, and what was the silly bugger doing racing a motorbike at Silverstone?'

On arrival at Northampton General Mr Cobb soon established the true identity of his patient and set about assessing the damage. By this time Barry was aware of the severity of the crash and was terrified that he was going to lose at least one of his legs. The surgeon was quick to assure him that this would not be the case.

'Barry was not in a very conversational mood when I arrived because he thought he might lose his legs. I had a quick look at the X-rays and decided that I would leave it to the Intensive Care Unit [ICU] to get him into shape. There was no question of having to amputate right away because he had a good blood supply and he was in excellent condition himself.

'It was always going to be complex and the main worry was that his knees would move again. They did move, and of course he got the aching and so forth from them, which was what you would expect. After shattering his knees the way he did they were never going to feel the same again. If you just have a simple break of the ankle you find, a couple of years later, that it will still ache after a lot of walking.

'I decided to operate in the morning. I didn't want to start emergency surgery on him because it might have killed him after so much trauma.'

Early the next morning Cobb and his team assembled in the operating theatre. Barry was wheeled in for the operation that was to bring him more column inches and film coverage than any race win or world title.

'It was a good thing that we did not operate on the night of the accident, because I think it would have been too exhausting. I had a very good team. A damn good senior registrar helped me, and the anaesthetist and ICU did a splendid job. The ICU had to get all his fluids into good shape and his electrolytes into a good buzz. The anaesthetist Matthew Styles kept the balance right between the fluids, electrolytes and blood throughout the seven-and-a-half hours.'

Although the X-rays had been carefully studied it was only when Barry's legs were actually cut open on the table that Nigel Cobb realised the severity of his injuries.

'X–rays are only shadows of things that contain metal, calcium and soft tissues. You don't really get a three-dimensional picture of the leg until you have opened it up and seen what is there. It gives you a good indication of what you are going to find but sometimes you get a lot of surprises.

'The legs were shot apart, and looked rather like a jigsaw puzzle. All the bits of bone were loose in an enormous bag of blood but fortunately there was no skin damage. When we opened the skin around his knees we found that the ligaments were all more or less loose and so we had to reconstruct the knee by fitting a shaping plate and then attaching the ligaments to the shaft of the tibia where it was not injured. They went up like an ice-cream cone and we fixed them to the top of the tibia plateau.

'Then we bundled all the bits into the space, closed up the stitches and it worked. There were two plates in each leg held together by twenty-eight screws.'

Everything was going to plan until the surgeon turned his attention to Barry's shattered left wrist.

'His wrist was an absolute bugger and it almost took longer than the legs. It was a devil – I just could not find a way to put it together. It suddenly struck me that maybe he had broken his wrist before. He had never told us because he was far more concerned about his legs, and we had never asked him. Once we realised that, we were able to put it together with screws and plates.'

Seven-and-a-half hours of intense concentration, interrupted by just a couple of breaks, and it was all over. Barry was wheeled back to the ICU and the surgeon prepared to face the press.

'You just don't notice how tiring it is. It's only at the end that you realise you are absolutely whacked. When we were finished the press were all around but I told them all to go away and come back the next day. We would get the press in every now and then. With Silverstone being close by there were always racers coming in, but nobody as spectacular as Barry. I remember operating on Jochen Mass. He was the same sort of physically fit and tough character as Barry. He had thighs the size of an elephant. When we opened him up we went through quarter of an inch of fat right into rich red meat that would whet your appetite.'

Nigel Cobb told the assembled press the next morning that he was pleased with the outcome of the operation. He was certain that Barry would not only walk again but also race if he wanted to, although he had had a very close shave.

'I had seen serious leg injuries like that before but the great thing about Barry's injuries was that he had been wearing proper protective clothing. Any ordinary motorcyclist that had an accident like that would have lost a leg. The extra protection saved his skin. With no skin damage the risk of secondary infection was small and that was what saved him.'

For a couple of days, that was enough for the media, who were camping out in the foyer of the hospital. When Barry was fit enough to leave the ICU interest hotted up again, but Nick Harris managed to get the scoop:

'I had assumed that, as Barry was in hospital, I wouldn't need to write his column that week. I was wrong. John Bowles, the chief sub at *Motor Cycle Weekly*, told me, "I don't give a stuff what state he's in, get it and phone it through to the printers by lunchtime because they've left a big space on the front page."

'I really didn't know what to expect or even where to go when I arrived at the hospital. Finding where to go proved no problem as at least twenty of Fleet Street's finest were hanging around the reception desk. There was a snigger when I asked the receptionist if I could see Barry, but Stephanie answered the phone and immediately invited me upstairs.

'Barry was lying surrounded by flowers and baskets of fruit, with cards and telegrams covering the floor. I was surprised that his legs weren't in plaster. He pulled himself up using the trapeze-style contraption above his bed and just about managed a weak smile. He then gave me his exclusive account of the crash before insisting I went into the next room to have a word with the rapidly recovering Jack Middelburg.

'I couldn't believe that Barry, who was in so much pain, could give *Motor Cycle Weekly* the exclusive interview when all the nationals were downstairs with open chequebooks. I'll never forget the headline: "Sheene: I'm sickened! Someone could have got killed out there, but little did I realise it was so nearly going to be me."'

From the moment he came round from the operation Barry had just two things on his mind. How soon could he get out of hospital and how soon could he ride a bike again? His shattered legs and wrist could take months or even years to heal properly.

Barry may have been no stranger to pain, but this proved to be one of the toughest tests of his eventful life. He faced it in typical style although his determination and bravery surprised even Nigel Cobb.

'About five days after the operation I went in to see him and said to him, "Barry, you have got to get these legs to bend 135 degrees or you will not race again." He replied, "I fucking know that."

'I called in again a couple of days later. Barry had his knees bent right up and was pulling his shin up towards his chin. He was almost there. I said to him, "great", but thought that it must be really hurting him. I asked him, "Does it hurt?" He took a breath and, through his teeth, said, "Of course it fucking hurts," and then carried on. He was a fanatical patient who helped himself so much with his physiotherapy. He always did what he was told very well. I think it must have been immensely frustrating for a man of his drive and determination to face the prospect of being stuck without any legs for six months.'

Once the operation was completed successfully the main worry was infection as Barry fought his way back to fitness. Once again, his excellent physical condition kept that risk to a minimum.

'We thought that given the extensive exposure we would get some breakdown in the skin and some infection somewhere but there was no infection at all. One tiny area on the skin wound went a bit moist but there was nothing at all of significance. That was really terrific and partly due to his state of physical health, as well as the way we managed to operate on him when he was in good condition and the good job the anaesthetist and ICU did for him.'

Best friend or not, Steve Parrish had work to do and was, as always, a very active participant in the van and caravan race from Silverstone to Anderstorp. Steve finished tenth in the 500cc Swedish Grand Prix but claimed a higher finish in the unofficial race to and from the circuit. He returned home to find Barry recuperating.

'Typically, I was straight off to the Swedish Grand Prix and when I returned he had moved to the Three Shires Hospital. Barry was causing mayhem. I was getting phone calls all the time about the various nurses and how I should get over there to check them out. That was a good enough reason to visit with the obligatory bunch of grapes.'

Stephanie was at Barry's side twelve hours a day, seven days a week.

'I was staying at the Heskeths' at Easton Neston near Towcester but they were away on holiday. I was at the hospital for such a long time every day I told the cook not to bother with anything for me. She would lay up a place for me on the big dining-room table with silver cutlery and a wine glass but the only food I ever got to eat was takeaways. I would leave before breakfast to be at the Three Shires by nine and never left before nine o'clock at night.'

To the outside world Barry was the perfect patient. To those closest to him, and especially Stephanie, Barry demanded undivided attention.

'Every morning when I arrived the Sister would be waiting outside for me. Barry would not allow them to do anything until I was there. I would have to go into his room, draw the curtains, open the windows to clear out the smell of smoke and empty a huge ashtray. Only then would Barry allow the nurses in the room.

'He would not let me go out and it was a really draining time. One day I wanted to go into Northampton, just to have my fringe cut, and he made such a fuss. He let me go back to Charlwood once and the nurses told me he didn't speak for the whole day.'

That was Barry. He needed people around him, Stephanie in particular. Franco and Iris were also there, having parked the motorhome in the hospital car park.

The exclusive Three Shires Hospital had never witnessed anything approaching the Sheene whirlwind before. There were constant visitors, sacks of mail, phone calls day and night and, of course, the man himself. Nigel Cobb remembers it well.

'Usually the Matron would greet me by saying "You will never believe what Mr Sheene has said today." One morning she stopped me in the doorway and told me what happened when they wanted to give Barry an enema. He didn't like that much and told Matron, "If this is what poofters get up to, count me out." It was always a case of what Mr Sheene did next. I used to enjoy it – it was great fun. He was so kind to everybody and so obliging. He didn't want people to be kept away if they wanted to see him. His mum and dad used to try to prevent him seeing too many people but he would see anybody that came.'

On his return from Sweden, Steve was ready to reap the benefits of the Three Shires with more than a little help from Barry. It was business as usual for the pair, with Barry's injuries no hindrance whatsoever.

'There were always fun and games. He enjoyed the bed baths very much. He liked nurses and he liked nurses' uniforms. There was always the banter going. Of course the nurses were going home and saying, "You'll never guess who pinched my arse today." That was the same if he was in hospital or out somewhere. He always wanted to know if they were wearing suspenders and we would always ask if we could give them a "blimp". It was like that all the time, nurses, policewomen at Silverstone and air hostesses. Lots of banter, lots of "blimping" and cracking good fun. Being in hospital made no difference.'

Lord Hesketh returned from his holiday and, like Steve, enjoyed his regular visits to the Three Shires.

'Barry was a great friend before he settled into domestic bliss. We spent a lot of time together in London, usually ending the evening in party HQ, Tramp. But, above all else, our friendship was based on the fact that his Silverstone accident happened while he was staying with us and subsequently was in various Northampton hospitals under the care of Mr Cobb and several extremely attractive nurses whom I had the pleasure of seeing every time I went to visit.'

The public's response to the accident was staggering. Northampton's sorting office almost buckled under the weight of mail arriving each day, both from home and abroad. Barry estimated that he received a total of twenty-five thousand letters, cards and telegrams with ten thousand of them coming from overseas. Barry sought help, including Steve's, to ensure as many as possible were answered.

'Barry really did appreciate all the support he was getting with so many people writing to him. Literally thousands and thousands of letters would turn up and Barry would delegate opening and answering them – email wasn't around in those days. Ken, Barry's accountant and secretary would write most of the letters, saying "Many thanks from Barry on your kind thoughts, which he appreciates very much." Barry himself would only answer the ones that sounded like they came from a good-looking bird. That said, he was good at telephoning people to thank them.'

Barry and Steve never talked about the accident although they did slate Silverstone for the lack of marshals on the fateful practice day and talked about how Barry should sue the owners. However, thoughts about just how close Barry had come to losing his legs or even dying were privately stored. Nonetheless, Steve knew.

'It was a massive scare to Barry and to all of us. Initially we thought that he would never race again, and might never walk again. It was a huge, huge scare. He was so relieved when Nigel Cobb kept coming round to say it was all looking good. We are all good at bottling things up. People said he was fearless, but nobody is fearless – you are scared. Barry was very concerned about his future.

'When you have a bad accident, it flashes by. You are in the ambulance, chugging along thinking, is this the end? Have I done it this time? Am I ever going to be able to race again? Am I ever going to be able to get good motorbikes again? It happened to me on many occasions and Barry was no different. He was just so relieved when it started working for him again.'

Once assured that Barry would live, walk and ride a motorcycle again Steve was not surprised by his quick recovery. The thought of someone else riding your bike and stealing your contracts while you are lying in a hospital bed has always been the perfect medicine for racers old and new. Barry was no exception, although he had a great deal more to lose than most.

'Barry was well aware he had to get himself back as quickly as possible. Doctors were constantly amazed by how Barry and other riders could repair themselves. It was a lesson to everyone because not many people want to heal that quickly – they just don't want to do it. We all knew that if we didn't get out there soon there would be somebody else on your bike doing it for you. That threat was enough, it was the last thing you wanted happening.

'It's the same today with Valentino Rossi, Loris Capirossi and Marco Melandri. They may not be any different physically, with the same bones, muscles and blood as other people, but racers have an inbuilt will just to do it. Your average bloke and your average doctor expect injuries to take two months to heal because that's how long it normally takes. Some patients will sit in front of the telly and not bother about healing. Whereas racers, and Barry in particular, are such determined people, physically very fit, eating a decent diet and, most important, with incredible willpower. Barry used to work himself so hard, exercising all day long getting the flexibility back into his knees and wrist. It was quite extraordinary, but then every racer is like that. It's your career and your body is the tool of your trade.'

Fortunately the crash had no way affected Barry's brain. In between the knee bending, enemas, bed baths and 'blimping' he was already planning his next move. It was not the move home to Charlwood that occupied his thoughts but the unlikely prospect of a ride on a motorcycle round Donington Park before the end of the racing season. Barry had pencilled in 3 October for his return to the track, at the John Player-sponsored 500cc World Cup meeting, just sixty-seven days after his accident. Steve recalls Barry's thinking.

'While he was in hospital he was always on the phone sorting out deals with someone. Barry was well aware he had got more publicity through the crash than he ever would have done winning the race. He knew his season was over but he was already working on the following year.

'He was soon planning his first time back on a motorcycle when other people would have still been laying in bed moaning about their luck. He organised it all with Robert Jackson at Yamaha. The plan was to go to Donington Park for the World 500cc Cup meeting and ride a lap on the Yamaha LC350 road bike with me on the back in case anything went wrong.'

Once the ride was organised, Barry set about ensuring everybody knew what was happening. It was not a particularly difficult task to secure maximum publicity, as Steve remembers.

'Barry phoned up his mates in the national press, including Leslie Nichol at the *Express* and George Turnbull at the *Telegraph*, telling them he was thinking of having a go at riding a bike again and of course they could not get enough of it. He told them he was not sure that he could do it but he was determined to try, when of course it had already been planned and organised – typical Barry.'

'Before the Donington ride there was the small matter of persuading Nigel Cobb to let him leave hospital and get home. He agreed, but also warned Barry of the consequences of doing something stupid, although his warning did not include riding a motorcycle round Donington Park.

Twenty-three days after the crash Barry was discharged. His departure from the Three Shires Hospital was like a showbiz wedding. Fleet Street's finest turned out en masse with their photographers, while all the television networks filmed the departure. Gary Newbon from ITV Sport was given the honour of pushing Barry's wheelchair out of the main doors into the car park to greet the assembled throng. Barry said all the right things about returning to the track, but also found time to try to seek out a national paper journalist who had suggested he was mad and irresponsible to even contemplate such a move. Unfortunately, the confrontation never occurred because the journalist had decided it was not the time or the place to discuss such a matter and didn't turn up.

Once at home Barry maintained his relentless fitness regime. Visits to a hotel at Gatwick for swimming in the morning were followed by long periods on the exercise bike to get the knees bending as the ligaments and shattered bones began to heal. Painkillers were used less and less as planning intensified for the big day at Donington.

The routine at Charlwood resulted in early nights for Stephanie:
'Franco and myself would lift Barry into a wheelchair and then into the bath in the morning. One day I forgot all about him – I was busy with the laundry downstairs and left him in freezing cold water. We would carry him downstairs and leave him in his office all day, then we would carry him back up the stairs and always go to bed early. He would want to get me in bed by half-past seven and as always he won. In the middle of summer I would be lying in bed in bright sunshine, missing *Coronation Street*. Even when he was fit and well he always wanted to go to bed early.'

Barry had always been fit and looked after himself, although the cigarettes did not help. He had always told his rivals that he never did any training and lived on forty fags a day and plenty of greasy food. He might not have been lying about the cigarettes but the rest was just a smokescreen to keep those rivals guessing. It was all part of the Sheene legend, but Steve knew the truth.

'Barry used to tell people that he never did any "bleedin' exercises", smoked forty fags a day, couldn't be bothered with all that training nonsense and still won races. He didn't want to tell anyone about his fitness because that was all part of the deal – if he told everybody he trained a lot, everybody would start training harder.

'In those days physical strength was not quite as necessary as it is today. The reason you need so much strength now is because the bikes have so much grip. He was as fit and strong as anyone, but nothing like as strong as the guys out there now. Nevertheless, Barry knew how important it was and behind the scenes did a lot to keep fit. He had a gym at Charlwood where he would always be doing pull-ups and sit-ups but he always had those skinny little legs. His upper body strength was massive and he worked very hard on his physical condition.

'Barry was not only intelligent but a massively tough character. On the intelligence side Barry would know exactly where to go for everything treatment-wise and what medication was available. This was years before the Web, but Barry was my Internet, and probably even quicker than a search engine. If I wanted something I just phoned up his private number at Charlwood. He had so many con-tacts – people in any industry – because of his way of networking. If he needed to fix something for himself, he had all these people round him that he could pick up on the phone and get anything he wanted.'

Slowly, the trips to the swimming pool, where, with the help of Stephanie, he would flop out of the wheelchair into the water, were replaced by short walks with the aid of firstly two crutches, then by two walking sticks and finally one.

Barry was determined to fly to Donington by helicopter. He later explained how he had persuaded the doctor, with more than a little help from Franco, to pass him fit to fly once again. Steve Parrish is not so certain that the alleged medical even took place.

'Barry flew up to Donington at the controls of the helicopter, which I'm sure was illegal. The CAA keeps your licence until you are fit and well. You would need a medical to say you are fit to fly and I'm not certain Barry had one.'

The original plan, hatched by Barry and Donington boss Robert Fearnall, was for him to attend the meeting and be driven round the track in the back of an open-top car to celebrate his comeback. As Barry's strength grew, and no doubt the size of the brown envelope increased, the actual bike ride was planned. Barry had told Robert that riding a bike would be easier than walking and, as always, he was proved to be correct, albeit with a little help from Steve.

'He flew into Donington and then was walking around on his crutches before getting on the bike. My job was to sit on the back and the reason was quite simple. If the bike stopped or something happened he could not put his feet down to steady it and so I was Barry's kiddy wheels on the back. I had never had so much applause in my life.

'We went on a pretty good lap, perhaps not lap record times but we were still bombing round. The adulation coming from the crowd was absolutely extraordinary. Barry's deal with Robert for some extra brown envelope money had certainly proved worth it because his presence at the track had doubled the crowd on the day.'

Back at both Northampton General and the Three Shires the staff followed Barry's progress with interest. They missed him, and none more so than Nigel Cobb, who fondly recalls his most famous charge: 'Barry was a great person and a perfect patient. He was also very thoughtful. Following the operation I went up to London to do a BBC broadcast with him. Afterwards, we looked around the set for a popular show and the producer asked for an autograph for his son. Barry wouldn't sign it until he was promised two tickets for the show, for me and my wife.'

Barry returned to Nigel Cobb's operating table some years later. After Stephanie and Barry stayed the night at his home in Northamptonshire it was back to the hospital where the surgeon removed the well-photographed plates and screws from his legs. Some of Barry's thinking had clearly rubbed off on his saviour:

'Once the bones have healed the plates are useless and, in some cases, they are a hindrance because they give rise to a mechanical effect between the bones, which are slightly elastic, and the rigid plate which can break off at the edge. It is better to take the plate out and leave the hole in the bone.

'Barry was only in and out to have that done. When we took the plates and screws out we divided them up. He had the ones from the right leg and I had the ones from the left. Later on he bought an artificial tibia and I screwed the plates on in the same position as the operation. I could have made a fortune by putting my share on eBay or something. I could have sold boxes of screws as nobody would have been able to identify them.'

Barry never forgot what Nigel Cobb had done on that July morning in 1982 and took every opportunity to repay him for saving his legs.

'Years later he said, "Whenever you go skiing and fly from Gatwick just leave your car at my place." We did that once, and then the next time we went down there Barry and Steph were away so we all piled into Franco's car to take us to the airport. Barry and Steph then arrived after flying overnight from South Africa and driving down from Heathrow. Barry told Franco we were his friends and so he was going to look after us. The luggage was swapped over and we set off to Gatwick in Barry's car. We didn't go the usual way, but through a little back rabbit hole into the departure lounge, which was absolutely packed. Barry told us to wait by an empty check-in desk and went off to have a word with somebody. We were standing there, looking like twerps when a girl came along, opened the desk, checked us in and then, as everybody else piled in behind us, closed up again.

'He then got us into the executive lounge and on the way there a young lad stopped him and asked him if he was Barry Sheene. He had a chat with the lad about his bike and signed an autograph, wished him luck and told him it was nice to have met him. Barry was dead tired. He'd just flown back from South Africa but still found time to talk to the lad, which was very different from other sportsmen.'

Barry and Nigel Cobb only fell out once. As often happens it was over money and the payment of bills. However, this was a reversal of the usual story and an indication of just what gratitude and respect Barry had for the surgeon.

'Barry was the only person who has complained about my bills. "What are you charging me this for?" he said. "You think that I can go round and tell people that I can get my legs fixed for that much? Look, I want a proper bill." He insisted that I charged him six times the normal rate because he wanted to have paid a decent price for the operation. Actually, I think it was one of Barry's bullshit stories and he really just wanted to show a bit of extra gratitude.'

Nigel Cobb has now retired and lives in a charming village outside Northampton with his wife, Eileen, who was the anaesthetist who applied the correct measures to keep Barry asleep when her husband removed the plates and screws from Barry's legs.

He will always be remembered as the surgeon who saved Barry Sheene's legs. That phone call twenty-five years ago may not have changed his life but it certainly brought him fame. While most people marvelled at his skill, sadly some people in his profession resented his elevation to the front pages.

'Fame – it was a two-edged sword. There was an awful lot of envy and jealousy. I didn't exactly get hate mail, but rather some offensive stuff, which was interesting.'

Wednesday 28 July 1982 was a day that Barry Sheene and Nigel Cobb would never forget. The surgeon can now reveal his celebrated patient's very first thoughts when he was drifting in and out of consciousness on that Silverstone tarmac:

'Barry confided to me the first thing he thought about when he shot off the bike in a ball of flame was his goolies.'

RETIREMENT

Barry Sheene was incapable of doing anything quietly. His departure from Suzuki and arrival at Yamaha was no exception.

There was no announcement or press conference, no 'Thank you Suzuki, but I think it's time to move on.' Instead there was a blatant dig at his old employer while shamelessly promoting Yamaha.

The first time the press or public knew about his defection came at the Lyceum Ballroom in central London when Barry walked on to the stage wearing a Yamaha T-shirt. The occasion was the bike-racing version of the Oscars, the 1979 *Motor Cycle News* Awards. Barry was there to collect the main prize of the evening, the Man of the Year award, and chose the moment to reveal where his loyalties now lay. Steve Parrish was there with him.

'That was Barry, Mr Controversy, and I'm sure he squeezed another fifty grand out of Yamaha when he wore that T-shirt on stage. Suzuki didn't even know they had lost him, or that he had done a deal with Yamaha. Barry didn't do it blindly, he knew exactly what was going on.

'He fell out with the Suzuki guys because they would not give him what he wanted. Also, Robert Jackson at Yamaha was selling more bikes than he knew what to do with and came up with an amazing deal for Barry.'

This final act of defiance came after months of wrangling and stand-off in which, for once, Barry came out second best. He wanted to run his Suzuki team from Charlwood but Suzuki refused. He told them he would leave, taking his sponsorship and Texaco money in particular, but they did not budge. Barry always believed they would, but he was wrong.

Martyn Ogbourne believes that if both parties, and Barry in particular, had just swallowed a little pride the matter could have been resolved but that was not the way Barry Sheene conducted business.

'If there had been more time it would have all calmed down, but nobody was prepared to break the ice. Suzuki wanted to run a team that wasn't based around Barry, who also wanted the bikes to be based at Charlwood and not in Croydon. At first Barry agreed but when he turned up to sign the contract with Maurice Knight he insisted a clause was put in to have the bikes based at his house.

'Barry told them he had an offer of works bikes from Yamaha, which he didn't. Suzuki refused, tempers got frayed and there was a stalemate between the two parties. Nobody called anybody. Franco phoned and said, "You've got to get them to do it. You can't do this to Barry." I went upstairs and asked them what was going on. They told me they could not sign him under those conditions. Maurice Knight was furious about the T-shirt and never paid Barry the last part of his contract.'

The messy end to the marriage cost Barry money but now he was in his element. He had the contacts to put together a superb financial package but the problem was the Yamaha bikes he received were not good enough.

Barry had burned more than a few bridges with Yamaha when he rode their 250 and 350cc machines in those ill-fated 1972 world championship campaigns. Barry initially thought he would get very much the same machinery as Kenny Roberts when he made the switch but he was wrong, very wrong. The machines he received from Mitsui, the British Yamaha importers, were standard production models. The 750 was OK but the 500 was nothing like the Roberts world championship-winning machine. The Akai and Texaco stickers may have brought in the cash but they would not make the machinery go faster.

It was a disaster for Barry who was riding as well as at any time in his career. He had some early success on the 750, winning first time out at Cadwell Park, but when he got down to the real business, the 500cc world championship, he soon realised he was bashing his head against a brick wall. Barry had made a big mistake and, according to Steve Parrish, probably the biggest one of his whole career.

'It turned out to be one of Barry's only major faux pas. I don't think he realised just how bad the standard Yamaha bikes were at that time. He got the out-of-the-crate stock machines initially, although he did eventually manage to persuade Yamaha to supply him with works bikes. The bikes he had in 1980 were like everybody else had. I remember Barry turning up at Cadwell Park for his first race not really knowing what was happening, although he did win a race. He simply underestimated just how bad the stock bikes were going to be.'

The 1980 500cc world championship was very disappointing. He ended the season a lowly fifteenth with only two top-ten finishes, in Spain and Italy. To rub salt into an already very painful wound the young American Randy Mamola, his replacement at Suzuki, pushed Roberts until the very last grand prix before finishing second. Kenny won his third consecutive title for Yamaha but on a very different bike to Barry.

Barry rode as hard as at any time in his career to try to reduce the deficiencies of the production Yamaha but it came at a cost. At the Paul Ricard circuit in France he battled with New Zealander Graeme Crosby, who had joined Mamola at the start of the year. He would close up behind that familiar Suzuki in the corners only to have to start all over again after the long straight as the Suzuki simply disappeared into the distance. A frustrated and angry Barry pushed just a little too hard and crashed, jamming his little finger under the handlebars as he slid along the track.

It was certainly not a crash of the same magnitude as Daytona or Silverstone but the accident caused the most excruciating pain and two months later he had to have the finger amputated.

However, that was not the final appearance of the finger. The next time it was seen in public, it was on Steve Parrish's dinner plate.

'We used to have competitions all the time and about everything. Sunday lunch at Charlwood we would see who could eat the most Yorkshire puddings. Stephanie, bless her, used to make about twenty-five to thirty for all of us, which included Franco, Iris and Uncle Arthur. We would put them in piles and see just how many we could get down, although Barry always used to cheat.

'This particular lunchtime we had the works, roast beef, Yorkshire puddings and all the vegetables you could imagine. Under the first big slice of beef was the end of the finger he had had amputated a month or so beforehand.

'When he first injured it, they managed to wire it back on to his hand in the hope that it would start growing again. Barry always said he never wanted to lose any parts of his body but it proved more trouble that it was worth. In the end he had it amputated and put in a jar of vinegar, where it sat at Charlwood until it appeared under my beef. It was a horrible shrivelled-up thing with a yellow nail on it. Barry could not stop laughing and claimed he had won the competition that weekend.'

The dreaded finger also caused Steve a freezing swim in the English Channel. He recalls a boat trip with Barry when he still had the finger attached.

'Barry would often refer to Steph as "my Doreen", so much so he named his boat after her. In 1980, he blagged a speedboat from a bloke who used to work for Shakespeare Boats. *My Doreen*, which was about eighteen feet long with a great big Mercury engine on the back, was delivered to Charlwood and we decided to take it down to Brighton on a trailer towed by a black Granada, which Ford had loaned to Barry. It was freezing cold but Barry wanted to launch his boat. He started to back the trailer down this very slippery slipway into the sea and I was standing outside directing him.

'Then the car and trailer started to slide down the slipway into the water and there was nothing Barry could do to stop it. The boat went in so far it started to float – still on the trailer – while the car was half in the water with the water pouring in through the boot lid and rear window. It was just after Barry had his little finger put back on following his crash at Paul Ricard and he was terrified of getting it wet because it would probably drop off again.

'The water was flooding in and he was screaming for me to release the trailer and boat from the car. I was fully clothed, up to my neck in freezing sea water trying to unhook the trailer as it dragged the Granada – and Barry – into the sea.

'In the end I managed to unhook it and, with water bubbling out of the exhaust, wheels spinning and blokes from the boatyard pulling, Barry got the Granada up the slipway, leaving me hanging on to the boat and trailer in the bloody cold water. The boat had started to float out to the marina despite still being fixed to the trailer. People kept going past on their boats saying, "Good afternoon". In the end the blokes from the boatyard managed to get a rope to me and tow us back in. Talk about going beyond the call of duty, that was a big one.'

Despite the world championship disasters, Barry was still a match for the home-based riders on the 750cc Yamaha and scored notable victories in the ITV *World of Sport* Superbike races at Donington, Scarborough and Cadwell. More important, he then impressed the Yamaha hierarchy both with his manners and riding ability at their end-of-season international meeting at Sugo in Japan.

Barry knew that a good performance in the event, which was regarded as a bit of a chore by established Yamaha stars like Roberts, could earn him a better bike the following year. Barry crashed in the second race, but still did enough on and off the track to ensure Yamaha let bygones be bygones and they duly came up with some more competitive machinery in 1981.

What Barry finally got from Yamaha was the previous year's model, which had brought world championship success. Kenny got a brand-new machine and needed it as Suzuki upped their challenge. Yamaha told Barry that once Kenny had sorted out the new machine he would get one too. That did not go down well, but with Freddie Spencer's top man Erv Kanemoto joining the Charlwood team prospects looked a lot brighter.

Barry was back in the hunt for podium finishes, if not victories, as was shown by his early season results, which included a third at Monza. Yamaha kept their promise and Barry got the new bike for the French Grand Prix at Paul Ricard. He was back on the podium with second place behind Marco Lucchinelli's Suzuki at Imola in a race cut short when a spectator was killed by lightning. He arrived for the British Grand Prix brimming with confidence but once again that Silverstone jinx struck.

The leader, Graeme Crosby, crashed going into Stowe Corner on the third lap and Barry had to lay his bike down to miss him but was promptly run over by Lucchinelli. Nobody was hurt but Barry was furious with Crosby and made a customary attack through the press on the New Zealander, who was very capable of fighting back.

Two weeks later the grand prix season ended on familiar territory for Barry, the Anderstorp circuit in Sweden. Nobody realised at the time that 16 August 1981 would prove to be the date of Barry Sheene's last grand prix victory.

Anderstorp was not a place to stir the heart. You approached it through a local trading estate and opposite the entrance was a dark, forbidding wood inhabited and policed by Scandinavian Hell's Angels. Smoke always rose from between the trees. The fires were there not only to keep the tree dwellers warm but no doubt also to produce some illegal alcoholic brew.

Roberts had already conceded the championship and after this final round Suzuki would regain the crown, either through Lucchinelli or Mamola. Italian Lucchinelli was a great friend of Barry's and looked odds-on to take the title. When it started to rain in the 30-lap race he decided to settle for a safe ninth place with Mamola dropping down the field. Barry had different ideas and sensed victory. He stalked the front-runner, Boet van Dulmen of Holland, before snatching the lead. It was close but Barry won by just eight-tenths of a second to share the victory celebrations and garland with Lucchinelli, the new world champion.

Little did anyone realise, but it would be the last time Barry – or indeed any British rider – topped a 500cc grand prix podium. The demise of Barry Sheene was the start of a long black period for British grand prix riders. It has now been over a quarter of a century since a British rider won as much as a premier class grand prix. Much has been written about the lack of opportunity and machinery given to British riders during this barren period. The sad fact is nobody has been good enough to replace Barry.

The 1981 season had been better all round for Barry. Improved Yamaha machinery brought him fourth place in the world championship and victories at home, notably at Donington, kept him in the manner to which he was accustomed. Yamaha were quite happy to keep writing big cheques because Barry continued to do a great job for them off the track. Like Suzuki before, they also agreed for Steve Parrish to join him in the team.

The year 1982 will always be remembered for Barry's Silverstone crash and quite rightly so. The horrendous accident and the way he fought through pain to ride again was the stuff of legend. What has been forgotten was just how well the former world champion had been riding that year, right up until that July afternoon.

He started the season on the same machinery as Kenny Roberts although the parity only lasted for the Argentine Grand Prix, held in a country about to be propelled into the world headlines. The grand prix community enjoyed the delights of Buenos Aires before the race got underway, but five days later war was declared with Britain. Flying home was difficult as Argentinian Airlines refused to fly beyond Madrid, as it feared its planes would be impounded in London.

The 32-lap race was an absolute cracker, with Roberts eventually fighting off Barry and the twenty-year-old American Freddie Spencer spearheaded Honda's long-awaited return to grand prix racing. Second place in the second round behind the Suzuki of Franco Uncini at the Salzburgring kept Barry right in the hunt. Kenny was third, riding the brand new V-4 Yamaha, which was very quick but its handling at high speed left much to be desired.

The riders boycotted the third round as they felt the Nogaro circuit near Bordeaux wasn't suitable to host 190 mph 500cc rocket ships. The fourth round produced the classic confrontation between Roberts and Sheene. Kenny came out on top but only after the toughest thirty-seven laps of his career round the two-mile Jarama circuit in Spain.

'My bike was virtually unrideable. I was setting up in the apex and aiming for the outside kerb and somewhere between the two the thing would start spinning. You were never quite sure whether the throttle was going to open or not. I just aimed the bike at the kerb, which was quite high, and pulled the trigger.

'The only reason I was doing that was because Barry was catching me and I rode 105 per cent every lap because in my opinion his Michelin tyres were better than mine and he kept coming and coming, cutting my lead by two to three tenths of a second per lap after I had stretched an early lead using the Dunlop tyres. I was riding the thing out of control.

'A lot of times I would race and never get in a sweat but in this grand prix I really broke a sweat. When I had finished the race this little Spanish guy came running up and said, "The king is here." There was nobody to hold my bike and it was hotter than hell. I was trying to pull my leathers down. The little guy kept yelling at me, "The king is here, the king is here." In the end I just shouted,

"Fuck your king", and away he went. They finally got somebody to hold the bike, but they would not let my mechanics through because of security. I honestly knew nothing about their fucking king and I could not care less. I had run very close to my physical and mental limit – I was done.'

Barry was furious when Graeme Crosby got the first go on the 'Roberts replica' and failed to finish at Misano. He was back to his best with third place in Assen, second at Spa-Francorchamps, where Spencer celebrated his first grand prix win, and another third at Rijeka. It was then on to Silverstone and the rest is history.

Barry's return to Suzuki was stage-managed in very much the same way as his departure had been revealed three years earlier. This time the audience was far larger and a bike replaced the infamous T-shirt. Barry rode a 500cc Suzuki on to the set for the BBC's *Sports Personality of the Year* in December 1982. It was a master stroke, the hero riding back to grand prix racing after those horrendous injuries at Silverstone – and on a Suzuki. Steve Parrish watched the whole plot unfold: 'Barry told Suzuki that the new deal could be announced on national television if they upped the fee by around a hundred thousand pounds. He rode the bike on to the stage, which was so typically Barry who had it all mapped out from the start for maximum impact. When it was obvious he was not going to get Yamaha works bikes Barry tested the water back at Suzuki. He was mates with Gerald Ronson, the big boss of Heron who owned Suzuki GB. As always Barry started at the top and worked his way down. Gail Ronson, Gerald's wife, was also a great friend of Stephanie.'

Heron Suzuki, and new managing director Denys Rohan in particular, wanted Barry back. While Yamaha stalled over re-signing a rider who was recovering from two shattered legs and who was never backwards in coming forward with his opinions about their bikes, the deal was struck. However, a familiar problem very soon emerged as Barry realised that the equipment was not up to the job of regaining world titles. After so much world championship success Suzuki was dropping off the pace, with Yamaha and Honda ploughing millions into their teams.

The British public was not interested in how competitive the Suzuki was going to be. They just wanted to see Barry back on a bike. Their wishes were granted in the sunshine of the South African Grand Prix at Kyalami on the outskirts of Johannesburg, eight months after the Silverstone crash.

After a couple of early tests in England, Barry arrived in South Africa a week before the race. The Holiday Inn at Sandton was a typical South African establishment of the time with a dress code in the restaurant and no fraternising with the black members of the hotel staff. The rules were like a red rag to a bull for Barry. He made the front pages of the local newspapers because he had the audacity to wear jeans in the restaurant. He parked his hired Rolls-Royce right outside the front door of the hotel and he talked to whoever he wanted.

The fact that Barry finished tenth in a race won by Freddie Spencer really didn't matter. Once again Barry had proved everybody wrong. He could push-start the bike, he could last thirty laps in the heat and he could still race with the best of them. It was a great day, ending with a fantastic party in the Holiday Inn.

Sadly, it soon became obvious that Barry's production Suzuki was no match for the works machines. It was sad to see him ride as hard as ever but struggle to finish in the top ten. It all got very messy, with teammate Keith Huewen taking on Barry, the master of spin, in the press and coming off worst. Barry got Harris Engineering to build him a frame and Suzuki promised him an ex-works engine but then changed their minds after some typical Barry comments in the Japanese press. Another problem was that many of the races in the early part of the European season were cold, which increased the pain in his legs and wrist.

His lowest point came at the British Grand Prix. It was expected that Suzuki would give him a works machine as Franco Uncini had been seriously injured in a horrendous crash at Assen. Old scars run deep, though, and Suzuki refused. The bike went to Boet van Dulmen and Barry was furious, convinced that Suzuki wanted revenge for comments he had made over the years.

The Silverstone weekend was an absolute disaster. Norman Brown and Peter Huber were killed in a hideous collision. The race was eventually stopped after an inexplicable delay and was then run in two parts. Once again the Silverstone officials made fools of themselves trying to work out the final results from two races. Barry was eventually awarded ninth place, one hundredth of a second behind van Dulmen. After the second race, thousands of fans climbed over the fences on to the track to salute Barry. It was a spontaneous show of support and affection and even Barry was humbled. That support had much to do with their hero continuing to race, although he had a few more painful times to endure.

The final blow for Barry came in the last grand prix of the season, at Imola. It was a classic showdown between the old and new grand prix generations. The new came out on top, as Freddie Spencer's second place was enough to give him the title. The old master Kenny Roberts had battled with the youngster throughout the season but even first place at Imola was not enough. All Barry could do was watch from fourteenth place. Soon after, Kenny Roberts announced his retirement from riding, only to return just a few months later as a team manager. It was the end of an amazing era in which the American had turned grand prix motorcycle racing on its head. The racetrack without the dirt tracker from Modesto around was a very strange place for a few years.

Towards the end of the year Barry's mood changed and he started to plan for the following season with the same enthusiasm and single-minded determination that had been the hallmark of his thirteen years of grand prix racing. The problem once again was the machinery. Suzuki had pulled the plug on their grand prix efforts but in a strange way this suited Barry, who relished the challenge.

He squeezed an ex-factory engine from Suzuki, got Harris to build the frame and sought sponsorship from DAF trucks. He was no longer the factory superstar but a man on a mission and one who, if the conditions were right, was still capable of producing some big surprises.

The first grand prix of the 1984 season took place in pouring rain at Kyalami. Barry was in his element. Despite a bad start he rode through the field, mastering the slippery track that acted as a leveller for non-factory machinery. He set the fastest lap and finished a superb third, almost catching second-placed Raymond Roche on the line. It was Barry at his best, and how he loved it! He prayed for rain at every other race. Unfortunately, not even Barry Sheene could influence the weather.

On the fast tracks he had no chance, but when it got slightly trickier and riding ability became a more significant factor Barry was able to fight for podium finishes. Despite that mile-long back straight at Paul Ricard, Barry coaxed the ageing Suzuki into fifth place and this was followed by a seventh a week later at Rijeka. He was right up with the leaders Mamola, Roche and Lawson at Assen when the old Suzuki cried 'enough'.

Barry arrived at Silverstone knowing deep down this would be his last British Grand Prix. He also knew that unless the heavens opened he had no chance of giving his loyal fans the victory they deserved.

Nonetheless, he produced a display of pure magic in the 28-lap encounter round the Northamptonshire circuit. It was such a shame, but no one realised at the time that this was Barry saying goodbye. For ten glorious laps he battled with the works bikes of Mamola, champion-in-waiting Eddie Lawson, Roche, Ron Haslam and Didier de Radiguès. He was catching them on the corners but losing out on the Hangar Straight and the crowd was in raptures. Barry was on the absolute limit of adhesion; the Suzuki was on the absolute limit of its power. Slowly the leaders pulled away with Barry knowing he would crash if he tried to go any faster.

It was stunning. Never has a fifth place been greeted with such joy by a home crowd.

It was a supreme effort, which he couldn't hope to repeat. He crashed at the Anderstorp circuit that had brought him so much success before. His grand prix career ended when he retired at Mugello with a broken ignition. Silverstone had been his last proper goodbye; those last two races didn't really count.

Even though Barry had given up grand prix racing he gave no hint of retiring. After all, he still had some British commitments. Little did the television viewers who tuned into the final round of the ITV *World of Sport* championship in between the wrestling and the football results realise, but they were watching history in the making. Barry competed as a professional racer for the last time on a chilly Saturday afternoon at Donington Park on 22 September 1984.

He disappeared in style, fighting a race-long battle with local hero Ron Haslam. For eighteen laps they swapped the lead, with Haslam finally taking the chequered flag by less than a second. Like everybody else, and perhaps even Barry, it never occurred to Ron that it might be his last race.

'You would never have guessed that this was going to be Barry's last race because he just never gave up. He was riding as hard as he ever did. I thought I had done enough to pull away but he kept pushing me and I thought he'd snatched it on the line. It was always great racing with Barry and it was sad it turned out to be the last time. Though if I had known that at the time I still wouldn't have let him win.'

In fact, Barry was actively trying to sort out some competitive machinery for 1985 while also turning his hand to four wheels. A few weeks after that last race on two wheels Barry returned to Donington at the wheel of a DAF truck, the star of the first truck meeting to be held at the Leicestershire circuit. Andrew Marriott – Count Jim Moriarty – was there.

'That event at Donington Park attracted a hundred thousand

fans and brought the Midlands to a standstill, even closing East Midlands airport. Barry's appearance, plus the fact the event was sponsored by the *Sun*, Radio One disc jockey Mike Smith was driving and Martin Brundle was making a racing comeback pulled such a massive crowd.'

It was not Barry's first or last dabble with four wheels but the experience never triggered the passion that made him such a great bike rider. Andrew Marriott recalls Barry's thinking.

'I helped organise a secret test for him and George Harrison with the Surtees Formula One team in 1977. He was seriously thinking about making a switch but it was not until he had retired from bike racing that he actually embarked on a four-wheel project. He drove the Akai-sponsored Audi touring car for Richard Lloyd but Barry never really got his head round it. He also had a go in truck racing and later went on to help Steve Parrish become so successful.'

Time was running out for Barry and he knew it. If there was no competitive machinery he would have to call it a day but he kept everybody waiting. He even told *Motor Cycle News* he was going to Honda, and rang the editor of the *Daily Mirror* to try to get Ted McCauley sacked when he dared suggest Barry was about to retire. Ted, however, was right.

On a freezing cold January afternoon in 1985 Andrew Marriott summoned the press to a plush Mayfair hotel. The whole family was there as Barry calmly announced it was all over. He was going to retire from the sport he had graced since an autumn afternoon at Brands Hatch in 1968, nearly seventeen years earlier. Andrew Marriott asked for questions from the floor but there was silence, either through sadness or shock.

It was time to move on. In addition to the car racing he co-hosted the *Just Amazing!* television programme with singer Kenny Lynch, as well as Jan Ravens and, later, Suzanne Danielle. He also had plenty of fun and games in the *Driving Force* series with the likes of Murray Walker, Roger Daltrey and Nigel Havers. He was still a big personality in Britain but it was not enough, and so decided to broaden his horizons by moving to Australia in 1987.

Barry always claimed that the warm weather soothed his aching limbs, and that the opportunity for investment lured him away. Andrew Marriott had a different theory: Barry had not been declaring those brown envelopes.

'He discovered Australia before he went to live there. He liked the weather and it was good for his health, but also Her Majesty's Special Tax Unit had something to do with the move. He did a deal to write out a cheque and clear off.'

The wrath of the taxman was confirmed by Linda Patterson, who received a fax from Barry in January 1987 telling her that his phone was being tapped and that she was not to make any comments about brown envelopes.

The Sheene family soon settled in Queensland. The sunshine was good for his health, property investments were going fine and a new career beckoned. He started broadcasting for the Sydney-based public broadcasting channel SBS which had the rights to grand prix bike racing. Things were changing in Australia owing to a certain Wayne Gardner. The Wollongong-based rider returned home to a hero's welcome when he became the first Australian to win the 500cc world championship in 1987. Suddenly bike racing was big business and television tycoon Kerry Packer stepped in. He bought the rights to grand prix bike racing to put on the number one sports show in Australia, Channel Nine's *Wide World of Sport*. He persuaded Barry – not that he needed much persuading – to join former Formula One world champion Alan Jones and the legendary Darrell Eastlake as the commentary team. Barry persuaded them they needed somebody to help on site, and Nick Harris was duly appointed.

'Dazza' Eastlake became an overnight legend in Australia after commentating from a broom cupboard on the success of an Australian weightlifter at the Brisbane Commonwealth Games. He knew little about grand prix racing in the early days but his loud, enthusiastic commentary was the perfect foil for the Pom. Throw in AJ – Alan Jones – and they had the whole of Australia tuning in.

At the opening grand prix of the 1989 season, at Suzuka in Japan, Darrell Eastlake quickly learnt all about his new commentating partner.

'It was the very first time I worked with Barry and it was my first grand prix. There were just three of us, Barry, the producer Mike Williams and myself. We took these big aluminium containers with us because we didn't know how much gear we would need. We arrived at Narita airport near Tokyo where Barry was picked up in a stretch limo and, typically, he just pissed off and left us. Five hours later, after two train journeys and three cab rides, Mike and I arrived at Suzuka to be told by Barry, "I'm the governor, I get the ride and you go by train." Everything just went from there.

'On the same trip he borrowed my camera. When I got home I took the film to be developed at my local chemist shop. Barry had taken thirty-six shots up the skirts of Japanese girls walking over the bridge above him. The chemist asked, "Who took these?" and I replied, "I'll give you just one guess." On the way home one of the air hostesses asked Barry to try to fix her camera. He took it to the toilet and came back with a stupid grin on his face. He then told me, "Wait until she gets home to have the pictures developed – Percy is on every one.'

That first grand prix for Channel Nine may have been an eye-opener for all concerned but the second, on home soil at Phillip Island, produced more classic Sheene antics, usually aimed at new boy Nick Harris:

'The whole team was on duty at the second round and schoolboy humour prevailed. They would tell me the wrong time for meetings with the director then deny all knowledge, or hide my race-day shirt and tell the car park attendant I didn't have a pass. They were brilliant – and when Alan Jones couldn't pronounce "Loris Capirossi" properly they just laughed even more.'

For Darrell it was something of an education. Life and limb were in constant danger. 'They built a new tunnel under the track to get from the infield to the paddock and Barry, plus Kevin Schwantz, Kenny Roberts and a few others, had a competition to see who could climb the highest up the wall when racing through the tunnel in a hire car. Barry got me to sit in the back to act as ballast because the competition, as always, was getting very serious. We got so high up the wall the car rolled over, got jammed in the tunnel and had to be pulled out by a tractor.'

The Australian viewers just loved them, the brash Australian commentator brought up on surfing and rugby league and the plain-speaking Pom who was a legend in his own right.

'Barry just went into everybody's hearts because he was so rare. He was such a fantastic character and had a wonderful manner. He didn't give any bullshit. If he didn't like a rider he would say so and he always knew when somebody was going to crash. He also helped a lot of Australian riders like Gary McCoy and Chris Vermeulen when they first went to Europe, which was fantastic and I respected him for that.

'He was such a lovable rogue and did some outrageous things. When we didn't go to races we broadcast from the studio in Sydney. Barry hung a pair of knickers on the wall behind us and they must have been there for five grands prix before Mike Williams saw them and went ballistic. They got taken down but before the next grand prix we found some big moustaches in the make-up room and put them on twenty seconds before we went on air. Mike Williams screamed down the headphones to get them off but it was too late and we had to keep them on. This time it was the boss David Hill who went ballistic.'

For six years the television audiences stayed high, helped by Mick Doohan replacing Gardner as the dominant force in the 500cc world championship. Barry was now a household name in Australia, with his television commentaries and commercials for companies such as Shell bringing him far more exposure than his two world titles ever did. In 1996 he moved another rung up the ladder.

Network Ten took over the rights to broadcast grand prix racing and Barry went with them. A year later, when they launched their ninety-minute Sunday afternoon *RPM Motorsport* programme Barry was the co-presenter, giving exactly the same treatment to V8 Touring cars, Formula One and Superbikes as he had to grand prix bikes. Once again both the audiences and the executives loved him, as did fellow commentator Leigh Diffey.

'You could not buy what Barry brought to Channel Ten and it was fantastic to work with him. He would always say before we went on air, "Let's have a laugh," and we always did. He used to call me Stiffy and it was just such a great time.'

Although the television work provided Barry with a challenge and adrenaline rush it was still not enough. Barry had a reputation for burning bridges and when he told Stephanie and later the press that he would rather have a frontal lobotomy than race a bike again he was asking for trouble. It all started innocently enough, with an appearance at the fantastic Centennial Classic event in 1998 at Assen. Barry was in his element, alongside old friends and enemies, as the who's who of grand prix racing delighted the crowds in demonstration races and parades. Barry rode the Suzuki on which he had won his very first 500cc grand prix twenty-three years before.

He then returned to Europe to 'race' a 1962 Manx Norton with Damon Hill at the 1998 Goodwood Revival meeting, finishing second and third in his two outings. The bug was beginning to bite and things had to be done the Barry way. He returned to Goodwood a year later, winning both races.

Barry bought a re-manufactured Manx Norton of his own, enlisted the help of top tuner Fred Walmsley and got serious. The bike was flown to Australia where he won at Phillip Island but also crashed. Barry then returned to Europe to continue racing at Goodwood and Donington.

In 2002 he came to Donington to compete in the Classic races at the British Grand Prix. He knew then that something was very wrong and promised to see the specialist when he returned home to Australia, but put those worries to one side to win both races. The years just rolled back.

Just a few weeks after being diagnosed with cancer he arrived at Goodwood to do battle for the very last time. He had lost weight, his face was gaunt but his wit and sheer brilliance had not yet been taken away.

After finishing second to Wayne Gardner's G50 Matchless in the first race Barry won the second to take the Lennox Cup on aggregate time. Barry said a final goodbye to the sport in the only way he knew how: crossing the line in first place.

LIFE AFTER BARRY

A pair of muddy motocross boots lie discarded on the immaculate paving stones in front of the garage doors of Manor House. The red glow of the fading sun is reflected in the waters of the river that flows past, making its way to the sea less than a mile away, while the lights on the high-rise apartments of Surfers Pardise twinkle in the distant twilight.

Behind those garage doors a lone figure works beneath the tank of his orange 125cc KTM off-road machine. This is eighteen-year-old Freddie Sheene's domain, just as it had been his father's before he died three-and-a-half years earlier.

The front page of the local newspaper is Sellotaped to the garage wall. Once again a Sheene is making the headlines for riding a motorcycle. The fact the story tells of local riders upsetting the neighbours rather than winning world titles matters little.

The passion, confidence and sheer cheek has a familiar ring to it. Turn back the clock nearly forty years across the world to Queen's Square, Holborn and it is Barry all over again. Back in the kitchen Stephanie misses the babble of voices from the garage as her son Freddie works alone.

'Freddie is doing things now that Barry was doing as a grown man and it's so sad seeing him out there in the garage, working alone on his bike. It so reminds me of the times that Barry and Franco would be out there working and arguing. It was great when Stavros visited us recently, to see him and Freddie laughing and joking together even if they were seeing just how far they could shoot onions across the river with Freddie's home-built gun.'

Freddie's love of motorcycles has already brought him the pain and the challenge that his dad met head-on so many times. He broke his left wrist and right femur when he fell from a motocross bike in 2005. In 2006, in true Sheene style he returned to the hospital to have the pins removed.

A closer examination of that newspaper cutting on the garage wall reveals another throwback to those school-hating days back in Holborn, as Stephanie discovered.

'I wondered why Freddie had this picture up in the garage, together with the article about local off-road motorcycle riders upsetting the neighbours with their riding. I looked at the picture and realised the unnamed rider was wearing a school blazer as he pulled the wheelie. I looked again and realised it was Freddie's school blazer. Enough said.'

Twenty-two-year-old Sidonie may not be showing her brother's desire to race motorcycles but she could only have one father. She works for the Australian Grand Prix Corporation in Melbourne, has never been afraid to express her views and speaks to her mum on the phone at least half-a-dozen times a day.

'Sidonie was the only person that could stand up to Barry, apart from his sister. He just could not fathom out or understand somebody who answered back. Barry was very good when the children were little. He didn't care about being woken up in the middle of the night and never grumbled.

'When Sidonie was thirteen she started answering back. Barry just could not handle it and I always had to negotiate between them. He hated her smoking and one day when she bent over he spotted a tattoo at the bottom of her back. He went mad, then just walked out of the house and drove off. Later Sidonie had four tattoos, including one of Barry's number seven, on the back of her neck.

'Barry would ask them to watch him on the telly but they hardly ever did. Sidonie would say, "Why bother? We see plenty of you at home." Freddie is like me and Sidonie is certainly very much like her dad in character.'

Sister Maggie agrees: 'Out of the two kids, Sidonie is much more like Barry. Freddie has a much kinder, quieter nature. He is more like Stephanie. Sidonie is a carbon copy of Barry and never lets anybody get away with anything but also, like Barry, can be immensely generous and loving. When I spend time with them I really see that.'

Inside the magnificent house there are framed pictures of Barry racing, Barry water-skiing, Barry just being Barry and Barry with the family filling every wall. The hallway is home to the machinery which made him famous: the two 500cc world championship-winning Suzukis, the 680cc and 500cc Suzuki twin plus a couple of Yamahas. Pride of place goes to the 125cc Suzuki upon which Barry won his very first grand prix.

Barry's office is lined with pictures, and a cabinet the length of the wall is packed with trophies, sponsors' caps and a fireman's whistle given to Franco when he was a fire auxiliary during the Blitz.

It's as if nothing has changed, but of course it has. Stephanie knows that better than anybody else.

'I've become a TV critic and a bit of a hermit. I've lost confidence in myself and, to be honest, just feel very contented to be home at this time of my life. I thought "What is the point of doing something alone when you are used to doing it with somebody else?"'

More than three years after Barry's death, Stephanie is slowly getting to grips with life without him. They had always floundered when the other was not around, although Barry never had to cope without Stephanie for more than a few days.

'When I went shopping I would deliberately leave the phone in the car. He would get so mad if he couldn't get me to pick up something that was often not all that important.

'When he travelled to England he would phone when he was getting off the plane, phone waiting for the luggage, have a moan to British Airways about the luggage delay, and then phone again waiting for the taxi. He would stay with Jules [Julian Seddon] and after a shit, shave and shower he would phone again.'

Barry's funeral was a private affair, although tragically one member of the family was not there to say goodbye to the son he worshipped.

'Franco could not get out of bed on the day of the funeral. His brain just would not accept that Barry had died and he blocked out the funeral. Franco is still alive and lives in a care home down the coast. He is ninety-five years old and often thinks that Barry is still alive.'

There is so much to do immediately after the death of a loved one. You could be sure that Barry was up there, as always checking that Stephanie was doing things the right way, or at least his way.

'Life after Barry died was certainly different. I was used to being told what to do. When he died I had to sit in the office checking the paperwork. At first just settling down took me months and Maggie stayed to help. I had to rise to the occasion, because to do what Barry had done so routinely I had to become a director instead of being directed.'

Part of the procedure was organising the departure of Barry's dream helicopter. Typically, when he realised he would never fly again Barry made specific plans for its final flight.

'Before Barry died he told me the only person he wanted to fly the helicopter away from our house was a pilot from Melbourne called Russell. I was at home with Maggie when he arrived and he seemed to spend hours in the hangar checking everything out.

'The helicopter finally emerged and Maggie and I went up into the tower at the top of the house to watch its final flight. As the helicopter climbed away from the house a rainbow appeared over the river and Russell flew under it. It was as if Barry was acknowledging that his dream helicopter had finally flown away.'

After a few months, memories of those Marks and Spencer white socks and those dreadful shoes from that very first meeting prompted Stephanie to go through Barry's clothes drawers.

'He would have gone mad seeing us throw so much stuff out. Later that night there was a frightening storm. I knocked on Maggie's door and we sat together, agreeing it was Barry showing us he was mad about us chucking out all the odds and sods he had collected.'

Further proof that Barry was still pulling the strings came in a visit to a clairvoyant by Maggie's daughter Paula. 'Paula went to a clairvoyant wearing the watch that Barry had given her for her twenty-first birthday. She told Paula a man in his fifties was coming through to her and it was the man who had given her the watch. He told her to tell the family how much he loved them and also that he was doing all his hobbies.'

Stephanie and Maggie had become good friends, even though this had not been the case in the early days of Barry's romance with the model. Both knew Barry better than anybody in the world and both loved him so very much.

Unlike Stephanie it had been a rocky road for his sister who watched the 'little shit' grow into a celebrity, carrying much of the baggage that goes with such elevated status. It was also a heartbreaking experience watching her parents pour so much affection on to their only son, often at the expense of their only daughter.

'I'm not a jealous person and I've never envied what Barry had but the only thing I got really hurt by was the fact that he had more of my mum and dad than I ever did.'

When Barry insisted on taking Iris and Franco with him to Australia in 1987 it was the final straw for Maggie.

'We really did fall out and I was very upset when he went

to Australia and took Mum and Dad. I certainly didn't care much for it. I never minded the fact that they lived with Barry because it was a two-hour drive to Wisbech or half-an-hour to Charlwood. When he took them to Australia that really did upset me. My mum did not want to go but she had to because my dad wanted to. She would say, "Could you imagine what Franco would be like if I told him I did not want to go?"

'Barry knew my mum really didn't want to go because of her first two grandchildren. It was very hard for her and she never really settled there. She never felt well the whole time they were there. They went in 1987 and a year later she came back to stay with me for three months. She came back several times before she was taken ill in 1990. She died a year later in Australia, which was pretty bloody awful. Barry flew me out there and I stayed with her for twelve months while she went through all the treatment. She was determined to come back to England for Christmas that year. She stayed with us and, though knew she was going to die, she wanted to be there for my birthday in early February. After that, she flew back to Australia and died on 2 June. I was not there when she died but I had said my goodbye.'

Following the death Maggie recalls that she and Barry just drifted apart.

'There were a couple of years or more when we hardly ever spoke to each other. Franco came back to stay with us and then he decided he was coming to live with me because he'd had enough of Australia. I think he thought he would come here and I would take over the role of Iris, but that was not my plan at all. He was my dad but I was not going to take over the role of Mum. He stayed a while but then went back to Australia and kept going backwards and forwards between the two countries until 2000.'

As is often the case, it was a family illness that brought Barry and Maggie back together again.

'We became friends again when Franco had a heart attack and was taken into hospital here. He kept telling people he had fallen off a bar stool but it actually happened in the night at our home. He came home and then had a couple of small strokes that really affected his memory. When he was fit enough to fly I took him back to Australia and he's never come back.'

Maggie's rekindled friendship with her brother also brought her closer to Stephanie.

'By this time I was making my regular visits to Australia – going for two weeks and staying for three months. It was really nice and that's when Stephanie and I hit it off. In fact, when Stephanie was living apart from Barry we started to get on really well.

'I didn't get on well with Stephanie to start with. I just didn't think she was my type of person at all. Barry changed in those early days with Stephanie, just as everybody who suddenly gets money changes. He was not the same person and I suddenly felt that I had nothing in common with him. He became much more materialistic and he always seemed to want to be with important people rather than his friends from club races. I suppose that's progress, but he was different. Later on he did come back.'

Barry did come back but there was still one thing upon which he never saw eye to eye with his sister. Franco had devoted his life to Barry's racing but when Maggie asked Barry for some help when her son Scott embarked on a racing career in Britain Barry refused.

'I was disappointed that he didn't help Scott with his racing. A couple of times I did ask for his help and he told me he couldn't. I have a theory why Barry was like that but I've never told anybody what it was: he couldn't have done what he did without my dad. Everybody needs a helping hand.

'I got upset that he opened doors for all these bloody Australians but not for his own nephew, the only nephew he had. Poor Scott, when he started racing everybody thought he was being helped by Barry but he really wasn't. It did upset me.'

Steve Parrish had already said his goodbyes back in Australia and was ready and relieved when that phone call from Stephanie told him Barry's pain was finally over. However, there was one final fax from the Queensland number, written in a familiar style. The only difference from the hundreds of faxes that had landed in Hertfordshire over the years was the handwriting. It was written by Stephanie but dictated by Barry.

'Years ago I asked Barry to write a foreword for the book I was going to write one day. When I got down to Australia to see him for the last time I was too embarrassed to remind him about it. He had far too much on his plate to worry about a stupid foreword for a book. I never thought it would get done but Barry reminded Stephanie just before he died and dictated it to her. He made it sound quite amusing. Barry always used to say, "Stavros, if you fell in a cesspit you would come out with a salmon on your head," and his foreword just summed up our friendship:

I first met Stavros in 1975 at Brands Hatch and we immediately got on like a house on fire and seemed to see eye to eye about everything. I invited him over to my place at Wisbech and I haven't stopped laughing yet.

I've never met anybody who could get themselves in and out of so much trouble. If he could have set up and put as much effort into preparing his bikes as he did with the intricate pranks he pulled on people, he would have been a world champion. As it was, he spent most of his time running away from trouble.

He was blindingly fast on four or six wheels, which he proved by winning those five European Truck Racing titles.

Whatever he does, bikes, trucks or television commentary, it's always fun for him and all those around him.

Gas it Wanker!

Barry

Back home in Britain, Barry's death was big news. For a week Steve found little time to grieve as he spoke to newspapers, television and radio stations about Barry. Even the Prime Minister, Tony Blair, passed on his condolences to Stephanie and the family during a speech in the House of Commons. Archive footage of that 1979 Silverstone battle with Kenny Roberts – and the two-fingered salute – flashed across British television screens.

Lord Hesketh, now a Tory peer, rekindled memories of those adrenaline-fuelled days with Barry and James Hunt. Hunt died ten years before Barry, when just forty-five years old, and Hesketh mourned the death of two friends, the like of which he would never see again.

'As I get older it becomes by and large clearer and clearer to me that the good guys die young and the shits go on forever. Both Barry and James had a charm, an innocence, a vulnerability even, which combined with raw talent, skill and a will to win places them for ever in the pantheon of sporting greats.

'They may not have made the money of modern champions but the fact that nearly thirty years on they are so fondly remembered tells you an awful lot.'

Only a week later, when the phones stopped ringing, did Steve start to miss his great friend. However, he was certain Barry would have already got everybody running about after him and everything organised to his liking in his new residence.

'For about two weeks after he passed away I kept expecting a fax to arrive: "Stavros you need to get up here, the gin and tonics have been poured, I've got loads of crumpet lined up and we've got the fastest bikes." I also wanted to send him faxes, although I've not got his number up there. I'm not a religious person but if there is anything up there Barry will have it all sorted out for us, so that's something for me to look forward to.'

Life was never going to be the same for Steve.

'It certainly put the skids under me and gave me a whole new outlook on life. It's something that is a reminder to us when we are moaning about an electricity bill or missing a flight that health is the most important thing in the world. Someone who had everything, who was my hero and who I thought was indestructible was in fact mortal.

'It was an education knowing Barry. He taught me how to get through life efficiently. He was a wheeler-dealer. He ducked and dived, steered things the way he wanted it. I could never expect to be as good but I learnt plenty of tips from him and they have stood me in good stead ever since. It was not that he was a greedy person, but it was competition. He would fix it to get something better than the other people and that's what he was all about.

'It was like having a brother, father and mate all rolled into one. For a long period of time I would think of Barry every time something happened and wonder how he would have coped with it. When something good happened or something funny happened I wanted to phone him up and tell him. But he was not there. Even now there are not many weeks that pass by when something crops up and I think about how Barry would deal with it.'

Steve helped organise and took part in many tributes to Barry, both in Britain and Australia. He even persuaded Freddie to ride pillion with him on the Barry Sheene ride to the 2004 Australian Grand Prix at Phillip Island.

However, it was a special event in Scarborough that provided the most fitting tribute. The Oliver's Mount race circuit high above the Yorkshire holiday resort was tight, hilly and bloody dangerous, but Barry had always raced there in front of enormous crowds. His battles with local hero Mick Grant were legendary.

Barry and Steve had always loved going to Scarborough and not only for the brown envelopes. The Saturday night get-together at the Spa Ballroom down on the front where the fans met the riders had reached spectacular proportions. Leaving Stephanie and Linda drinking gin and tonics in the comfort of the hotel bar they would 'wander' down for a couple of hours as part of their obligation to the organisers. The problem was that their interpretation of just wandering down was a little different to most. As were Barry and Steve's ideas about meeting the fans, especially the women. Steve recalls many happy memories.

'Scarborough was a place where all sorts of things went on.

Generally it was never a championship meeting and so it was a fun weekend where we would earn a few quid. Neither Barry nor I particularly liked road circuits but there was something about Scarborough. Of course, it was dangerous but we would only ride it at around eight-tenths, which was usually enough for Barry to win races up there. We were like two schoolboys bunking off. Generally it was drizzling on the Friday afternoon of practice and so Barry and I would give it a miss and go down in the town to the lingerie shops instead. We would go in and pretend we were going to buy something but really we were trying to have a peep through the curtains at somebody trying on the underwear. It was pretty ridiculous, but it was another one of those challenges.'

Following Barry's death the Scarborough organisers had a commemorative plaque made and invited Steve and many other leading riders to its unveiling by the Duke of Edinburgh. Steve did not let his old Spa Ballroom partner down, even in royal company.

'Barry would have absolutely loved it. The Duke of Edinburgh turned up to unveil a plaque to Barry on the start and finish line – not down at the Spa Ballroom. As always when royalty are involved, we were briefed what to do before he arrived. He had two bodyguards with him and the first person he was to meet was world champion Phil Read. As always I had my remote-controlled fart machine with me and it fitted perfectly between one and two cylinders underneath the fuel tank of Phil Read's TT-winning red and white Formula One Honda.

'I told Mick Grant and Jamie Witham what I had done but we didn't tell Phil. Sure enough, at noon Prince Philip arrived and with outstretched hand went to meet Read. As their hands touched off it went. It was set for a rip-roaring fart and that's what it was. Witham buckled over in laughter, and went down to hide behind the bikes. The best part was the two bodyguards, who looked at each other and winked. Phil Read didn't know where to look. Barry would have just loved it. He was always egging me on to do things and he was up there egging me on as always when the Duke of Edinburgh arrived.'

A couple of years before Barry died he had flown up to Scarborough with Steve to cause another 'scandal', but this time it involved pensioners rather than girls.

'We flew up to Scarborough to ride in the Gold Cup memorial meeting. Barry was riding a 500cc Cagiva, the same model as those Randy Mamola and Eddie Lawson had ridden in the world 500cc championship. Barry picked me up from my house in Hertfordshire in an Agusta 109 helicopter. We scurried up towards Scarborough and stopped at Humberside to refuel where our problems started. Apparently we flew into Humberside air space without the correct permission. Barry got a huge bollocking over the radio and was told to report to the control tower immediately after our landing. I helped with the refuelling and by the time I got to the control tower Barry was signing autographs and everything was smoothed over and all the women from air traffic control were getting kisses.

'That was the first thing sorted out, but the Agusta doesn't have a big fuel tank and so we had to get to Scarborough pretty quickly. We flew over Scarborough looking for the Rea Hotel that, according to Barry, was two miles north of the town. We didn't have any coordinates but Barry insisted it was easy to find because it had lovely big gardens that would be perfect for landing.

'After twenty minutes circling round the area, the big twin-engine helicopter gobbling up the fuel, we were starting to panic a bit and were getting lower and lower. Suddenly Barry reckoned he could see the hotel and down we went. I checked Barry was sure and, as always, he told me that it was the right place.

'I was not so sure, especially as when we started to land everybody looking up was either in a wheelchair or was over ninety-five years old. Barry was concentrating so hard on landing this big helicopter he did not notice. We landed and I was dispatched to check if we were in the right place. I was like Anneka Rice, ducking under the rotor blades and running towards the wheelchairs. The first person I got to told me we had landed in the Miners' Union Retirement home and certainly not the Rea Hotel. I started giggling, did a 180-degree turn and began running back to the helicopter. On the way I was accosted by the gardener, who told me in no uncertain terms that we had wrecked their bowling green. It had just been laid, not even marked out, and we had landed right smack in the middle of it.

'I looked across and saw the wheels of the Agusta had sunk right into the grass. I told him that it had really soft tyres and it would be OK, which was of course a load of bollocks. Then another old boy on walking sticks arrived and asked if Arthur had arrived. I told him it was Barry Sheene, and who was Arthur? "Arthur Scargill," he replied. "He comes here once a year and they land the helicopter just over there."

'I couldn't speak but managed to get back in the helicopter and somehow through the tears of laughter shouted at Barry just to take off, take off and don't ask any questions.

'We discovered the hotel just over the hill, where the local press were waiting. They had seen us disappear to land at the Miners' Union home and presumed we had crashed and were already writing the story about the world champion in a helicopter crash when we landed. However, we did make the front page of the local newspaper for wrecking the bowling green.'

A few months before Barry's death Nick Harris was asked to record a short obituary for the BBC. 'I honestly didn't know how to react, but they assured me that other people who'd been asked to record an obituary for other terminally ill people felt equally confused. I felt that if I didn't do it someone else would, and it wouldn't be right. I owed it to Barry.

'They wanted less than a minute, ready to go out on their news bulletins when Barry died. Less than a minute about Barry Stephen Frank Sheene's fifty-three years on the planet was a tall order. Writing it was hard enough, but going into the studio to record it was far worse. I kept expecting Barry's voice to come through the headphones, saying "Nickel Arse, you can't say that . . . you must mention this . . . who's that bird behind the glass recording all of this?" No voice came through the headphones. I recorded it all in one go and hurried away. God forbid Barry ever found out.

'Phone calls early in the morning scare us all. When the phone rang in the darkness on 10 March I need not have picked up as I knew what I was going to be told. I put on the radio, ready for the news. Barry's death was announced and my voice piece cued. I was glad I'd done the right thing. But someone pressed the wrong button and there was silence. Barry, as ever, had the last laugh.

'The phone didn't stop ringing, with calls from journalists and old friends. My generation had grown up with Barry Sheene and the prospect of growing old without him was so very sad.'

It's easy to understand why so many people of Barry's generation mourned the premature loss of somebody who played such a big part in their growing up in the 1970s. For the older grand prix paddock generation stories about Barry still filled most dinner times and late-night drinking sessions.

In many ways Italian Valentino Rossi is the Barry Sheene of the twenty-first century. He is blindingly fast and brave, a master of mind games, has a wicked sense of humour, a total belief in his own ability and a loyalty and love of close friends and family.

He had already won the MotoGP world title when the teams arrived at Phillip Island for the 2003 Australian Grand Prix. Just twelve months earlier Barry had flown in with Freddie for what turned out to be his final farewell to the MotoGP community at the windswept but beautiful location overlooking the choppy Bass Strait in Victoria.

Australia was remembering one of her favourite adopted sons with typical passion. Over seven hundred motorcyclists had ridden in a convoy from up-state Victoria to commemorate Barry's life and to raise money for charity. They finished with a lap of the 2.764-mile circuit. Five-time world champion Mick Doohan braved the torrential rain and gale-force winds to complete a lap on the Manx

Norton, which had brought Barry his final emotional victory at Goodwood. However, it was Rossi's tribute that would have delighted the departed Englishman the most.

After winning the controversial 27-lap race riding the Repsol Honda, Rossi's celebration lap turned into a personal tribute to a man he never raced against but who he readily admits was his inspiration.

'In the morning we "borrowed" a sheet from the hotel and put a big number seven in Barry's style on it. When we arrived at Phillip Island it was a strange feeling to realise that Barry was not there and so when I won the race I wanted to remember him by riding the lap with his flag. Barry was my hero and when he died it was very difficult.'

Barry had been a rival and great friend of Valentino's father Graziano. Like those younger members of the MotoGP paddock he had grown up on stories of their exploits.

'I have very good memories of Barry . . . when I was very young, together with my father Graziano, at Donington Park in 1995 when he was racing with the Classic bike and I was there for the first time riding in the European Championship.

'He was a good friend of Graziano and when he came to speak to me it was a great emotion because Barry Sheene was not just a fast rider but a rider who changed the image of motorcycle racing throughout the world. He was so very cool. He had lots of friends and always arrived in the Rolls-Royce and reminded me of the Beatles. He was the first cool rider in the story, not just fast and a world champion.

'Later I spent a lot of time with him in Australia. For many years I would have dinner with him and Mick Doohan at Phillip Island. I saw Barry in the February of the previous year when we were testing at Phillip Island. He was in good shape and we spent a lot of time together. He died in such a short time it's difficult to understand why.

'When he knew he had very little time we went to dinner and as always he gave out so much energy and was smiling and so positive. That's why he was such a great guy. His wife Stephanie is incredible. She was a heroine in the past for all the mechanics and Graziano.

'I'm happy because with my style I've done something similar to Barry. I think in our own way we changed the image of the rider, showing he is just not a crazy man who constantly risks his life. Barry Sheene inspired me very much and I've tried to do the same as him. It left a big hole when he went.'

In the race before the famous celebration lap, Rossi had been penalised ten seconds for overtaking under a yellow flag. The infringement just spurred the Italian on to greater things, and he later admitted that he had been forced to race at 100 per cent for the whole race for the first time that year, en route to his eighth victory of the season.

His two fingers to officialdom, the ability to ride so fast for so long and the use of a hotel sheet was certainly very cool and, also, so very Barry Sheene. His father's great friend would have been very proud.

Gary Nixon remembered Barry for many different reasons: all those girls in the 1970s, his blinding ability and, most of all, his kindness and friendship when the going got tough for the American. However, when a cheque arrived not long after Barry's death, he couldn't believe it.

'This DHL parcel arrived and it didn't say who it was from. Inside was a cheque for ninety-five thousand American dollars. It could only have come from Barry. What a friend! I always just did what I could for him but it was never enough. He was the best guy I ever raced against. Roberts was good but Sheene, you never worried about him doing anything stupid. He was one of the few guys that I would really trust both racing and also driving around in the Rolls-Royce or Mercedes.'

Not everybody felt the same way about Barry. He was such a complex character. On the one hand he could organise ninety-five thousand dollars to be dispatched after his death to an old friend but on the other would take every advantage he could and at nearly anybody else's expense.

Andrea Coleman had shared much of her life with Barry, first as paddock children, then as the wife of one of his great rivals and then teammate and latterly as the co-founder of the enormously successful Riders for Health charity. It was a love–hate relationship, as Andrea admits.

'Barry and I never got on. I would tell him to shove it and he would tell me to shove it. We were always battling one way or another and then we would make up, but soon be swearing at each other again.

'I did respect his riding and what he did for motorcycling. I don't really know if I would call it selfishness but he had a very, very strong ego. I feel in some ways he was a very sad person and quite a hurt person with a chip on his shoulder.

'He was very insecure. I remember on one occasion Barry asking me if it was true that Kenny Roberts couldn't read or write. I asked him, "What has that got to do with anything?" and Barry said, "It shows what kind of a person Kenny is." I have no idea where he got the idea from, but I simply replied that if you can ride a motorcycle like Kenny Roberts you don't have to read or write. Barry was constantly looking at ways of undermining other people, particularly competition, because he did not like other strong people. That's why he found me hard to deal with.

'He was smiley, jolly and nice, especially to fans, but when I think of Barry I feel sad for him. That's not because he's dead – I've always felt that way about him and I'm still annoyed about him. He was always fantastic with our two girls but we never got on. I was close friends with Kenny and I was always protective of him when Barry was trying to chip away.

'Everybody was slightly in awe of Barry because of his ability but also annoyed with him because he really was an annoying person. Barry was also very funny and there was plenty to talk about when he was around. He certainly enlivened the whole environment. What a mixture.'

Andrea's husband Barry was the organiser of the World Series breakaway that did so much to alter the structure of grand prix motorcycling in the early 1980s. He was a great friend of Barry's bitter rival Kenny Roberts and was still a journalist for the *Guardian* when he first met Barry. He witnessed all sides of Barry's complex character and liked what he saw.

'It was my privilege to write about Barry, but I sometimes wrote things he did not like. Once I wrote something about him and he didn't speak to me for a whole year, but we made it up in the end. You just don't get people like him every five minutes, you just don't. Neither Kenny nor I are going to say Barry was an angel, but we both miss him. He was extraordinary. The cheeky chappy cockney hero was the sort of stuff that went in the *Sun* and it was always amusing to see Barry on the front and back pages. It was gratifying to see all that but there was a great deal more to him. He was an amazingly gifted sportsman.'

Twenty-nine years ago Kenny Roberts arrived in Europe to spoil Barry's party but to many people that first season-long duel seems like yesterday. Certainly both Kenny and Barry Coleman have never forgotten those fiery days of competition, press speculation and, of course, Barry's mystery illness in 1978.

'On a rare occasion I was beating Kenny at golf the other day and he put his ball into the bushes at the eighteenth. He asked me how he was going to explain this rare defeat by me. I suggested jet lag but then he smiled and said it must be Barry's mystery virus. He does not forget. We agreed how much we missed Barry.'

The squadron of Barry's three closest friends missed their Wing Commander more than most. They all knew Barry so well and understood his insecurity, those moments of intolerance, and enjoyed his humour and loyalty. He was special and they loved him.

After fifty-two years of pushing so hard down every conceivable avenue, Barry was ready for a change. Stephanie and he had never been happier, the children were growing up and of course there was that new helicopter to fly.

The squadron had been looking forward to life with the Wing Commander in his fifties. It was certainly not going to be a routine of pipe and slippers. The fact they were not given the opportunity to find out has brought them much sadness, as Jeremy Paxton explains:

'I felt the tortuous part of his journey had been achieved. He was a very soft guy but he realised if he showed that soft underbelly he would get kicked too often. He would have become very comfortable in his skin, mellow and very satisfied in his fifties. Grandchildren would have come along and he was denied this.

'So many people say Barry lived seven lives and it was fine for him to get to fifty-two years because he did more in his life than anybody else but that's not the point. His life was cut short. I chose never to believe that friends died until this point because it really reminded me of my own vulnerability.

'Barry and Franco were just the same. Barry absolutely loved his dad. There was this incredibly soft and compassionate side to Barry. I think he was an absolute romantic and I think he was really out there after love. He loved real friends that he could be himself around. He could be himself around me, Raj and Stavros, but I'm not convinced he could be himself around many other people. We were as close to family as you could get. We shared everything together. It was an amazing relationship and we all held him in our arms before he died. He was the sweetest man at the end of his life and an absolute darling.'

Being such a close friend to Barry was never an easy ride for the squadron. They knew what to expect when matters were not to his liking. For Jeremy that's what made him so special and in some ways is what they all miss the most.

'Barry was very complex, an incredible human being in so many ways. When he had horsepower he had fuckin' horsepower but when he was insecure, he was insecure.

'When he was angry you had to run for cover because he would think of fifteen ways to dig your heart out. When he was generous he was incredibly generous. Coping with all that when it kicks off is complex and sometimes Steph did not have the tools to do that. If you understood him there would be enough good there to make you really want to be with him.

'There was Barry the celebrity who's been written about. The world champion with the glamorous wife, but it's all a little superficial. In my later years of knowing him I got to really understand the person. The deep, complex and often very insecure side of Barry.

'You can compare him to some of the greatest leaders because he was charismatic, determined, focused and almost anal in his attention to detail. It was very important that everything was just so. It was mixed with a very insecure side to his personality. In the end it was very important to him that he was well thought of and was seen in a particular light.

'Insecurity is often seen as a character failing but it can be a tremendous strength, it can be what drives people. Most incredibly clever and talented people are insecure. I think Barry was driven by a fear of failure.'

Jeremy, Steve and Julian had all squirmed in restaurants, airports and hotels as Barry insisted things should be right. They had learnt that nothing but the best would do Barry, whether the choice of tyres on a racing motorcycle or the temperature of the wine in a restaurant. Jeremy, like the other two, learnt how to deal with it.

'You could easily paint him as someone who was a complainer by nature, but he wasn't. He really understood human nature and he knew the only way to make a point stick was to exaggerate it, reinforce it, underline it and say it again. He was anything but chilled and absolutely clear on every detail. Combined with that natural talent was the focus and determination to get every detail precisely right. He was intolerant in the end of human beings that could not respond to the level of service or detail that he required.'

The squadron gave Barry the support and security he needed. In return he gave them all his love.

'An amazing human being, a fantastically good friend, but one who really needed a huge amount of support. Barry was an incredible bloke but you could not have a world of Barry Sheenes. It would be war – he was needed in the minority and that's why he achieved so much at so many different levels. Just look at his commercial instincts. Barry had a nose for a deal and if he had wanted to be much bigger and much wealthier I've no doubt he could have been but he also wanted freedom. He really appreciated and treasured freedom and was not going to conform.

'Barry had his own very unique style. The step down from "remarkable" is "very good"; Barry didn't want to be very good at anything, he wanted to be fucking remarkable. He had amazing power and energy. I loved that about him and miss being around him. I miss him for the reasons of companionship, humour, awkwardness and his uncompromising stance on matters that he totally believed in, for being completely impossible, for kissing me and saying, "I really love you." Barry had every single piece of humanity in him.'

Darkness had descended over the river behind Manor House, the water lapping gently against the small jetty that had so often been the starting point for the jet-skiing antics of Barry and the squadron. Freddie was entertaining yet another young lady in the flat once occupied by Franco and Iris. Sidonie was on her way to Phillip Island to help organise the memorial ride for her dad at the forthcoming Australian Grand Prix. Stephanie and Clive's son, Roman, was watching television.

Their mother Stephanie sat alone, surrounded by memories.

The final words should go to Stephanie:

'I loved him to death and I miss him terribly. He died too young and getting old on your own is hard. I had been with Barry since 1976, and after that there had never been another man in my life. Success just happened at the right time and there has been nothing to compare with it. They were good times, coinciding with the prime of his successful years. They were such happy days. It was all down to Barry – he was the hero.'

RACE RESULTS

DNF   Did Not Finish
DNS   Did Not Start
DSQ   Disqualified

WORLD CHAMPIONSHIPS

1970	Spanish Grand Prix	Montjuich Park	125cc	2
1971	Austrian Grand Prix	Salzburgring	125cc	3
	German Grand Prix	Hockenheim	All classes	DNF
	Isle of Man TT		125cc	DNF
			250cc	DNF
	Dutch TT	Assen	125cc	2
	Belgian Grand Prix	Spa-Francorchamps	125cc	1
	East German Grand Prix	Sachsenring	125cc	2
			250cc	6
	Czechoslovakian Grand Prix	Brno	50cc	1
			125cc	3
	Swedish Grand Prix	Anderstorp	50cc	4
			125cc	3
	Finnish Grand Prix	Imatra	125cc	1
	Italian Grand Prix	Monza	125cc	3
	Spanish Grand Prix	Jarama	50cc	2
			125cc	3
	Final Placing	*125cc World Championship*		*2*
1972	German Grand Prix	Nürburgring	250cc	DNF
			350cc	DNF
	French Grand Prix	Clermont-Ferrand	250cc	DNS
			350cc	DNS

	Austrian Grand Prix	Salzburgring	250cc	4
	Italian Grand Prix	Imola	250cc	DNS
			350cc	DNS
	Swedish Grand Prix	Anderstorp	250cc	DNF
			350cc	DNF
	Spanish Grand Prix	Montjuich Park	250cc	3
1973	Finnish Grand Prix	Imatra	500cc	DNF
1974	French Grand Prix	Clermont-Ferrand	500cc	2
	German Grand Prix	Nürburgring	500cc	DNS
	Austrian Grand Prix	Salzburgring	500cc	3
	Italian Grand Prix	Imola	500cc	DNF
	Dutch TT	Assen	500cc	DNF
	Belgian Grand Prix	Spa-Francorchamps	500cc	DNF
	Swedish Grand Prix	Anderstorp	500cc	DNF
	Czechoslovakian Grand Prix	Brno	500cc	4
	Final Placing	*500cc World Championship*		*2*
1975	Austrian Grand Prix	Salzburgring	500cc	DNS
	German Grand Prix	Hockenheim	500cc	DNF
	Dutch TT	Assen	500cc	1
	Belgian Grand Prix	Spa-Francorchamps	500cc	DNF
	Swedish Grand Prix	Anderstorp	500cc	1
	Finnish Grand Prix	Imatra	500cc	DNF
	Czechoslovakian Grand Prix	Brno	500cc	DNF
	Final Placing	*500cc World Championship*		*6*
1976	French Grand Prix	Le Mans	500cc	1
	Austrian Grand Prix	Salzburgring	500cc	1
	Italian Grand Prix	Mugello	500cc	1
	Isle of Man TT		500cc	DNS
	Dutch TT	Assen	500cc	1
	Belgian Grand Prix	Spa-Francorchamps	500cc	2
	Swedish Grand Prix	Anderstorp	500cc	1
	Finnish Grand Prix	Imatra	500cc	DNS
	Czechoslovakian Grand Prix	Brno	500cc	DNS
	German Grand Prix	Nürburgring	500cc	DNS
	Final Placing	*500cc World Championship*		*1*
1977	Venezuelan Grand Prix	San Carlos	500cc	1
	Austrian Grand Prix	Salzburgring	500cc	DNS
	German Grand Prix	Hockenheim	500cc	1

Italian Grand Prix	Imola	500cc	1
French Grand Prix	Paul Ricard	500cc	1
Dutch TT	Assen	500cc	2
Belgian Grand Prix	Spa-Francorchamps	500cc	1
Swedish Grand Prix	Anderstorp	500cc	1
Finnish Grand Prix	Imatra	500cc	6
Czechoslovakian Grand Prix	Brno	500cc	DNS
British Grand Prix	Silverstone	500cc	DNF
Final Placing	*500cc World Championship*		*1*
1978 Venezuelan Grand Prix	San Carlos	500cc	1
Spanish Grand Prix	Jarama	500cc	5
Austrian Grand Prix	Salzburgring	500cc	3
French Grand Prix	Nogaro	500cc	3
Italian Grand Prix	Mugello	500cc	5
Dutch TT	Assen	500cc	3
Swedish Grand Prix	Anderstorp	500cc	1
Finnish Grand Prix	Imatra	500cc	DNF
British Grand Prix	Silverstone	500cc	3
German Grand Prix	Nürburgring	500cc	4
Final Placing	*500cc World Championship*		*2*
1979 Venezuelan Grand Prix	San Carlos	500cc	1
Austrian Grand Prix	Salzburgring	500cc	6
German Grand Prix	Hockenheim	500cc	DNF
Italian Grand Prix	Imola	500cc	4
Spanish Grand Prix	Jarama	500cc	DNF
Yugoslav Grand Prix	Rijeka	500cc	DNF
Dutch TT	Assen	500cc	2
Belgian Grand Prix	Spa-Francorchamps	500cc	DNS
Swedish Grand Prix	Karlskoga	500cc	1
Finnish Grand Prix	Imatra	500cc	3
British Grand Prix	Silverstone	500cc	2
French Grand Prix	Le Mans	500cc	1
Final Placing	*500cc World Championship*		*3*
1980 Italian Grand Prix	Misano	500cc	7
Spanish Grand Prix	Jarama	500cc	5
French Grand Prix	Paul Ricard	500cc	DNF
Dutch TT	Assen	500cc	DNF
Belgian Grand Prix	Zolder	500cc	DNS
British Grand Prix	Silverstone	500cc	DNF
Final Placing	*500cc World Championship*	*14*	

1981	Austrian Grand Prix	Salzburgring	500cc	4
	German Grand Prix	Hockenheim	500cc	6
	Italian Grand Prix	Monza	500cc	3
	French Grand Prix	Paul Ricard	500cc	4
	Dutch TT	Assen	500cc	DNF
	Belgian Grand Prix	Spa-Francorchamps	500cc	4
	San Marino Grand Prix	Imola	500cc	2
	British Grand Prix	Silverstone	500cc	DNF
	Finnish Grand Prix	Imatra	500cc	DNF
	Swedish Grand Prix	Anderstorp	500cc	1
	Final Placing	*500cc World Championship*		5
1982	Argentine Grand Prix	Autodromo de la Cuidad	500cc	2
	Austrian Grand Prix	Salzburgring	500cc	2
	French Grand Prix	Nogaro	500cc	DNS
	Spanish Grand Prix	Jarama	500cc	2
	Italian Grand Prix	Misano	500cc	DNF
	Dutch TT	Assen	500cc	3
	Belgian Grand Prix	Spa-Francorchamps	500cc	2
	Yugoslav Grand Prix	Rijeka	500cc	3
	British Grand Prix	Silverstone	500cc	DNS
	Final Placing	*500cc World Championship*		5
1983	South African Grand Prix	Kyalami	500cc	10
	French Grand Prix	Le Mans	500cc	7
	San Marino Grand Prix	Monza	500cc	9
	German Grand Prix	Hockenheim	500cc	DNF
	Spanish Grand Prix	Jarama	500cc	DNS
	Austrian Grand Prix	Salzburgring	500cc	13
	Yugoslav Grand Prix	Rijeka	500cc	13
	Dutch TT	Assen	500cc	DNF
	Belgian Grand Prix	Spa-Francorchamps	500cc	DNS
	British Grand Prix	Silverstone	500cc	9
	Swedish Grand Prix	Anderstorp	500cc	DNF
	Italian Grand Prix	Imola	500cc	DNF
	Final Placing	*500cc World Championship*		*14*
1984	South African Grand Prix	Kyalami	500cc	3
	Italian Grand Prix	Misano	500cc	DNF
	Spanish Grand Prix	Jarama	500cc	7
	Austrian Grand Prix	Salzburgring	500cc	10
	German Grand Prix	Nürburgring	500cc	10
	French Grand Prix	Paul Ricard	500cc	5

Yugoslav Grand Prix	Rijeka	500cc	7
Dutch TT	Assen	500cc	DNF
Belgian Grand Prix	Spa-Francorchamps	500cc	9
British Grand Prix	Silverstone	500cc	5
Swedish Grand Prix	Anderstorp	500cc	DNF
San Marino Grand Prix	Imola	500cc	DNF
Final Placing	*500cc World Championship*		*6*

NATIONAL CHAMPIONSHIPS AND AWARDS

1969	ACU British Championships	125cc	2
1970	ACU British Championships	125cc	1
1971	ACU British Championships	125cc	1
		250cc	2
1972	Shellsport 500 Championship	500cc	2
1973	Shellsport 500 Championship	500cc	1
	Motor Cycle News Superbike Championship		1
	Motor Cycle News Man of the Year		
	King of Brands		
1974	Shellsport 500 Championship	500cc	1
	Motor Cycle News Superbike Championship		1
1975	*Motor Cycle News* Superbike Championship		3
	Motor Cycle News Man of the Year		
1976	Shellsport 500 Championship	500cc	1
	Motor Cycle News Superbike Championship		1
	Motor Cycle News Man of the Year		
1977	Shellsport 500 Championship	500cc	1
	Motor Cycle News Superbike Championship		1
	Motor Cycle News Man of the Year		
1978	Shellsport 500 Championship	500cc	1
	Motor Cycle News Superbike Championship		1
1979	*Motor Cycle News* Man of the Year		

Year	Event	Location	Class	Result
1983	Shell Oils 500 Championship		500cc	7
	Motor Cycle News Masters Championship			12

NATIONAL MEETINGS AND HOME INTERNATIONALS

Year	Event	Location	Class	Result
1968		Brands Hatch, March	125cc	DNF
			250cc	3
		Brands Hatch, April	125cc	1
			350cc	1
1969	Hutchinson 100	Brands Hatch	250cc	4
	Race of Aces	Snetterton	350cc	2
			125cc	2
1970	Hutchinson 100	Brands Hatch	250cc	4
	Race of Aces	Snetterton	500cc	DNF
1971		Mallory Park, March	125cc	1
			250cc	1
			350cc	1
	Post-TT	Mallory Park, June	500cc	2
	British 'Grand Prix'	Silverstone	125cc	1
			250cc	1
			500cc	2
1972	Race of Aces	Snetterton	250cc	1
			350cc	1
			500cc	2
1974	British 'Grand Prix'	Silverstone	500cc	1
	Race of the Year	Mallory Park		1
1975	Race of the Year	Mallory Park	750cc	1
1976	Transatlantic Trophy Races			1, 2, 3, 13
	Race of the Year	Mallory Park		2
1977	Transatlantic Trophy Races			1, 2, 2, 3, 4, 11
	Race of Aces	Snetterton		4
	Race of the Year	Mallory Park		DNS
	Gauloises Power Bike	Brands Hatch		5

1978	Transatlantic Trophy Races		1, 2, 3, 3, DNF, DNF
	Race of Aces	Snetterton	1
	Race of the Year	Mallory Park	1
	Gauloises Power Bike	Brands Hatch	1
1979	Transatlantic Trophy Races		1, 1, 1, 2, DNF, DNF
	World of Sport Superbike	Donington Park	1
	AGV Nations Cup	Donington Park	1, 1, 1, 1
	Race of the Year	Mallory Park	2
1980	Transatlantic Trophy Races		4, 5, 8, 16, DNF, DNF
	World of Sport Superbike	Donington Park, April	DNF
	World of Sport Superbike	Donington Park, June	DNF
	World of Sport Superbike	Donington Park, August	1
	Gauloises Power Bike	Brands Hatch	DNF
	Race of the Year	Mallory Park	1
1981	Transatlantic Trophy Races		1, 3, 6, 7, DNF, DNF
	World of Sport Superbike	Donington Park, April	1
	John Player Gold Cup		3
	World of Sport Superbike	Donington Park, June	1
	World of Sport Superbike	Donington Park, August	1
	Winter World Cup	Donington Park	1
	Race of the Year	Mallory Park	2
1982	Transatlantic Trophy Races		1, 1, 1, 1, 1, 2
	World of Sport Superbike	Donington Park, April	DNF
	John Player Gold Cup		2, 2
	World of Sport Superbike	Donington Park, June	DNF
	John Player International		3, 6
1983	Transatlantic Trophy Races		4, 5, 6, 7, 8, 8
1984	Transatlantic Trophy Races		9, 9, 10, 11, 11, DNF
	World of Sport Superbike Challenge		6

INTERNATIONAL MEETINGS

1975	Daytona 200		750cc	DNS
1976	Daytona 200		750cc	34
	Chimay International		500cc	1

1977	Daytona 200		750cc	DNS
		Long Beach	750cc	3
	Grand Prix des Frontières	Chimay	750cc	1
			500cc	2
1978	Grand Prix des Frontières	Chimay	750cc	1
			500cc	1
	AGV Cup Imola		Highest individual score	

FIM FORMULA 750 RACES

1973	European Championship	Rouen	DNF
		Imola 200	DNF
		Clermont-Ferrand	1
		Anderstorp	3
		Hameenlinna	2
		Silverstone	DSQ
		Hockenheim	4
		Montjuich Park	2
	Final Placing	*F750 European Championship*	*1*
1974	Daytona 200		DNF
	European Championship	Imola 200	5
		Silverstone	1
1975	European Championship	Magny-Cours	1
		Anderstorp	1
		Silverstone	1
	Final Placing	*F750 European Championship*	*2*
1976		San Carlos	DNF
	Imola 200		3
		Nivelles	DNF
		Nogaro	DNF
		Silverstone	DNF

CLASSIC BIKE RACING

1998		Goodwood	2, 3
1999		Goodwood	1, 1

Barry

2000	Phillip Island	1, 1, DNF
	Donington Park	DNF, 2
	Goodwood	DNF, 2
2001	Phillip Island	3, 3, DNF
	Eastern Creek	3, 3
	Donington Park	4, 1
	Goodwood	1, 1
2002	Phillip Island	2, 2, 2
	Eastern Creek	5, 4, 6, 2
	Donington Park	1, 1
	Goodwood	2, 1

INDEX

Adelaide, Australia 91–3
advertisements 97–8
Agostini, Giacomo: on Barry's illness 15–16; as Barry's rival 63–4, 66, 67, 68, 70, 102; on Barry's talent 39–40, 41; on deaths 62
Agusta 109C (helicopter) 1–2, 7–8, 15–16, 89–90, 188–9, 196–7
AJS Triumph (motorcycle) 25, 30
Akai 168, 179
AMA Grand National Championship 103
American riders 78, 102; *see also* Hennen, Pat; Roberts, Kenny; USA
Anderstorp, Sweden: 1971 Grand Prix 37; 1974 Grand Prix 70; 1975 Grand Prix 67; 1976 Grand Prix 72–3, 1977 Grand Prix 77; 1981 Grand Prix 135, 171–2; 1982 Grand Prix 156; 1984 Grand Prix 96, 178; travelling to 36, 104
Andrews, Eamonn 124
Argentine Grand Prix 172–3
Armco barriers 57, 58, 88
Armes, Colin 144
Armes, Marie 144–5, 146, 149
Ashwood Hall *see* Wisbech, Cambridgeshire
Assen, Holland: Centennial Classic 183; *see also* Dutch TT
Australia: Barry's retirement in 16, 19, 116, 124, 131–2, 180, 189–90; Barry's television work in 130, 180–3; Classic meeting 15, 183; Formula One car grand prix 91–3; helicopter flights in 16, 89–90; increased popularity of bike racing in 180; tributes to Barry 198–9
Australian Grand Prix 20, 181–2, 194, 198
Austrian Grand Prix (Salzburgring): 1974 69; 1975 66; 1976 71; 1977 58, 76; 1978 104; 1979 110; 1982 173; dangers 59
Auto-Cycle Union 54, 115, 128, 144

Baker, Steve 76, 77, 78
Ballington, Kork 52–3, 59, 60
Bandol, France 123–4
Barrie, Ritchie and Lynne 119
barriers: Armco 57, 58, 88; straw bales 54, 62
BBC 163, 197
Beattie, Daryl 19
Beckham, David and Victoria 123, 125
Belfast Motorcycle Show 127
Belgian Grand Prix (Spa-Francorchamps except 1980): 1971 37; 1975 66–7; 1976 72; 1977 76–7; 1978 105, 108; 1979 boycott 111; 1980 (Zolder) 62; 1982 174; Barry's record lap 41; dangers 59, 111
Berger, Gerhard 92, 130, 131

Best, George 123–4
Blackburn, Tony 119
Blair, Tony 192–3
Bobtons model agency 83
Bowles, John 154
Brands Hatch, Kent 40, 59; Barry's crash at
    42; Barry's debut at 31; mechanical
    preparations at 75–6; Piers Forester
    killed at 88; Shellsport Championship
    79; Stars of Tomorrow Competition 84;
    Superbike Championship 74, 78–9
Breuss, Rudolf 11
Breuss diet 11–12, 13
British Grand Prix (Silverstone): 1974 70;
    1977 77–8; 1978 106–7; 1979 60, 112–14;
    1981 141, 171; 1983 175–6; 1984 177–8;
    2001 15; 2002 preview event 5; classes
    139; *see also* Silverstone
British Leyland calendars 125–6
British racing: 125cc championship 34, 35;
    benefits for Barry 40, 73; lack of success
    of British riders 172; *see also* Shellsport
    500 Championship; Superbike races
Brno, Czech Republic 2–4, 37–8, 70, 77;
    poor safety at 54, 56–7
Brooklands, Surrey 25
Brookman, Martin 55–6
Brown, John 147
Brown, Norman 176
Brundle, Martin 179
Brut advertisements 97
BSA motorcycles 25; Bantam 31
Bultaco motorcycles: Barry rides 31, 32, 34;
    Barry visits factory 30, 35; Frank Sheene
    and 24, 25, 30, 32, 35; Phil Read rides 28
Bulto family 35
bump-starting 66

Cadwell Park, Lincolnshire 50, 65–6, 68,
    73, 168, 170
Cagiva (motorcycle) 196
Callas, Maria 23
Capirossi, Loris 159
Carr, Cliff 69
Carruthers, Kel 104–5
Cecotto, Johnny 56, 77

Centennial Classic (Assen) 183
Channel Nine 180–2
Charlwood, Surrey house: Barry buys 124;
    Barry's parents live at 124, 169, 190;
    Barry's recuperation at 161, 162; Barry's
    wish to run team from 167; helicopters at
    89, 90; 'the squadron' at 94–5, 99, 129;
    Sunday lunch at 169; telephone calls 98
Chelsea, London 82, 85–6, 87, 120
Chimay, Belgium 59, 74, 105
Clermont-Ferrand, France 69
Cobb, Eileen 165
Cobb, Nigel 148, 151–4, 155–6, 157, 158,
    160, 163–5
Coleman, Andrea 201
Coleman, Barry 60–1, 202
Cooper, Henry 82, 97
Cooper, Vernon 128
Co-operative Society 97
Cosmopolitan 119, 121
Cromer, Dan 82
Crosby, Graeme 136, 168, 171, 174
CSS Marketing Company 81, 96–8
Cvitanovich, Frank 65
Czech Republic Grand Prix (Brno) 2–4
Czechoslovakian Grand Prix (Brno) 37–8,
    54, 70, 77; poor safety at 54, 56–7

DAF trucks 177, 178–9
Daily Mirror 121, 179
Daltrey, Roger 179
dangers 32, 44–5, 50–1, 52, 53–5, 56–9, 76,
    107; and faster motorcycles 58–9;
    protests and improvements 60–2
Danielle, Suzanne 179
Davies, Linda xi, xii, 128, 129, 137, 138
Daytona, USA: Barry's crash at 63, 64–5, 76,
    82, 103, 118
deaths 33–4, 45–50, 62, 86, 88
de Radiguès, Didier 177
Derbi motorcycles 35, 36, 37
Desert Island Discs 93
de Vries, Jan 37, 38
Dianese leathers 55
Diffey, Leigh 183
Dodds, John 42

Donington Manor Hotel 128
Donington Park, Derbyshire 8–9, 15–16,
    128, 199; 1979 season 114; 1981 season
    172; and Barry's return after crash 160,
    161, 162–3; Classic races 183–4;
    MotoGP championship 4–5; Superbike
    races 170, 178; truck racing 178–9
Doohan, Mick 19, 127, 182, 198–9
drinking (by riders) 52–3
Driving Force 179
drugs 85–6, 87
Dutch TT (Assen): 1971 38; 1972 41; 1975
    63–4, 66; 1976 71–2; 1977 76; 1978 105;
    1979 111; 1982 174; pay 54

Eastlake, Darrell 180–1, 182
Easton Neston, Northamptonshire 156
Ekerold, Jon 59, 142
Empire Ballroom, London 30
Enstrom 280 Turbo (helicopter) 89

Fabergé 119; advertisements 97
factory riders 53–4
Falklands War 173
fans 40, 158
Fearnall, Robert 163
Ferrari, Virginio 111, 112, 113, 114
FIM (Féderation Internationale de
    Motorcyclisme) 57, 60, 61; Formula 750
    European Championships 42
Findlay, Jack 69, 72
Finnish Grand Prix (Imatra): 1971 37; 1975
    67, 68; 1977 77; 1978 105–6; 1979 112;
    dangers 59; travelling to 36
Fletcher, Ken 137, 147
Fogarty, George 113
'Fols' *see* Paxton, Jeremy
Forester, Piers Weld- 82, 84–5, 87–8, 120,
    128
Formula One car grands prix 91–3, 94
Formula 750 European Championships 42
French Grand Prix: 1976 (Le Mans) 71;
    1977 (Paul Ricard) 76; 1978 (Nogaro)
    104; 1979 (Le Mans) 114; 1980 (Paul
    Ricard) 168–9; 1981 (Paul Ricard) 171;
    1984 (Paul Ricard) 177

Gardner, Wayne 180, 182, 184
Gary Puckett and the Union Gap 118–19
German Grand Prix 99; 1975 (Hockenheim)
    66; 1977 (Hockenheim) 76; 1978
    (Nürburgring) 107–8, 109; 1979
    (Hockenheim) 111
Giacobetti, Francis 125
Gobbi, Tito 23
Goodwood, West Sussex 12, 100, 183, 184
Goon Show, The 81,90
Gould, Rodney 40
Graham, Stuart 35
Grant, Mick 65, 73, 74, 78–9, 194, 195
Guardian 60
Guy, Chris 46

Hailwood, Mike 34, 40, 52
Harley Davidson motorcycles 103, 104, 105
Harris, Nick xii, 63, 64, 73–4; and Barry's
    Silverstone crash 147, 154; joins
    commentating team 180, 181; records
    Barry's obituary 197–8
Harris Engineering 175, 177
Harrison, George 91–3, 97, 123, 131, 179
Hartog, Wil 62, 76, 106, 113, 114
Hartzog, Marianne 121
Haslam, Ron 177, 178
Havers, Nigel 179
helicopters: Agusta 109C 1–2, 7–8, 15–16,
    89–90, 188–9, 196–7; Barry flies to
    Donington Park for comeback 162;
    Barry's gains pilot's licence 89; Enstrom
    280 Turbo 89; Robinson R22 90
helmets 54–5, 137
Hengelo, Holland 39
Hennen, Pat 74, 76, 77–8, 79, 102, 104,
    105
Herne Hill, London 25
Heron Suzuki 110, 174
Herron, Andrea xi, 50, 52, 123
Herron, Tom 47–9, 52, 60, 110, 114
Hesketh, Thomas Alexander Fermor-, 3
    Baron (Lord Hesketh) 74, 121, 150, 156,
    157–8, 193
Hill, Damon 92–3, 94, 98–9, 183
Hill, David 182

Hockenheim, Germany 66, 76, 99, 111
Holiday Inn, Sandton 175
Holt, John 14
Honda Britain 48
Honda Gold Wing (motorcycle) 5
Honda team 173, 175, 195, 199
Huber, Peter 176
Huewen, Keith 175
Hunt, James 71, 74, 96, 123–4, 193

Idle, Eric 123
Igoa, Patrick 140–1, 142, 149
Imatra, Finland *see* Finnish Grand Prix
Imola, Italy: Barry's car crash in 103; Guido
    Paci killed at 86; Imola 200 race 102;
    Italian Grands Prix 66, 76, 111, 176;
    Nations Grand Prix (1974) 69; non-
    championship events 52; poor treatment
    of riders 59–60; San Marino Grand Prix
    (1981) 171; toilets 104–5
International Marketing Group (IMG) 61,
    120
Isle of Man TT: Barry refuses to race in
    40–1, 66, 71; Barry visits when young
    28–9; dangers 40–1, 53–4, 128; Frank
    Sheene competes in 25; protests against
    60, 66; removed as world championship
    circuit 71, 75, 105; Steve Parrish
    competes in 59, 87–8, 96
Italian Grand Prix: 1971 (Monza) 39; 1973
    (Mugello) 71; 1975 (Imola) 66; 1977
    (Imola) 76; 1978 (Mugello) 104; 1979
    (Imola) 111; 1981 (Monza) 171; 1982
    (Misano) 174; 1983 (Imola) 176; 1984
    (Mugello) 178
Itom motorcycles 24, 25, 34
Ivy, Bill 34

Jackson, Robert 160, 167
Jansson, Borje 38
Japanese Grand Prix 181
Jarama, Spain 37, 38, 39, 104, 173–4
Jawa motorcycles 34
John, Elton 94
John Player World Cup (500cc) 160
Jones, Alan 180, 181

Judy (Stephanie's friend) 119
Just Amazing! 179

Kanemoto, Erv 171
Karlskoga, Sweden 105, 111–12
Keegan, Kevin 82
Knight, Maurice 167
Kobenzl Hotel, Salzburg 121
Kojak 81
KTM 185
Kyalami, South Africa 175, 177

La Famiglia, Chelsea 82
Lansivuori, Teppi 72
Lavado, Carlos 56
Lawson, Eddie 177, 196
leathers 53, 54, 55
Le Mans, France 71, 114, 128
Lennox Cup 184
Lewis, Paul 46
Lloyd, Richard 179
London: Barry's childhood in 23–30; Barry's
    home in Putney 122, 124; Chelsea 82,
    85–6, 87, 120; nightclubs 118, 119, 120,
    121, 158
Lowe, Chris 59
Lucchinelli, Marco 141, 171, 172
Lynch, Kenny 179

McCauley, Ted 121, 179
McCormack, Mark 61
McCoy, Gary 182
Mackay, Don 75–6
McLean, Clive 65, 118–19, 120
McLean, Roman 118, 119, 128, 143, 205
Mallory Park, Leicestershire 39, 40, 68, 78,
    79, 114–15
Mamola, Randy 147, 168, 172, 177, 196
Manor House *see* Surfers Paradise
Manx Norton (motorcycle) 12, 58–9, 183,
    198–9
March, Earl of 12
Marie (Stephanie's friend) 119
Marlboro 97–8
Marriott, Andrew ('Count Jim Moriarty')
    81, 96–8, 99, 178–9, 180

Mass, Jochen 153
Matchless (motorcycle) 30, 184
medical facilities 39, 45, 55, 56, 146
Melandri, Marco 159
Mexico 13
Michael of Kent, Prince 87–8
Middelburg, Jack 134, 141–3, 146, 147, 149,
    154
Milligan, Spike 81
Misano, Italy 174
Mitsui 168
money *see* pay
Montjuich Park, Spain 35, 36, 42
Monza, Italy 39, 171
'Moriarty, Count Jim' *see* Marriott,
    Andrew
Mortimer, Chas 34, 35
Morton, Peter 119
MotoGP championship 4–5, 198
Motor Circuit Developments 59
Motor Cycle News 59, 179; Lifetime
    Achievement Award 14; Man of the Year
    Award 42, 68, 166; Superbike series
    65–6, 70, 73, 74, 78–9, 110
Motor Cycle Weekly 154–5
Motorcycle Racing 147
Motorcycling 32
Mugello, Italy 71, 104, 178
MV Agusta (motorcycle) 15, 40, 54, 63, 67,
    68, 70
My Doreen (boat) 169–70

Nations Grand Prix (1974) 69
Network Ten 183
Newbold, Allison 123
Newbold, John xi, 46, 71, 72, 74, 123
Newbon, Gary 161
Newcombe, Kim 54
Newey, Adrian 133
Nichol, Leslie 160
Nieto, Angel 3, 35, 36–7, 38–9
1970s 44–5, 56–7
Nixon, Gary 69–70, 76, 86–7, 124, 128, 137,
    200
Nogaro, France 104, 173
North West 200 race 30, 47–8, 60

Northampton General Hospital 146,
    147–50, 151–6, 163
Norton motorcycles 5, 25; Manx Norton 12,
    58–9, 183, 198–9
Nürburgring, Germany 50, 59, 107–8, 109

Ogbourne, Martyn 75, 76, 106, 110–11, 112,
    115, 146, 167
Oulton Park, Cheshire 59, 122

Paci, Guido 86
Packer, Kerry 180
Page, Stuart 11
Parkinson, Michael 97–8, 124
Parrish, Ruth 95–6
Parrish, Steve ('Stavros'): on Barry's fitness
    161–2; and Barry's helicopter 1–2, 7,
    196–7; and Barry's illness and death 1–2,
    9–10, 14–15, 16, 17, 18–20, 21–2, 191–5;
    on Barry's marriage 122–3; on Barry's
    relations with Suzuki 166–7; and Barry's
    Silverstone crash and recuperation 137,
    145–6, 148–9, 150, 156, 157, 158–9, 160;
    bobsleighing holiday 87–8; crash at San
    Carlos 56; on deaths of teammates
    45–50; as driver for Barry 84; on faster
    bikes 58–9; on fear and reaction to
    crashes 158–9; and fee negotiation 59;
    first meets Barry 84; friendship with
    Barry xii, 81, 85; and girls 85, 128, 129;
    helps Barry at Donington comeback
    163; impersonates Barry in qualifying
    session 114–15; and launch of *My Doreen*
    169–70; marriage 95–6; and North West
    200 race 47–9; origin of nickname 81;
    and partying lifestyle 52–3, 85–6; as
    pilot 90; and practical jokes 91, 169;
    races for Suzuki 55, 74, 75, 76, 77–8, 79,
    110, 114; races for Yamaha 172; races in
    Swedish Grand Prix (1982) 156; on
    safety and treatment of riders 55–9;
    Scarborough trips 194–7; tests
    Nürburgring in Rolls-Royce 107–9; and
    truck racing 179; undertakes 'rescue
    mission' with Barry 94–5; visits Freddie
    Sheene 186

parties, paddock 52–3
partying lifestyle 74, 85–7
Patrick, Mick 50
Patrick, Viv 50
Patterson, Linda 96, 98–100, 118, 180
Paul Ricard, France 76, 123, 168–9, 171, 177
Paxton, Jeremy ('Fols') 80–1, 88–9, 90–3, 132, 203–5
pay 45, 50–1, 53, 54, 56, 57, 59, 76; appearance money 57–8, 67; collecting 59–60; fee negotiation 59; protest movement leads to increase in prize money 60–1; start money system scrapped 61, 62
Philip, Prince, Duke of Edinburgh 195
Phillip Island, Australia 181–2, 194, 198–9; Classic meeting 15, 183
Pickfords 131
Pietri, Roberto 143, 146
Piper Aztec (aircraft) 89
Playboy Club, London 119, 121
Pons, Patrick 60
Potter, Dave 46
practice sessions 139
press 98–9, 118, 120–1, 123, 124, 147, 153–5, 160–1
Putney, London 122, 124

Race of the Year: 1970 70; 1979 114–15
RAF Kemble 80
'Raj' *see* Seddon, Julian
Ravens, Jan 179
Read, Madeleine 67–8
Read, Phil 66–7, 69, 70, 72, 195; on dangers 53–4; friendship and fallout with Barry 28–9, 67–8, 71
Richardson, Ralph 124
Riders for Health 201
Rijeka, Yugoslavia 111, 174, 177
Roberts, Kenny: 1977 season 78; 1978 season 101–10, 135; 1979 season 110–14, 193; 1980 season 168; 1981 season 141, 172; 1982 season 135, 172, 173–4; 1983 season and retirement 176; and Barry's crash 143–4, 147; Barry's frustration over

superior machines of 136, 168, 170, 171; and Barry's illness 3–4, 12–13; friendship with the Colemans 201, 202; misses Barry 202; and Phillip Island prank 182; on treatment of riders 51–2, 60, 61–2
Robinson R22 (helicopter) 90
Roche, Raymond 177
Rohan, Denys 174
Rolls-Royce cars 36, 95, 107–9, 124, 199, 200
Romero, Gene 103
Ronson, Gail 174
Ronson, Gerald 105, 174
Rossi, Graziano 5, 199
Rossi, Valentino 4–5, 37, 56, 159, 198, 199–200
Rougerie, Michel 72
Royal College of Surgeons, London 24, 25
Royal Opera House, London 23–4
RPM Motorsport 183
Ryan, Paul and Barry 119
Ryuyo, Japan 69–70, 75

Saarinen, Jarno 40
Sachsenring, East Germany 34, 36, 54, 56–7
safety *see* barriers; dangers; deaths; medical facilities
St Joris, Belgium 57–8
St Martin-in-the-Fields school, London 23–4
Salzburgring, Austria: Barry and Stephanie go public in 120–1; dangers 59; *see also* Austrian Grand Prix
San Carlos, Venezuela: Barry's successes at 76, 103, 110; poor facilities 55–6, 58
Sarron, Christian 60
SBS 180
Scarborough, Yorkshire 59, 170, 194–7
Scargill, Arthur 197
Schumacher, Michael 92, 94
Schwantz, Kevin 182
Scott, Selina 99
Seddon, Julian ('Raj') 81, 82–3, 88, 89–91, 93–4, 188, 204; as Barry's agent 80, 83; and Barry's illness 17, 19, 89–90;

friendship with Stephanie 80, 125–6; as photographer 80, 83

Seddon, Patsy 91

Sharif, Omar 125

Sheene, Arthur (uncle) 24, 124, 169

Sheene, Barry Stephen Frank

PERSONAL LIFE: ability to overcome adversity 26; appearance 121, 122–3; asthma 27, 28, 29, 34, 138–9; cancer and death 1–22, 183–4; celebrity status 123–5; character xiii, 100, 198–205; childhood 23–30; and defenestration of television set 128; dislike of authority 25–8, 81–2, 128, 175; drink-driving ban 84; early jobs 30–1; early romance with Lesley Shepherd 34–5, 43; eating habits 120, 121, 138, 169; eczema 26; education 23–4, 27–8, 30; first car 29; fitness 161–2; friendship with 'the squadron' 80–100, 202–5; funeral 188; and girls 30, 32, 42, 43, 52, 83, 85, 86–7, 99–100, 128–30, 157, 194–5; good at languages 30, 96; and helicopters and flying 1–2, 7–8, 15–16, 89, 162, 188–9, 196–7; hoarding tendencies 88; home in Putney 122, 124; home in Wisbech 82, 84, 121, 122, 124, 190; humour and pranks 90–1, 92–3, 94, 99, 122, 169, 181, 201; insecurity 201, 203, 204; intelligence and toughness 162; jealousy of Stephanie 125–6; launch of boat 169–70; liking early nights 161; lucky clothes 137; meets Stephanie xi, 87, 117, 118–22; lives at Charlwood with family 89, 90, 94–5, 98, 99, 124, 129, 161, 162, 167, 169, 190; musical tastes 93–4; obsessive nature 126–7, 136, 138; partying lifestyle 74, 85–7; relationship with his children 186–7; relationship with Stephanie 112, 116–33, 187–8, 204; reluctant to spend money but rewards services 83, 88–9, 131, 165; 'rescue mission' 94–5; retirement in Australia 16, 19, 116, 124, 131–2, 180, 189–91; Rolls-Royce cars 95, 107–9, 124, 199, 200; and sexual assault allegation 130, 131; as smoker 4, 27, 30, 31, 81, 138–9, 161; social skills 83–4, 97; as Steve Parrish's best man 95–6; suffers from ME and depression 132; tax problems 180; tributes to 194–5, 198–9; visits Bultaco factory 30, 35; as water-skier 88–9, 91, 94; wedding 117–18

RACING CAREER: 1968 debut races and victories 31; 1970 grand prix debut (125cc) 35; 1971 season and first grand prix victory (125cc) 35–9; 1972 season and change to 250 and 350cc Yamahas 41–2; 1973 season and change to biggest classes 42; 1974 season and dangers of RG500 Suzuki 69–70; 1975 season: first 500cc victory, crash and quick return to racing 63–9; 1976 season and first world championship win 71–4; 1977 season and second world championship win 74–9; 1978 season and illness 103–10, 202; 1979 season 111–15; 1980 season and loss of finger 168–71; 1981 season and last grand prix victory 171–2; 1982 pre-crash season 172–4; 1982 Silverstone crash and recuperation 42, 55, 116, 117, 134–65, 174; 1983 season 175–6; 1984 season and last professional races 177–8; 1985 retirement 130, 179; 1998 appearance in Classic events 183–4; appoints management company 96–7; attitude to the press 98, 99; awards and honours 14, 42, 68–9, 124, 166; commercially astute 97–8; and dangers 54–5, 58, 60–2; Daytona crash 63, 64–5, 76, 82, 103, 118; and deaths of other riders 33–4, 45–7, 49–50, 88; decides on racing career 32–3; deliberately delays start of race 75–6; dissatisfaction with Suzuki, and eventual split 74–5, 101, 106, 111, 115, 166–7, 168–9; dislike of Pat Hennen 76, 78; early crashes 39, 40, 42;

Sheene, Barry Stephen Frank – *continued*
  RACING CAREER: – *continued*
    early experience as mechanic and
    gofer at grands prix 30, 32–3; early
    interest in motorbikes 26, 28–9; early
    transport and accommodation 33, 36,
    42; falls out with Phil Read 67–9; and
    fans 40, 158; femur injury 64, 66;
    forces management changes at Suzuki
    74–5; helmet 54, 137; helps Australian
    riders 182; importance of British
    racing to 40, 73–4; influence on
    changes in the sport 45, 52; insistence
    on the best motorbikes 71; insistence
    on good medical treatment 39; knee
    injury 68; leathers and protective kit
    54–5, 137; linked with James Hunt 74;
    magazine column 33, 154–5; pay 45,
    51, 54, 57, 58, 59, 60, 67, 73–4, 163;
    races for Yamaha 41, 42, 134–5, 136–7,
    141–3, 166–75; races on 750cc
    motorbikes 42, 74; refuses to race in
    Isle of Man TT 40–1; removal of
    femur pin 76; removal of plates and
    screws 163–4; returns to Suzuki but
    given poor bikes 174–7; rivalry with
    Kenny Roberts 101–10, 136, 168, 170,
    171; Ryuyo crash 70, 75; skill at
    publicity 60; sponsorship 45, 51, 85,
    177; as sports commentator 130,
    180–3; and telephone calls 98–9, 133;
    television appearances 65, 76, 97–8,
    124, 179, 182; tries car racing 179; tries
    truck racing 178–9; and World Series
    movement 60–1
  Sheene, Frank (Franco) (father): and
    Barry's crash 146, 148, 157, 161; and
    Barry's death 21, 188; and Barry's
    dispute with Suzuki 167; and Barry's
    MBE 124; and Barry's wedding plans
    117; in Blitz 187; and Bultaco
    motorcycles 24, 25, 30, 32, 35;
    disapproval of Don Mackay 75; dislike
    of publicity 124; dotes on Barry 26–8,
    121, 126, 203; encourages Barry's
    interest in motorbikes and racing 26, 29,
    30, 31, 32, 33, 35, 64; as engineer for the
    Royal College of Surgeons 24, 25;
    illness and care in old age 188, 190–1;
    injured by crashing bike 105; lives with
    Barry at Charlwood 122, 124, 169;
    marriage and children 24, 25; as
    motorcycle mechanic 24, 25, 29, 31, 32,
    33, 34; moves to Australia with Barry
    131, 189–90; as road racer 24–5; role as
    Barry's mechanic ends after mistakes
    110–11; smuggles Barry out of Mallory
    Park 114
  Sheene, Freddie (son) 10, 18, 20, 21, 125,
    131, 187; and motorbikes 185–6, 194
  Sheene, Iris (mother): and Barry's crash
    149, 157; and Barry's MBE 124; death
    190; disapproval of Don Mackay 75;
    dotes on Barry 26, 27, 121, 126;
    involvement in motorcycle racing 29,
    33, 138; lives with Barry at Charlwood
    122, 124, 169; operation 31; marriage
    and children 24, 25; reluctantly moves
    to Australia with Barry 131, 189–90;
    takes offence over Barry's secret
    wedding 117
  Sheene, Margaret *see* Smart, Margaret
  Sheene, Sidonie (daughter) 4, 10, 21, 124,
    186–7
  Sheene, Stephanie (wife): background and
    first marriage 118–19; on Barry's
    character xiii, 100, 205; and Barry's crash
    and recuperation 135–6, 137, 143, 145,
    146, 148, 149–50, 156–7, 161, 162; and
    Barry's friends xii, 80, 84; and Barry's
    girls 128–30; and Barry's illness and
    death 5–6, 10, 13, 16, 21, 22; birth of
    Freddie 125; entertains at Charlwood
    94–5, 169; first experience of racing
    xi–xii, 123; first sees Barry on television
    65, 118, 120; on Freddie 185–6; humour
    126; on life after Barry 187–9; meets
    Barry xi, 87, 117, 118–22; modelling
    career 118, 119, 120, 121, 125–6; and
    move to Australia 131; popularity with
    mechanics 200; first pregnancy (with
    Sidonie) 96; relationship with Barry 112,

116–33, 187–8, 204; relationship with Maggie 188, 189, 191; responsible for helmet 137; responsible for tickets and cigarettes 138; responsible for timekeeping 123, 137–8; supportiveness 132–3; temporary separation 131–3; wedding 83, 117–18

Shellsport 500 Championship 70, 74, 79, 110

Shepherd, Lesley 35, 43, 67, 84, 86

Silverstone, Northamptonshire: Barry's 1982 crash at 42, 55, 116, 117, 134–65, 174; dangers 54; as fast circuit 139; Heskeths and 121; John Player meeting (1971) 40; practice sessions 139; replaces Isle of Man 75; *see also* British Grand Prix

Simon, Paul 123

Singleton, Dale 98

Smart, Margaret (Maggie) (*née* Sheene, sister): on Barry's children 187; and Barry's illness and death 6–7, 8–9, 12, 17–18, 20, 21; blanked by Iris after husband's win 121; childhood 23, 24, 25, 26–7, 29, 31, 33; first marriage 33; marriage to Paul 41–2; relationship with Barry 189–91; relationship with Stephanie 188, 189, 191

Smart, Paul 6, 21, 40, 41, 69, 121

Smart, Paula (niece) 6, 17–18, 189

Smart, Scott (nephew) 8–9, 17, 191

Smith, Mike 179

Snetterton, Norfolk 59, 110

South Africa 41

South African Grand Prix 175, 177

Spa-Francorchamps, Belgium: Barry's record lap at 41; dangers 59, 111; *see also* Belgian Grand Prix

Spanish Grand Prix: 1970 (Montjuich Park) 35–6; 1971 (Jarama) 37, 39; 1973 (Montjuich Park) 42; 1978 (Jarama) 104; 1982 (Jarama) 173–4

Spencer, Freddie 171, 173, 174, 175, 176

Spondon Engineering 136–7

sponsorship 45, 51, 85, 177

Sports Personality of the Year 174

'squadron, the' 80–100, 202–5

Stadelman, Hans 76

Starr, Ringo 83, 123

Stars of Tomorrow Competition 84

'Stavros' *see* Parrish, Steve

straw bales 54, 62

Styles, Matthew 152

Sugo, Japan 170–1

Sun 99, 118, 179, 202

Superbike races: *Motor Cycle News* 65–6, 70, 73, 74, 78–9, 110; *World of Sport* 170, 178

Surfers Paradise, Australia 16, 19, 116, 124, 131–2, 180, 189–90

Surtees 179

Suzuka, Japan 181

Suzuki motorcycles: Barry's 125cc machine 35, 40; Barry's 750cc machine and crash 64–5; Barry's collection 187; in Classic events 183; RG 500 69–70, 71, 72, 115

Suzuki team: 1976 season 71, 72; 1977 season 74–6, 77, 79; 1981 season 171, 172; Barry's dissatisfaction with 74–5, 101, 106, 111, 115; Barry's dispute with Phil Read 68; Barry leaves and is replaced by Mamola 166–7, 168–9; Barry returns to, but bikes not adequate 174–7; Franco Uncini rides for 135; management changes 74–5; Steve Parrish rides for 55, 56, 59, 74–5; test track 69; Tom Herron joins 47, 49; *see also* Heron Suzuki

Swedish Grand Prix: 1971 (Anderstorp) 37; 1974 (Anderstorp) 70; 1975 (Anderstorp) 67; 1976 (Anderstorp) 72–3, 1977 (Anderstorp) 77; 1978 (Karlskoga) 105; 1979 (Karlskoga) 111–12; 1981 (Anderstorp) 135, 171–2; 1982 (Anderstorp) 156; 1984 (Anderstorp) 96, 178; travelling to 36, 104

Talladega, USA 86

tax 180

Texaco 96, 102, 167, 168

Texas Heron 71

Thames Television 65

This is Your Life 124

Thorpe Park, Surrey 88

Three Shires Hospital 117, 151, 156–61, 163
timekeeping 123, 137–8
toilets 104–5
Took, Barry 151
Tramp nightclub, London 118, 120, 158
Transatlantic Trophy 70, 74, 78, 98, 102
transport and travel 33, 36, 42, 104
treatment of riders 50–60; protests lead to improvement 60–2; *see also* dangers; medical facilities; pay
Triumph motorcycles 29; AJS 25, 30
TT (Tourist Trophy) races *see* Dutch TT; Isle of Man TT
Turnbull, George 160
Tuxworth, Neil 48

Uncini, Franco 135, 173, 175–6
USA: grand prix racing in 102, 103, 104; *see also* American riders

V-4 (motorcycle) 134–5, 136–7, 139, 141–3, 173
V8 Supercars 130
van Dulmen, Boet 112, 172, 176
Van Veen Kreidler 37, 38
Venezuelan Grand Prix (San Carlos): Barry's successes at 76, 103, 110; poor facilities 55–6, 68
Vermeulen, Chris 182
Vogue 119, 121

Waibel, Alfred 140, 141, 144
Walker, Murray 179
Walmsley, Fred 183
water-skiing 88–9, 91, 94
Waterford Road, Chelsea 85–6, 87

Weld-Forester, Piers *see* Forester, Piers Weld-
White, Rex 74, 75, 76
Wide World of Sport 180–2
Wilkinson, Charlie 73
Williams, John 71, 72, 73, 74, 75, 77, 78
Williams, Mike 181, 182
Wisbech, Cambridgeshire (Ashwood Hall) 82, 84, 121, 122, 124, 190
Witham, Jamie 195
Woodman, Tony 30
Woollett, Mick 32–3, 38, 41
world championship: 125cc 36; Barry wins 72, 77; contractual obligations 57; Kenny Roberts takes away 107, 114; after World Series threat 61–2; *see also specific events*
World Cup, John Player (500cc) 160
World of Sport 99; Superbike races 170, 178
World Series movement 45, 60–2, 202
Wright, Merv 74, 75, 76

Yamaha motorcycles: 750cc 170; LC350 160; two-stroke 63–4, 69; TZ750 85, 88; V-4 134–5, 136–7, 139, 141–3, 173
Yamaha team: Barry rides for 41, 42, 134–5, 136–7, 141–3, 166–75; Bill Ivy rides for 34; factory riders' pay 54; Giacomo Agostini rides for 63–4, 66, 67, 68; Kenny Roberts rides for 78, 103, 109, 111, 135; Piers Forester rides for 85, 88
Youens, Georgina 85
Young, Lewis 32
Yugoslav Grand Prix (Rijeka) 111, 174, 177

Zolder, Belgium 62